A VERY MODERN
COMPANY

A VERY MODERN
COMPANY

——◆——

A HISTORY OF THE

Worshipful Company of
Chartered Secretaries and Administrators

1976-2012

The Worshipful Company of
Chartered Secretaries and Administrators

Published in Great Britain in 2013 by The Worshipful Company
of Chartered Secretaries and Administrators.

10 9 8 7 6 5 4 3 2 1

A CIP catalogue record for this book is available from the British Library.

Hardback ISBN: 978-0-9926019-0-4

Text design and typesetting: Carrdesignstudio.com

Printed in Great Britain.

The Worshipful Company of Chartered Secretaries
and Administrators

Saddlers' House
40 Gutter Lane
London
EC2V 6BR

www.wccsa.org.uk

PICTURE CREDITS

Gerald Sharp Photography: 6, 21, 22, 23, 24, 26, 27, 30, 33, 34 (top), 35, 36, 40, 43 (top), 44, 67,
78, 90, 91, 92, 97 (top), 119, 120, 121, 122, 123, 128 (left), 194, 198; Clarissa Bruce: 10, 13, 15, 188,
189, 191, 192, 193, 195, 196; Richard Best: 24; The Stationers and Newspaper Makers' Company: 43;
The Carpenters' Company: 77; Kiki Nortey: 101; Crown Copyright: 173; Jamie Smith: 219;
© The London Museum: 221; Clive Totman: 222, 223, 229

CONTENTS

———————

PREFACE

By the Right Honourable The Lord Mayor
Alderman Roger Gifford

I am delighted to have been asked to write the preface to this history of the Worshipful Company of Chartered Secretaries and Administrators. It was one of my predecessors, Sir Kenneth Cork, who encouraged three professional Institutes to form Livery Companies. All three have flourished but none more so than the Chartered Secretaries and the fact that their history has to be written after just thirty years reflects this.

The team behind the publishing of the book has achieved its aim of making a permanent record of the Company's activities over the last three decades. They have also made the book an interesting one to read, not just for the Company's own members but to all those involved with Livery Companies and the City.

My congratulations to the Company. I hope you will enjoy reading this History of a Modern Company as much as I have.

Roger Gifford
Mansion House
December 2012

SYLVIA IRENE MAUD TUTT

This history of the Worshipful Company of Chartered Secretaries and Administrators is dedicated to the late Sylvia Tutt, Master 1983/84 and the first female Master of any Livery Company. Past Master Tutt was a great supporter of the Company and it was her generous benefaction to the Company on her death in December 2011 that has made the publishing of this book possible.

INTRODUCTION

By Past Master Rory Jackson

CHAIRMAN OF THE HISTORY GROUP

This is the third attempt at writing the History of the Worshipful Company of Chartered Secretaries and Administrators. At the beginning of 2012 we agreed that a professional writer would be exorbitantly expensive but the task was too great to impose on one Liveryman and so we formed a small group to oversee the History but asking the best placed Liverymen to write individual chapters.

I am delighted to say that all those we approached took up the challenge and the history is now written.

We had two aims in mind; first to have a definitive record of the Company from its formation in 1977 to the end of 2012 and second to have a readable book which would be of interest to all members of the Company. This does mean that there is some duplication but we felt this was acceptable in order to make each chapter complete.

The Company in its short life not only changes its Master each year, but has also changed Clerks nine times and moved offices three times and records especially in the early years are not complete. This means there are gaps, for example, in the names of the winners of the Company's medals to Servicemen, and we could well have a wrong date or something. Please do contact us if you can fill in any of the gaps or your keen eye sees anything that is not totally accurate. I am glad to say that with the introduction of the Annual Report, our magazine *Integrity* and a fully staffed office, today's records are more complete and accurate.

The book is dedicated to Past Master Sylvia Tutt. I sat next to her at the Installation Dinner in October 2011, the last occasion she attended a Livery function, and outlined our plans for writing a history of the Company. She was full of enthusiasm and I know would have fully supported a small amount of her generous bequest to the Company being used to get the History in print.

Finally I must thank the members of the History Group, Michael Dudding, Charles Ledsam, Christina Parry, John Robertson and Brian Sole for all their patience and endurance in getting the book to the printers, and to all our writers for without them the history would never have been written.

Rory Jackson
October 2013

CHAPTER ONE

THE FORMATIVE YEARS

1976-1993

By Liveryman Brian Sole

THE FORMATION OF "MODERN LIVERY COMPANIES"

During the 1970s, Sir Kenneth Cork, a past Lord Mayor of the City of London, advocated changes in the City. He was keen for new Livery Companies to be formed. One of the requirements of a new Livery Company has always been that it should not fail for lack of support. The Court of Aldermen has to be satisfied that a number of people of good repute have come together as a body; have held together for a sufficiently long time, usually at least seven years, and can satisfy various conditions.

Based on the premise that all professionally qualified members of recognised Institutes were of good repute, Sir Kenneth proposed a method of "fast tracking". He approached the Institutes of the Chartered Surveyors, the Chartered Accountants and the Chartered Secretaries and Administrators to suggest that they might form Livery Companies. The challenge to the Institute of Chartered Secretaries and Administrators

(ICSA or "the Institute") was taken up in 1976 by a handful of eminent members, largely under the initiative of Mr John F Phillips, a former Secretary of the Institute and a Past President.

The Petition to be granted to the Chartered Secretaries and Administrators had to be sponsored and this was undertaken by Sir Edward Howard Bt. and submitted to the Lord Mayor, Sir Robin Gillett Bt. and to the Court of Aldermen, on 19 April 1977. The Grant of Livery was made on 19 July 1977, thereby creating the new company as the 87th in the order of precedence in the list of Livery Companies in the City of London. A full description of the ceremony, and the luncheon which followed, is included on pages 7-12 of Past Master Sylvia Tutt's book *A Mastership of a Livery Company*, published in 1988.

As it happened, ICSA was the last of the three Institutes approached by Sir Kenneth Cork to form a Livery Company. The Lord Mayor joked that had the Chartered Secretaries been faster with their paper work, they could have been first!

THE HISTORICAL BACKGROUND TO LIVERY COMPANIES

It is known that many guilds (or mysteries) were actively supporting and regulating their trades or crafts in the 12th century and some may have existed prior to 1066. One of the earliest known Royal Charters was granted to the Weavers' Company in 1155. Their original Charter was displayed at the City's Livery exhibition "Butcher Baker Candlestick Maker" during 2012. Guilds existed from the Middle Ages in London and other cities in England, Ireland and Scotland as well as many cities in Europe.

The term "mystery" originally derived from the Greek "mysterion" meaning "initiation". The Romans adopted the word as "mysterium" which translates as "professional skills". The word "Guild" derived from early Germanic languages; "gilde" in German means "association". However the derivation is probably from the Old Norse word "gildi" subsequently adopted by the Saxons as "guild". In medieval times "livery" referred to the clothing, food and drink given to the officers and retainers within large households, including colleges and guilds. Gradually the term was applied to the distinctive clothing and badges, which were symbols of privilege and protection, worn by the guild officers. The guilds came, in time, to be known as Livery Companies. Every Livery Company has retained its distinctive clothing and it remains the custom to wear ceremonial dress on official occasions.

The guilds flourished into the 17th century. Many invested money in the Merchant Venturer Companies, such as the East India Company, which sought exclusive rights of trade with overseas countries. A decline came about caused by tradesmen and craftsmen setting up businesses outside the City walls and, not being subject to City laws and livery restrictions, quickly became more competitive than those within the City. Another cause of decline was the constant demand for money by the Tudor and Stuart monarchs to finance wars. The Livery Companies were an easy target. Charters were withdrawn from the companies and new ones issued for large sums of money.

Pressure to change was brought on the Livery Companies by the Industrial Revolution, and inter alia, the extension of the franchise, which allowed middle classes and the working man to vote under the three Reform Acts of 1832, 1867 and 1884. This led to the development of new trades and the growth of the professional and middle classes. From about 1870 the Livery Companies began to increase support for education and the training of young people. These efforts were so successful that this led to the revival of some of the older companies and early in the 20th century other trades and professions began forming new Livery Companies.

Liverymen of the City of London play their part in the government of the City and participate in many functions of the City and Corporation. They are entitled to attend the meeting of Common Hall in the Guildhall to elect the Lord Mayor each Michaelmas Day (29 September) and to elect the two Sheriffs of the City on Midsummer Day (24 June). Becoming a Liveryman, however, is a lifetime commitment: "Once a Liveryman, always a Liveryman".

THE MEETINGS OF THE COMPANY OF CHARTERED SECRETARIES AND ADMINISTRATORS

After a Council meeting of ICSA on 3 November 1976, certain Council members, eight in all, began the first tentative steps to form a Livery Company. John Wedgwood took the chair with Barry Barker acting as Secretary. John Phillips submitted the first draft Ordinances for the new Company, which would be involved principally with charitable, educational and social activities. Freemen of the Company would have to be members or licentiates of the Institute. The objects were to complement, and not duplicate, those of the Institute.

It was resolved that a guild be incorporated as the Company of Chartered Secretaries and Administrators. Present at this meeting were Messrs Brent, Eley, Gardiner, Herbert, Mason, Phillips, Rutherford and Wedgwood. Subsequently the following 13 members were deemed to be the Company's Founder Members as at 3 November 1976, Messrs Wedgwood (Founder Master), Phillips (Founder Senior Warden), Eley

(Founder Junior Warden), Bounds, Brent, Clarke, Croydon, Gardiner, Jacques, Marwood, Mason, Roberts and Rutherford.

A second meeting took place on 17 November 1976 but clearly preparations for the formation of the new Company had been taking place for some months. The draft Ordinances of the Company, having been revised by Linklaters & Paines, the Company's Solicitors, were approved and ready for submission to the City Solicitor and Comptroller for their comments. Mr Geoffrey Gardiner had made various comments by letter about the proposed Trust Deed drafted 11 March 1976. Linklaters & Paines had given broad approval to all the points he had raised.

LEFT: *The Founder Master, Mr John Wedgwood CBE.*

In addition, the draft of a petition to the Lord Mayor of London for the grant of a Livery and the draft of a Constitution and Ordinances of the Livery Company, also dated 11 March 1976 were considered. Mr Phillips and Mr Barker were authorised to agree final versions of all the documents with Linklaters & Paines. Present at this meeting were Messrs Clarke, Eley, Herbert, Jacques, Mason, Phillips, Roberts and Wedgwood.

THE FIRST MEETINGS OF THE COURT OF ASSISTANTS

Matters were progressing quickly and the third meeting took place immediately after the Institute's Finance and General Purposes Committee meeting on 19 January 1977. A revised draft of the Ordinances of the Company dated 12 January 1977 was amended at the meeting and finally approved. The meeting was then deemed to be a meeting of the Assistants of the Company and the following elections became effective, until successors were elected to office in July 1978.

Master: Mr John Wedgwood; Senior Warden: Mr John Phillips and Junior Warden: Mr Stanley Eley.

Mr Barry Barker was elected as the first Clerk of the Company and was requested to consider recommending the names of fit persons to act as Assistant Clerk and Beadle.

He was also requested to write to those not present who had indicated agreement to serve as Assistants. On receipt of their confirmations to serve, they too would be deemed to have been elected from the date of the meeting. The fine for election to the Court was set at £150 but no fine was prescribed for the admittance as Freemen of those members who had agreed to form the first Court of Assistants. The quarterage for the period to 31 July 1978 was set at £10 per annum and would thereafter fall due annually on 1 August.

It was considered that a suitable number of Court Assistants was 20, although later this was increased to 24. The final resolutions at the meeting were to authorise the Master and Wardens to sign the petition to the Court of Aldermen which was to be submitted by Linklaters & Paines and to set the minimum number of members of the Livery Company at not less than 30 and a maximum of 300.

Present were Messrs Brent, Clarke, Eley, Gardiner, Herbert, Marwood, Mason, Phillips and Wedgwood.

APPROVAL TO BECOME A LIVERY COMPANY

There was no further Court meeting until 13 October 1977. At that meeting it was reported that the Court of Aldermen had approved the Company's petition to become a Livery Company of the City of London, subject to certain conditions, on 19 July 1977. The formal presentation to the Company of Letters Patent had been arranged for 12 January 1978 at a special meeting of the Court of Aldermen at Mansion House. Many matters were resolved at the meeting on 13 October, including:

(a) The fine for admission to the Freedom of the Company was set at £20, but not payable by the members of the first Court;

(b) The wording of the Certificate of Freedom of the Company;

(c) The form of Declaration for admittance to the Livery;

(d) The form of Declaration for admittance as a Court Assistant;

(e) The initial quarterage was set at £10 per annum, subject to review after July 1978;

(f) Windsor Herald at the College of Arms to be asked to undertake the engrossment on vellum of the Letters Patent at a fee of £350; £200 to be paid at once and the balance on completion;

(g) To initiate at once the Grant by Letters Patent of the Kings of Arms of Armorial Bearings, subject to agreement by the Council of the Institute of the use of part or parts of their Armorial Bearings and to ask Windsor Herald of Arms to act for the Company. The cost was estimated at £1,300 but likely to be higher;

(h) To increase the number of Court Assistants from 13 to 20;

(i) To appoint Mr. Brian Abethell as Beadle at a salary of £250 plus expenses and Mr. Robert Simmonds, FCIS Citizen and Scrivener, as Honorary Deputy Clerk;

(j) To issue an invitation to Mr P L Oliver FCIS to become the Company's Auditor;

(k) To open a Bank Account with Lloyds Bank City Office;

(l) To pay Linklaters & Paines its professional charges of £1,145.40;

(m) To purchase appropriate books of record at an estimated cost of £300;

(n) The Master, Wardens and Clerk to proceed with the purchase of robes of office for the Master, Wardens, Clerks, Beadle and three Liverymen at an estimated cost between £900 and £1,600;

(o) To defer the purchase of a mace, estimated at between £900 and £1,600.

The Clerk reported that approximately 250 enquiries had been received from members of the Institute and a few more continued to arrive each day. The Master confirmed that membership of the Company would be open to all qualified members of the Institute.

It was recorded that the Junior Warden had represented the Company at Common Hall on Michaelmas Day 1977 at the Election of the Lord Mayor. In keeping with the custom regarding the order of the Masters of the Livery Companies in the procession, Mr Stanley Eley had led the procession as the newest Company and had by the kindness of another Livery Company borrowed a robe.

THE FIRST ADDITIONS TO THE COURT OF ASSISTANTS AND OTHER APPOINTMENTS

At the start of the Court meeting on 15 December 1977 the Master reported that he had invited Dr Roy Harris, Mr Peter Newton, Mr Alfred Purse, Miss Sylvia Tutt and Major Kenneth Vink to serve on the Court and he was pleased to welcome them to their first meeting.

The Deputy Clerk reported that an order had been placed with William Northam & Co, to supply black lightweight panama gowns for the Master, Wardens, Clerks, Beadle and three Liverymen at an estimated cost of £1,300. The actual cost, reported 8 February 1978, amounted to £1,187. The gowns were decorated in velvet oak-leaf lace and tufts in the Livery colours of light blue and gold.

The Deputy Clerk also reported that the Master had submitted a document, known as a Memorial, to the Earl Marshal, His Grace the Duke of Norfolk, who supervises the work of the College of Arms, requesting the desire of the Company for Armorial Bearings. A colour sketch of Armorial Bearings prepared by Windsor Herald was displayed and an explanation given of the arms, crest and supporters. It was decided that the lion should bear a scroll and pendant rather than a pen and inkhorn and that a motto should be selected.

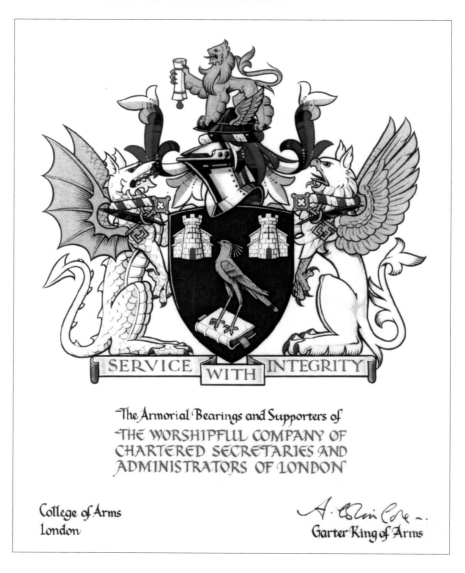

SERVICE WITH INTEGRITY

The Armorial Bearings and Supporters of
THE WORSHIPFUL COMPANY OF
CHARTERED SECRETARIES AND
ADMINISTRATORS OF LONDON

College of Arms
London

Garter King of Arms

Mr PL Oliver had agreed to undertake an audit of the Company's accounts and it was resolved that he should examine and report on the accounts for the period ending 31 July 1978. This prompted Mr David Marwood to query what sort of accounts would be prepared, whether there was an annual budget and whether there was to be a drive to recruit new Freemen. The Master and Wardens gave a rather guarded reply. They indicated that it was not usual to publish accounts to the Livery and financial information would be confined to the Court. Running expenses would be met from all fines because in the early days the annual fine "was certainly insufficient". The target for membership was 150 – 200 and it was likely that the annual fine in the following year would be between £20 and £30, if the Company was to be financially sound.

The cost of hiring accommodation for functions at three Livery Halls had been ascertained with charges amounting to between £1 and £3 per head. The Senior Warden suggested that the Apothecaries' Hall and the HQS Wellington should also be considered. The Clerk was asked to draft a programme for the next meeting consisting of an Inaugural Dinner in March/April, a Reception for the incoming Master in July, following the Court meeting and a Ladies' Dinner in November.

Then followed the more formal procedures of the meeting.

The Master and Wardens made and signed their Declarations as Master and Wardens respectively. Those Assistants who had been welcomed at the start of the meeting made their Declarations as Liverymen, signed the Livery Roll and were clothed with the livery. They then made their Declarations as Assistants and signed the Assistants' Roll. Four of the seven were later to became Masters of the Company, Mr David Marwood, (1981/82), Mr Kenneth Jacques (1982/83), Miss Sylvia Tutt (1983/84) who enjoyed the distinction of being the first Lady Master of any Livery Company and Dr Roy Harris (1992/93).

In addition, the Court confirmed the election of the Clerk: Mr Barry Barker, the Deputy Clerk: Mr Robert Simmonds and the Beadle: Mr Brian Abethell BEM and they were clothed in their livery. Finally, 21 members in attendance, having been duly elected and paid the customary fines were admitted before the Court, made their Declarations, signed the

Livery Roll, were clothed in the livery and were presented with Livery Certificates. Three of those who signed were later to serve as Masters, Mr Ken Parry (1989/90), Mr Francis Bergin (1993/94) and Mr Richard Sermon (2006/07).

PRESENTATION OF THE LETTERS PATENT AND FURTHER APPOINTMENTS

The presentation of the Letters Patent of the Company by the Lord Mayor, Air Commodore Sir Peter Vanneck, to the Master Mr John Wedgwood and the Wardens took place at Mansion House on 12 January 1978. The Court of Aldermen, Assistants and Liverymen of the Company were present at the Ceremony. All enjoyed a Luncheon at which the Senior Warden, Mr John Phillips, proposed the toast to the Lord Mayor and Aldermen. The Lord Mayor then proposed a toast to the Company and the Master responded. It was described as an auspicious day in the first Newsletter of the Company. The Master reported he had received many letters of thanks from the Lord Mayor and official guests and expressed his own satisfaction at the success of the occasion.

LEFT: *(left to right) The Lord Mayor, Mr John Phillips, the Founder Master, Mr Stanley Eley and Mr Barry Barker.*

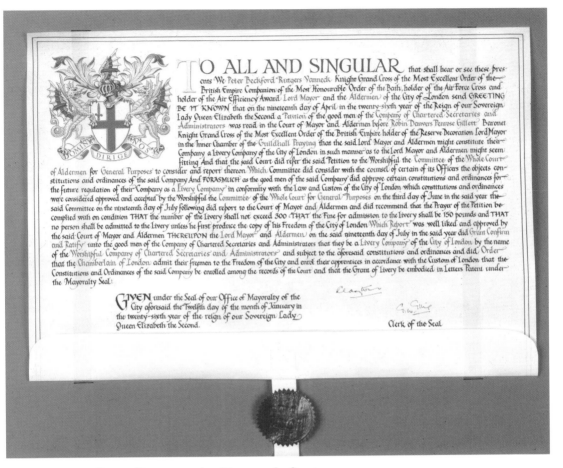

ABOVE: *Letters Patent granting Livery to the Company.*

The Liverymen present had made a contribution towards the cost of the event but, as anticipated, the cost to the Company amounted to between £500 and £600. Photographs taken by the official photographer were circulated for viewing.

The Deputy Clerk reported that he had written to Windsor Herald on 25 January 1978 requesting minor changes to the sketch of the Armorial Bearings. The motto chosen was "SERVICE WITH INTEGRITY".

It was resolved to appoint the Master and Wardens plus Mr Kenneth Jacques, Dr Roy Harris, Mr Peter Newton, Mr Dennis Roberts and Miss Sylvia Tutt as the Managing Trustees of the Company's Charitable Trust. Mr Geoffrey Gardiner suggested it was time to consider making contributions for charitable purposes but it was agreed to discuss this at the next meeting. The Master reported that he had invited the Rev Dr Newell Wallbank, Rector of St Bartholomew the Great to act as Honorary Chaplain and he had agreed to accept the position. The Court confirmed the appointment.

The Deputy Clerk queried whether members of the Institute resident overseas could be considered for membership. He specifically mentioned Rio de Janeiro, Botswana and New Zealand. The Senior Warden could see no problem in admitting overseas members, provided they could fulfil the citizenship qualification. At a later meeting Miss Tutt was concerned that, if too many Liverymen lived a long way from the City of London, they would merely become "names on a list". The Master confirmed that the main aim was to encourage membership in the United Kingdom, primarily from those who intended to support the functions.

Messrs Bounds, Mason, Newton, Roberts and Rutherford made their declarations as Liverymen, signed the Livery Roll and were clothed in the livery and then made their declaration as Assistants and signed the Assistants' Roll.

PROGRAMME OF FUNCTIONS IN THE FIRST YEAR

The Company's programme of functions commenced with attendance at the United Guilds Service at St Paul's Cathedral on 17 March 1978, by taking an allocation of eight seats. The inaugural Livery Dinner at the Apothecaries' Hall followed on 5 April, when the Master presented to the Company a sterling silver Loving Cup which is described in more detail in Chapter Eight. A service was held at the Priory Church of St Bartholomew the Great on 19 July, conducted by the Rector and Hon. Chaplain

RIGHT: *The Loving Cup presented by the Founder Master.*

of the Company, The Reverend Dr Newell Wallbank, followed by a reception at the Institute's Headquarters at 16 Park Crescent and finally a Ladies' Dinner on 21 November 1978 at Painters' Hall. There was an attendance of about 150 at this Dinner. The principal guests were Mr Colin Cole, the Garter King of Arms and Master of the Scriveners' Company; Lord Peart, Lord Privy Seal; Professor Alan Gillett, Master of the Surveyors' Company all accompanied by their ladies and Sir John and Alderman Lady Donaldson.

GRACE

By the Honorary Chaplain, The Reverend Dr. N. E. Wallbank, M.A., Mus.D., Ph.D.

Harpist, Miss Anne Ross
Singers from the choir of St. Bartholomew-the-Great
(Director of Music : Andrew Morris)

Menu

At the Reception
Madeira
Club Prestige Brut

Muscadet de Sevre
et Maine

Mousse of Salmon
Sauce Verte
Melba Toast

Roast Foreribs of Scotch Beef
Horseradish in Tomato

Mouton Cadet
Selection Rothschild

Broccoli Spears with Hollandaise Sauce
Braised Leeks
Chateau Potatoes

Taylors L.B.V. Port

Morello Cherries in Liqueur
Hazelnut Bombe

Brochette Diane

Camus VSOP
or
Liqueurs

Coffee
Petits Fours

GRACE

to be sung by all present

For these and all Thy mercies given
We bless and praise Thy Name, O Lord,
May we receive them with thanksgiving,
Ever trusting in Thy Word!
To Thee alone be honour, glory,
Now and henceforth, for evermore.—Amen.
Laudi Spirituali, 1545

On the withdrawal of the cloth the ceremony of the LOVING CUP takes place.

Toasts

THE QUEEN

Proposed by . . . . The Master

QUEEN ELIZABETH, THE QUEEN MOTHER
THE DUKE OF EDINBURGH
THE PRINCE OF WALES
AND THE OTHER MEMBERS OF THE ROYAL FAMILY

Proposed by . . . . The Master

THE WORSHIPFUL COMPANY OF
CHARTERED SECRETARIES AND ADMINISTRATORS
AND THE MASTER

Proposed by . . . . A. Colin Cole, Esq.
Garter King of Arms
Master, Scriveners' Company

Reply by . . . . . . The Master

THE GUESTS

Proposed by . . . . . The Senior Warden
Reply by . . . . The Rt. Hon. the Lord Peart
Lord Privy Seal

THE CLERKSHIP

Proposed by . . . . . . The Master
Reply by . . . . . . The Hon. Clerk

The Worshipful Company of
Chartered Secretaries and Administrators

Ladies' Dinner

at
PAINTERS' HALL
on
Tuesday, 21st November, 1978

Master :
J. F. PHILLIPS, C.B.E., LL.M., F.C.I.S.

Senior Warden :
S. J. S. ELEY, F.C.I.S., F.T.I.I.

Junior Warden :
T. E. D. MASON, B.Com., F.C.I.S., Comp.I.G.E.

Hon. Clerk :
R. M. SIMMONDS. F.C.I.S.

THE APPOINTMENT OF ROBERT SIMMONDS AS CLERK

At a meeting of the Court on 3 May 1978, the Clerk, Mr Barry Barker, requested the Court to release him from his duties in view of the pressure of Institute affairs. His resignation was accepted and Mr Robert Simmonds,

the Deputy Clerk, was appointed to the position. Mr Robert Simmonds (left) was to continue as the Clerk until 5 July 1984 and throughout this period acted as Editor of the Newsletter. From the outset, he demonstrated his deep affection for the City by providing entertaining articles on Livery history in each issue of the Newsletter, in addition to keeping members informed on current affairs. He was appointed Honorary Clerk Emeritus on retirement in in July 1984.

The Founder Master, John Wedgwood, reflects the high esteem in which Mr Robert Simmonds was held in the following tribute shortly after his death:

"'When some men discharge an obligation, you can hear the report for miles around'. That was one of Mark Twain's more cynical observations and if there was a man to whom such a comment would least apply, it was surely our dear Honorary Clerk Emeritus, Bob Simmonds. 'Least apply' because here you had a man who discharged his obligation to society (with bountiful interest) in a manner totally unassuming and without self-esteem. He was one of that rare breed of men who achieve many important things, but little notoriety.

"Our Company's indebtedness to Bob is reflected in the terms of the resolution passed by the Court when he retired from the office of Hon. Clerk. 'He has been its (the Company's) guide, counsellor and friend, applying his great personal interest in the customs of London, and their historical origin and development, to his services to the Company.

"Much of the goodwill, engendered in the City towards our foundling Company was created by Bob Simmonds as our outstanding representative amongst Clerks and City officials who, like us, admired his scholarship and diligence and the validity of his advice. As a fellow administrator and manager in a lifetime of service in the electricity supply industry, I like to feel that his insistence on accuracy and attention to detail, and his keen sense of service, were honed in the tough environment of that vital industry, in which he played such an important role.

"Add to this an impish sense of humour and you have someone whose effect on those around him was always beneficial. When you left his company after a meeting, you felt good and somehow content with what it was you had decided. And to see the smile of satisfaction on his face when one of his office bearers had struck just the right note in an important speech, or had introduced a personal touch, which had carried the day, was a most reassuring sight to behold.

"Bob's scholarship revealed itself in those delvings into Guild and City history, which we enjoyed so much in his entertaining and informative Newsletters. Do you remember his amusing reference to the 'flat' observation of municipal institutions that 'Company Clerks may rank amongst the higher class of educated and intelligent men'. Indeed, they may, and our Hon. Clerk Emeritus was one of the finest examples we know.

"We are all sad at Bob's passing because every one of us liked him, admired his splendid work and had a deep affection for him. We thank his charming wife, Olive, and their family, for the wonderful support they gave him, and we extend to them our heartfelt sympathy. We shall all miss this lovable man very deeply, but we shall ever be grateful for his memorable legacy to us and to the City; the warm fellowship, sense of service, and spirit of benevolence which are the hallmarks of the Worshipful Company of Chartered Secretaries and Administrators."

Reverting to the Court meeting of 3 May 1978, the Court considered quotations for a Master's badge and Past Masters' badges. The purchase of a Master's badge and collar at a cost of £1,200 plus 12½% VAT was approved in principle plus 25 Past Masters' badges and collars at a cost of £42 each plus VAT.

LEFT: *The Original Master's badge.*

The Master reported on the success of the Inaugural Livery Dinner at Apothecaries' Hall on 5 April 1978. The Senior Warden, on behalf of the Court, thanked the Master for his presentation to the Company of a silver Loving Cup at the Dinner.

The Hon. Chaplain's invitation to hold a Church Service for the Company at St Bartholomew the Great was accepted. A coach or coaches would be hired to take members attending the Church Service to Park Crescent for a reception afterwards.

Arising from a paper on the finances of the Company presented by the Junior Warden, it was resolved to increase the quarterage to £25 per annum from 1 August 1978.

THE PROCEDURE FOR BECOMING A LIVERYMAN OF THE WORSHIPFUL COMPANY OF CHARTERED SECRETARIES AND ADMINISTRATORS

The Clerk normally conducts an interview with any member of the Institute who wishes to join the Company and has submitted a written curriculum vitae. Subsequently, the applicant attends a meeting of the Past Masters so that they can satisfy themselves that the candidate is a fit and proper person to become a Liveryman. The applicant can raise any questions about the Livery Company. The Clerk then communicates with the applicant, proposing a date when the applicant can attend a meeting of the Court in order to become a Freeman of the Company. The Clerk will also set out the fees and fines payable.

On presenting himself to the Court the applicant makes a declaration before the Court. He or she is requested to sign the Freedom Roll and is presented with a certificate conferring on him or her the Freedom of the Company.

The next step is to contact the Chamberlain's Court at Guildhall to arrange a date to be admitted as a Freeman of the City of London. A person of any nationality, of good character and over the age of 21 years, may apply to the Corporation of London, Guildhall, for the Freedom of the City of London upon payment of a fee. After approval by the Court of Aldermen, the applicant is invited to make an appointment for the Freedom Ceremony. This involves reading the Declaration of a Freeman, signing the Declaration Book and being presented with a document entitled "Copy of Freedom City of London".

Having been granted the Freedom of the City of London, Freemen of the Company are expected to apply to be clothed with the livery of their Company within the next 12 months. At this ceremony, having paid the fine and made a Declaration, the new Liveryman of the Worshipful Company of Chartered Secretaries and Administrators is presented with the livery medal, a certificate, and a tie if male or a brooch if female. The award of the livery medal commenced in 1980; it is worn on formal occasions, to distinguish Liverymen from guests.

ACCOMMODATION

The Objects of the Company include a clause "to purchase, take on lease, hire or otherwise acquire and maintain, a Hall, Institute, Library or other building or premises, and any real or personal property within the City of London for the furtherance of the objects of the Company". This is a clause included in the Objects of many Livery companies. Mr. George Challis, Hon. Clerk from July 1984 to October 1994, strongly resisted proposals to consider the purchase of a Hall for use by the Company. The cost of the upkeep of a Hall is so great that only the wealthiest of Livery Companies can afford it.

Initially, the Institute had provided a desk in the Library for the Deputy Clerk and another desk for an agency typist. The Master, John Wedgwood, prepared a paper on the subject of accommodation for the Court meeting held on 8 February 1978. He considered the existing arrangements were unsatisfactory. He charged the members of the Court to suggest "solutions which will enable the Company's accommodation arrangements to match its position as a Livery Company". The Clerk protested that the Institute was already short of accommodation for its senior staff and that there was no alternative accommodation available for the Company.

The Deputy Clerk was asked to explore the possibilities of obtaining accommodation in the City. He reported back on 3 May 1978, that improved accommodation would be available on the 4th floor of the Institute's building in the autumn, despite the Clerk's earlier remarks. The Court accepted this offer with thanks. However the offer was amended to an office on the first floor of the Institute from 1 October 1978 on a leave and licence basis for one year. The licence fee was £1,250 per annum, and increased to £1,500 per annum from 1 February 1981. This covered the costs of heating, lighting and office services and facilities for four Court meetings and one reception per annum. An alternative but higher quotation offering fewer facilities had been received from the Clerk to the Ironmongers' Company.

Thanks to the initiative of Sir Lindsey Ring, Governor of The Honourable The Irish Society, it was resolved at a meeting of the Court on 2 July 1981 to transfer the Company's administration to a room on the 2nd floor of the Irish Chamber in Guildhall Yard, with use of the Court Room six times per year, at a licence fee of £750 per annum plus a charge for other services. The move to the Irish Chamber was completed on 23 October 1981 and occupation by the Company continued for the next 10 years.

In 1992 the offices of the Company were moved to St. Dunstan's House in Carey Lane. The accommodation was not ideal and a further move to Saddlers' House, at 40 Gutter Lane just off Cheapside took place in December 1997. The hire of accommodation from the Saddlers' Company has proved to be convenient and successful.

ABOVE: *The Irish Chamber, Guildhall Yard.*

EARLY MASTERS

Mr John Wedgwood 1976/78

The original Court of Assistants consisted of senior members of the Institute and of their profession who saw it as their prime objective to promote and nurture the Company in its development. The normal progress to becoming Master is by election by the Court of Assistants, first as Junior Warden and then as Senior Warden. The Master holds office for 12 months and has a heavy programme of engagements to fulfil. Although this leaves little time to make changes in Company affairs, most Masters made their mark in the development of the Company.

A Resolution of Thanks to John Wedgwood was passed at the Court meeting of 10 January 1979 and began "That there be recorded this expression of the deep gratitude of the Company to John Alleyne Wedgwood for the distinguished service rendered by him as the first Master from the formation of the Company on 3 November 1976 until he relinquished office on 11 October 1978." Reference was made to his personal qualities and that "he combined a respect for and an appreciation of history and tradition, with a lively modern outlook towards the importance of the City of London in the economic and social life of the country".

Outstanding occasions during John Wedgwood's time as Master were recorded, including the petition for constituting the Company as a Livery Company, heard by the Lord Mayor and the Court of Aldermen on 19 July 1977 and the grant of Letters Patent by the Lord Mayor at Mansion House on 12 January 1978. His initial objectives at the time of his election "the growth of the Company and the standard of management and excellence of the first social functions organised by the Company", were achieved due to the energetic leadership and cordial friendliness which he displayed on all occasions.

Subsequently each Master on relinquishing office was presented with a Resolution of Thanks.

Mr John Phillips 1978/79

John Phillips succeeded John Wedgwood. He was a barrister by training who had sat and passed the Institute's examination at a later age than most. He served a second term as Master in 1986/87 as a result of the stroke suffered by the Senior Warden, Sir Lindsay Ring. George Challis recalled an incident at the Livery Banquet in Mansion House when small wagers were being placed on the length of speeches. As John Phillips rose to his feet, the City Marshal whispered "This will be a long one: 30 minutes!" Others shook their heads because, customarily, nobody speaks for more than 6 minutes. The City Marshal had the last laugh. John Phillips spoke for 28 minutes, to the embarrassment of many!

The Resolution of Thanks to John Phillips referred to the grateful thanks of the Company for the distinguished services rendered by him in pioneering the formation of the Company in the year to 17 October 1979. For many years he had sought to establish a closer association between the Institute and the City of London and his efforts "were crowned with success upon the grant of Livery to the Company by the Court of Aldermen on 19 July 1977, thus securing a permanent link between the

ABOVE: *Sir Kenneth Cork as Lord Mayor.*

profession and the City". He had presided over the Company's functions "with dignity, charm and wit and his masterly speeches at the Ladies' Dinner in Painters' Hall on 21 November 1978 and at the Livery Dinner in the Mansion House on 22 March 1979 will long be remembered. He brought added prestige to the Company by his attendance at ceremonies of the City Corporation and functions of other Livery Companies and City institutions." His part in the Company's affiliation with the Royal Army Pay Corps was also highlighted.

Mr Stanley Eley 1979/80

Stanley Eley's first pleasant duty was to present and invest Mr Phillips with a Past Master's collar and badge. He congratulated Mr Phillips on becoming the first Master of the newly formed Arbitrators' Company and also on his appointment to the Court of the Scriveners' Company.

Mr. Eley initiated discussions with Sir Lindsay Ring, Lord Mayor of the City of London 1975/76, leading to his admission to the Freedom and Livery of the Company at a special meeting of the Court on 17 March 1980 in the United Oxford and Cambridge University Club, Pall Mall. At the same meeting on 17 March Sir Lindsay Ring made the Declaration and signed the Assistants' Roll.

At another special meeting of the Court of Assistants, held at Guildhall on 30 September 1980 Sir Kenneth Cork, Lord Mayor of the City of London 1978/79, was admitted to the Company as the first Honorary Freeman.

Mr Robert Simmonds, FCIS had not applied to become a Liveryman of the Company but in recognition of his services as Hon. Clerk he was clothed with the Livery, made the Declaration and signed the Roll at the Court meeting held on 1 July 1980.

At the Court meeting on 1 July 1980 the Court accepted Major Vink's suggestion for the Company to provide a livery medal to all who signed the Livery Roll after 31 December 1980. Liverymen elected prior to that date could purchase a medal.

The Resolution of Thanks placed on record the Company's warmest thanks and appreciation to Stanley James Sidney Eley "for his untiring and devoted services for the benefit of the Company, particularly in respect of the successful conclusions leading to the Association with the Royal Army Pay Corps, and also the satisfactory outcome of his personal appeal to Liverymen to contribute, by way of covenant or otherwise, to the Company's Charitable Trust Fund." There was reference to his charm and dignity with which he presided over Company functions and in particular the Ladies' Dinner on 23 October 1979, the Livery Dinner at the Mansion House on 21 March 1980 and the signing of documents of Association with the Royal Army Pay Corps at the Duke of York's Headquarters, Chelsea, on 6 March 1980. He too had added to the high esteem in which the Company was held and further enhanced its standing, and that of the profession of Chartered Secretary and Administrator in the City of London and elsewhere.

Mr Thomas Mason 1980/81
(known as Ted because of his initials)

During Mr Mason's term of office, an order was placed for a 1½ inch die with the Company's Coat of Arms and for 250 metal livery medals to be produced by Toye Kenning Ltd. 120 medals were sold to Liverymen and the cost of the balance was written off. It was agreed to establish a Master's Sub-Committee of the Court consisting of Past Masters and Wardens to consider the relationship with the Institute and the selection of candidates in all stages of progress through the Company.

Financial matters included an increase in quarterage for Liverymen from £30 to £40 for 1981/82 and increases in the honoraria to the Clerk and the Assistant Clerk to £1,500 and £500 respectively.

The Armorial Bearings of all the Livery Companies are displayed in Guildhall. The Lord Mayor unveiled the Company's own shield and those of seven other new Livery Companies at a special ceremony in Guildhall on 18 September 1980. Over 30 members of the Company were present.

Liveryman Cyril Ridd generously presented the Company with a pair of 15 inch French four-candle candelabra circa 1860 at a Court meeting on 23 April 1981. Although the candelabra were stolen during a break-in at the premises of the Institute, they were recovered and are still in use on special occasions.

The Company's administration was transferred from the Institute's offices in Park Crescent to the Irish Chamber. The Clerk reported to the Court on 7 January 1982 that the move had taken place smoothly on 23 October 1981. This achieved the aim of moving the Company into the City's financial area but made it more difficult to maintain good relations with the Institute.

Mr Alan Brent's resignation from the Court of Assistants had to be accepted following receipt of a letter confirming that he was resident in the USA and had no intention of returning to the United Kingdom. Mr William Rutherford's resignation was accepted with regret; the Court's appreciation of his services since the formation of the Company being placed on record at a Court meeting held on 22 April 1982.

The Resolution of Thanks to Mr Mason recorded the Company's warmest thanks and appreciation to him for the services rendered to the Company, particularly during his year of office as the fourth Master from October 1980 to September 1981. "He laid emphasis on the ideals of charity and service and, as an example, was particularly concerned with the promotion within the Company of "Practical Action", an organisation sponsored by Sir Kenneth Cork to help train the youth of the country during a period of great unemployment".

The Resolution continued with reference to the many functions of other Livery Companies and City of London events he had attended, supported by Mrs Mason on appropriate occasions. "His year as Master had been particularly marked by his dignified conduct in the Chair on all occasions and by the friendliness with which he presided over the Company's various functions, especially the Ladies' Dinner on 9 October at Clothworkers' Hall and the Livery Dinner at the Mansion House on 10 July 1981". The final paragraph referred to his personal qualities, which had helped to enhance the profession of Chartered Secretary in the City of London and elsewhere.

Mr David Marwood 1981/82

Notable events during Mr Marwood's term of office included the investiture of Miss Sylvia Tutt as Junior Warden. This was the initial step towards Miss Tutt becoming the first Lady Master of any Livery Company. The Clerk reported receipt of a letter from Buckingham Palace acknowledging the Illuminated Address sent by the Company on the occasion of the marriage of Prince Charles and Lady Diana Spencer. However, an approach to Prince Andrew to become an Honorary Liveryman of the Company was rejected by Buckingham Palace. The Clerk also reported that the Company's Petition dated 7 July 1980 had been approved by the Court of Mayor and Aldermen on 16 February 1982, subject to an amendment requiring the annual appointment of one or more qualified auditors to examine and report on the accounts.

Presentations of a silver goblet by Past Master Phillips, a silver Loving Cup by Past Master Mason, a silver inkwell, two silver pen holders and a quill pen by Court Assistant Harris and a Beadle's staff, or wand, by Past Master Eley for the treasure chest of the Company were made at Court meetings.

The original ornamental Master's badge had proved to be too heavy. A replacement was commissioned. It proved to be most satisfactory and was admired when worn for the first time at a Livery Dinner.

David Marwood has been a keen swimmer all his life. In 1995, he was pleased to organise for the first time the Company's participation in the "City Dip". This involved members of each participating team swimming a total of 5,000 metres. The Company had the youngest swimmer, Katy Thorpe, at age 12 years who was the daughter of the then Liveryman Adèle Thorpe. David Marwood continued to organise participation until 2000, when the Company raised the large sum of £6,200. In 2005 he swam again, covering 1,600 metres in 68 minutes.

The Resolution of Thanks placed on record the Company's grateful recognition and thanks to David Marwood for the services he rendered to the Company during his year in office as the Company's fifth Master.

"As a founder member of the Company Mr. Marwood has been and is a most conscientious Liveryman and Member of the Court of Assistants. He has constantly borne in mind the well-being of the Company and the need to integrate it fully into the life of the City of London.

"During a year of great pressure from his business commitments (as Company Secretary of ICL) Mr Marwood spared no effort to promote the image of the Company for the benefit of all within and outside the Livery. Particular mention should be made of his efforts in promoting the highly successful Summer Concert at the Barbican Centre in June 1982, which raised £8,000 for the Charitable Trusts of our own and four other participating Livery Companies."

The Resolution confirmed that Mr Marwood assisted by his charming wife Jean had spread the good name and aims of the Company throughout the City. Mr Marwood's participation in the elections of the Lord Mayor, and his Sheriffs, at Guildhall and the United Guilds Service at St Paul's Cathedral were noted in addition to his attendances at the Inaugural Dinner of the Worshipful Company of Arbitrators and at the ceremony at Guildhall to confer honorary Freedom of the City of London on the Prime Minister of Singapore, Mr Lee Kuan Yew. He had sought to strengthen the links between the Royal Army Pay Corps by making three visits to Worthy Down.

Mr. Marwood set out to involve as many Liverymen as possible in Company affairs.

"This he successfully achieved with the introduction of Court luncheons and the innovation of an Assembly of

RIGHT: *The replacement Master's badge.*

Liverymen held at the close of his own year in office. The friendly and dignified manner in which he presided over the Company's functions was much appreciated especially at the Ladies' Dinner at Carpenters' Hall in October 1981, the Livery Dinner at the Mansion House in March 1982 and the Annual Church Service and Reception in July 1982".

Mr Kenneth Jacques 1982/83

During Mr Jacques' term of office a number of administrative matters arose. The Clerk presented a paper on age distribution within the Company and a record of attendance by Liverymen. The Clerk was requested to write to those who had never attended any function and reported later that 12 of the 22 members had responded with reasons for non-attendance.

The Master's suggestion that a Livery tie be designed was agreed by the Court and carried through to fruition.

Arising from a request by the Bank of England, it was suggested that the Company obtain an official seal. It was agreed that future investment stock and share transactions be registered by the Master and Clerk of the Company and that the Clerk be authorised to sign bank mandates on behalf of the Company. Past Master Phillips hoped that the Company would eventually be incorporated by Royal Charter and that would be the time to obtain a seal. Dr Leslie Tutt, brother of Court Assistant Sylvia Tutt, produced a paper on commutation of quarterage, which was considered by the Court on 6 January 1983. Liverymen were asked for comments in the Newsletter but only eight members responded. It was agreed that the matter lie on the table; there was insufficient interest to justify proceeding.

The Senior Warden presented the budget for 1983/84, which was agreed subject to an increase of £100 p.a. in the honorarium to the Beadle. The quarterage for 1983/84 was raised by £5 to £45 p.a.

Past Master Marwood kindly presented the Master with a lady's chain and pendant to be worn by the lady of the Master during his year of office. He also presented to the Company a cut glass and silver decanter together with a book entitled "The City" by Jacques Lowe and Sandy McLachlan published in 1982.

The Resolution of Thanks to Mr. Kenneth Jacques commenced with the placing on record of the Company's "warmest thanks and appreciation for the outstanding services rendered by him to the Company during his year of office as the sixth Master from 1 October 1982 to 6 October 1983." It continued "Since the formation of the Company in 1977 Kenneth Jacques, a founder member, has been a most conscientious Liveryman and Member of the Court of Assistants and has contributed wholeheartedly to the proper development of the Company.

"During his term of office as Master, Kenneth Jacques carried out all his duties with distinction. His conduct in the Chair, the manner in which he presided over the Company's functions, and the way in which he represented the Company at many events of fellow Livery Companies and other organisations, was both dignified and naturally friendly. On many occasions he was accompanied by his wife, Audrey, who by her full support and her personal charm made her own distinctive contribution to such a highly successful year. The Company also wishes to place on record its grateful appreciation to her.

"As Master, Kenneth Jacques worthily maintained the charitable work of the Company. His very effective speeches at the Company Ladies' Dinner at Clothworkers' Hall in October 1982, at the Livery Dinner at the Mansion House in March 1983, and many other occasions, were most cordially received. The Company also wish to thank him for the manner in which he presided at the Annual Church Service and Reception in July 1983.

"Of particular note was the laying of the Company's Foundation Stone at the London World Trade Centre in February 1983 and the introduction during his year of the very successful Master's Luncheons, which were very well attended by many highly

distinguished guests. Moreover, in attending the Passing-out Parade at Worthy Down, and in other ways, he sustained the close links existing between the Company and the Royal Army Pay Corps.

"Amongst his numerous other activities as Master, the many occasions on which Kenneth so ably represented the Company at ceremonies and functions in Sheffield and of the Company of Cutlers in Hallamshire are particularly to be recorded. His extensive work in developing further the friendly relationships between the City of London and the City of Sheffield deservedly merit high praise and thanks."

The slate plaque Foundation Stone laid by Kenneth Jacques was returned to the Company when the World Trade building was demolished and now sits in our storage room in the basement of Saddlers' Hall waiting for a suitable display opportunity – perhaps, one day, in our own premises?

Miss Sylvia Tutt 1983/84

Sylvia Tutt enjoyed the distinction of becoming the first lady to be the Master of a Livery Company and was the author of the book *A Mastership of a Livery Company*, in which she described in detail her activities in her year as Master of the Company.

At Master Sylvia Tutt's first Court meeting, Past Master Wedgwood announced that it was five years since he became Master and, in accordance with a Court Minute, he would now become an Honorary Court Assistant. Past Master Phillips described the day as one tinged with sadness as he paid tribute to the first Master of the Company. He proposed that Mr. Wedgwood be granted the title "Founder Master" and that the title be added, in suitable fashion, to his Past Master's collar and badge. This was resolved with acclamation. Past Master Jacques then presented Mr. Wedgwood with a silver champagne goblet, suitably inscribed on the case. Mr. Wedgwood also resigned as the Managing Trustee of the Charitable Trust, whilst remaining a Trustee. Past Master Phillips succeeded to the vacated position.

The target figure of 200 Liverymen was reached and there was a long discussion on the future development of the Livery Company.

The Master presented Mr G H Challis ACIS AIB, Citizen and Tobacco Pipe Maker and Tobacco Blender, to the Court and it was resolved that he be appointed Honorary Clerk designate.

Thanks were received from The Honourable The Irish Company for the gift from the Company of a silver inkstand and quills in recognition of the harmonious relationship between the Society and the Company since the establishment of the Company's administration in its building.

The Livery Dinner held on 23 March 1984 at the Mansion House was a very special occasion for Miss Sylvia Tutt. The guests of honour were the Lord Mayor, Lady Mary Donaldson, and Sheriffs. The Junior Warden, Mr Leslie Croydon, proposed the

ABOVE: *The Hon. Clerk, Mr George Challis.*

Civic Toast with the reply from Lady Donaldson who proposed the toast to the Company. The Lord Mayor emphasised that it had taken over 800 years to bring together the first lady Lord Mayor and the first lady Master of a Livery Company.

A summary of The Resolution of Thanks to Miss Sylvia Tutt reads as follows:

It was RESOLVED

That the Worshipful Company of Chartered Secretaries and Administrators hereby records its grateful thanks and sincere appreciation to

Miss SYLVIA IRENE MAUD TUTT

for the outstanding and unique services rendered by her to the Company particularly during her year of office as the seventh MASTER from 6 October 1983 to 11 October 1984.

Since joining the Company in 1977 Sylvia Tutt has also served the Company wholeheartedly as Liveryman, Member of the Court of Assistants, Junior Warden and Senior Warden.

Miss Sylvia Tutt was the first lady ever to become Master of any Livery Company throughout the many centuries of livery history. Her distinguished term of office was memorable not only for the Company but also for the livery of the City of London and indeed for the professional and business community of the United Kingdom and other countries of the Commonwealth where Chartered Secretaries & Administrators live and serve.

As Master, Sylvia Tutt greatly enhanced the reputation of the Company by her devotion to its purposes, by carrying out all her duties with such high distinction and by her gracious and charming bearing and personality. Her speeches at the Company's Ladies' Dinner at Drapers' Hall in October 1983 and at the Livery Dinner at the Mansion House in March 1984, at both of which so many highly distinguished guests were present, were particularly effective and most cordially received. The Company also wishes to thank Miss Tutt for the manner in which she presided at the Annual Church Service and Reception in July 1984 and her highly successful inauguration of a Court Dinner at Bakers' Hall in January 1984 and a Livery Reception on HQS Wellington in September 1984.

During her term as Master, Sylvia Tutt represented the Company at events of the Corporation of London, of fellow Livery Companies and of other organisations on numerous occasions. At many of such functions she was invited to speak on behalf of the Company and the dignity of her presence and the impact of her excellent speeches on these occasions further valuably added to the reputation of the Company.

As Master, Sylvia Tutt worthily maintained the charitable work of the Company. She also enhanced the valuable connections which the Company has with the Royal Army Pay Corps in attending the Regimental Dinner in the Headquarters Mess also the Passing-out Parade at Worthy Down.

The election of Miss Sylvia Tutt as Master of the Company was a further landmark in a career which demonstrates the highest standard of service to womankind and to the profession of Chartered Secretary and Administrator and which commands the utmost respect and gratitude to all.

The Court of Assistants desire that a lasting record of its grateful recognition and sincere appreciation be made by illuminating the above resolution on vellum and by presenting Miss Tutt with a framed engrossment."

Mr Robin Clarke 1984/85

At the October 1984 Court meeting details of the agreement with Rank-Xerox to give the Charitable Trust £5,714 p.a. for a period of 4 years were reported.

After 4 years in office Mr Albert Hamilton-Hopkins resigned as Hon. Assistant Clerk to take up the position of Vice-Chancellor of the Order of Lazarus and a resolution was passed at the July meeting expressing the Company's high appreciation for his distinguished service. He was succeeded by Mr John Ieuan Jones JP.

Not having our own Hall means that the Master or Clerk has to seek venues for all Luncheons and Dinners. There were complaints from Court members about the quality of the food following the Court Dinner in July 1985. The Master had to point out that the Hall chosen was the only one available that could seat up to 120 on the date of the event. In addition there had been problems selecting the menu because of the attendance by a multi-faith group of people.

It was decided that from 1986 the March Mansion House function would become a Ladies' Banquet and that official invitations would be sent to the Lady Mayoress and the Sheriffs' ladies.

Following the Master's visit to Royal Air Force Support Command on 26 April 1985, the Clerk was requested to open informal discussions with other Livery Companies on links with the Armed Forces, and to report back to the Master, on the possibility of forming an association with the Royal Air Force Administration Branch.

Mr Leslie Croydon (1985/86)

At the Court meeting 9 January 1986 the Chairman of the Charitable Trust warned that the Trust was financially sound but that income was likely to decline in the short to medium term. It was proposed that an approach be made to all Liverymen who had not previously supported the Trust.

Past Master Sylvia Tutt presented the Company with an inscribed rose bowl to commemorate her year in office. Past Master Eley declined to take the chair of the Charitable Trust, due to ill health and he also resigned as a Trustee, at the April meeting. The Master reported a record attendance of 289 at the Mansion House Dinner on 21 March 1986.

The Hon. Clerk reported that the Company had registered under the Data Protection Act, 1968.

A Court meeting was held at Armoury House on 19 May 1986 to sign formal Letters of Association with the Royal Air Force. The Letters were read by the Hon. Clerk and then signed by the Master, the Hon. Clerk, the Head of the Royal Air Force Administration Branch and the Head of the Secretarial Specialisation. A presentation of two Loving Cups was then made to the Company. The Royal Air Force party consisted of Air Marshal AG Skingsley, Air Vice-Marshal Mason, Air Commodore M Tompkins and Group Captain JH Constable, who later became Master of

LEFT: *Sir Lindsay Ring as Lord Mayor.*

the Company just prior to his early death. The President of ICSA, Mr Bernard Brook-Partridge, and Vice-Presidents were also present.

At the Court meeting on 10 July 1986, the Senior Warden, Sir Lindsay Ring, was elected as Master for the next year. However, at the following Court meeting on 9 October 1986, Sir Lindsay had to withdraw on the advice of his doctor. The Master and the Wardens decided that the Court should elect the replacement. Both Past Masters Phillips and Tutt put their names forward and after a secret ballot, Past Master Phillips was chosen. He proceeded to invest Mr Ronald Bounds as Senior Warden and Mr Dennis Roberts as Junior Warden.

Mr John Phillips (1986/87)

100 members and guests attended the Church Service and Reception held on 18 July 1986. Once again there was criticism of the slow catering service and the Hon. Clerk was requested to speak to the caterers about the problem.

On 9 April 1987 Past Master Clarke presented badges to be worn by the Senior and Junior Wardens and Court Assistant Colonel George Cauchi presented a badge to be worn by the Clerk. The Mansion House Dinner had an attendance of 290. The Hon. Clerk suggested that one or two Court Assistants should in future look after the important guests, after the Master had received them.

On 9 July 1987 it was resolved that the quarterage remain at £50.

Past Master Sylvia Tutt reported details of a book she was writing to describe her year in office. She hoped that her publication would not inhibit or discourage the Founder Master and the Hon. Clerk proceeding with a history of the Company. Despite her comment, Founder Master John Wedgwood and the Hon. Clerk, Mr Robert Simmonds, reported at the next meeting that, having sought the views of the Court, they had suspended for the time being work on the history of the Company, to be entitled "The First Ten Years".

The retiring Master addressed the Court and invested Mr Ronald Bounds as the next Master.

Mr Ronald Bounds (1987/88)

A former member of the Court had suggested that the Company produce a special certificate for the founder members of the Company. Past Master Eley responded by saying that the proposal had been mooted in the past but it had been decided not to proceed.

The Hon. Clerk reported that a Livery Companies Dinner was to be held to commemorate the Australian Bi-Centenary and that 20 places had been allocated to the Company.

The Hon. Clerk also reported that he had been asked to act as Secretary to the committee assisting Mr Simon Block for election to the shrievalty in June 1988. It was later reported that Mr Simon Block and Alderman Francis McWilliams had been elected as Sheriffs for 1988/89.

On 14 March 1988 a Court meeting was held at Watermen's Hall to sign Letters of Association with the Supply and Secretariat Branch of the Royal Navy. The Master welcomed the Royal Navy party, consisting of Rear Admiral BT Brown, Captain JGB Musson RN, Commander RG Lockwood RN and Commander MHJ Peters RN and expressed his appreciation for having a link with all three administration/logistics branches of the Armed Forces. Admiral Brown responded by saying that it was a valuable association for the Royal Navy.

At the Court meeting on 7 April 1988, Past Master Croydon presented three goblets to the Company to commemorate his year in office. It was his intention that the goblets would be used by the senior member of each of the associated branches of the Armed Forces at formal dinners.

Mr Dennis Roberts (1988/89)

At the October meeting, the retiring Master, Mr Ronald Bounds, addressed the Court and invested Mr Dennis Roberts as Master for the next year. Mr Roberts proceeded to invest Mr Kenneth Parry as Senior Warden and Mr Donald Durban as Junior Warden. Past Master Phillips asked if a method could be devised whereby the incoming Master was installed at the Livery

Assembly instead of at the Court meeting. A procedure was approved by a meeting of the Past Masters and introduced at the Livery Assembly in October 1989.

At the Court meeting on 19 January 1989, the Hon. Assistant Clerk reported a switch of investments, from which a capital gain of £3,733 had arisen. A discussion on investments followed and it was agreed that an investment sub-committee should be formed with the Senior Warden as Chairman plus Court Assistants Francis Bergin and Geoffrey Gardiner.

The Chairman of the Trustees of the Charitable Trusts, Mr Geoffrey Gardiner, reported on the activities of the Trustees and requested that the Court reaffirm that the main thrust of support would be preferred to be directed at the General Trust whilst recognising that the support of the educational trust would be seen as one of its primary functions. The wording of this minute was amended at the following Court meeting under Matters Arising to read: "the educational trust would be seen as its primary function". The Court did not give the affirmation requested and the request was raised again at the Court meeting on 13 April 1989, but again without formal agreement.

The aims of the original Trust Deed of 1978 had been found to be too narrow and a second General Charitable Trust Fund had been created in 1983. However problems of interpretation continued to arise. A more detailed explanation of the working of the Charitable Trusts is given in Chapter Four.

The Master reported that the Livery Dinner on 21 October 1988 had been well attended but, as forecast, the financial outcome was bad. There was a loss of £1,281.

A further financial loss was reported at the April Court meeting. The deficit arising from the Ladies' Banquet on 31 March 1989 was reported as £541 "with the possibility of some small bills to come". The Hon. Assistant Clerk considered this "to be satisfactory in the light of the number of guests relative to the total attendance".

The Company was also having trouble in collecting quarterage arrears. A slight improvement was reported but a further attempts had to be made to reduce the arrears.

The Investment Sub-Committee's first report to the Court resulted in a discussion and the recommendation that Cazenove be appointed to handle the investments of both the Company and the Charitable Trusts was accepted. The Master reported his resignation from the Charitable Trust and indicated his intention to resign from the General Charitable Trust. It was agreed to appoint Mr Francis Bergin as a Trustee of both the Charitable Trust and, in due course, the General Charitable Trust.

The Chairman of the Trustees reported that the Lecture sponsored by Rank Xerox held on 1 March 1989 at the City University had been very successful and reflected great credit on the Company.

Recommendations to make donations of £1,000 to the Lord Mayor's Appeal and four other smaller donations plus donations of £250 each to Naval and Army charities were approved by the Court. The Chairman also confirmed that there were standing instructions to make regular donations to the Clergy Orphan Corporation and the Sheriffs' and Recorder's Fund.

The Junior Warden reported favourably on the first meeting of the Livery Liaison Group (LLG) on 17 March 1989. Arrangements had been made to provide stewards who assisted at the Mansion House Dinner. The Master considered that the Dinner had been well organised but the attendance at 222 was disappointing. Volunteers had helped at the Livery Exhibition at Guildhall and the Church Service. However the reception after the Church Service resulted in a deficit of £907, due to the low attendance of 74 members and guests and the difficulty in estimating the charges at Farmers' Hall. It was agreed that the annual Church Service was an essential part of the Company's programme and every effort should be made to encourage support for the Master and the Hon. Chaplain.

The Hon. Clerk reported on a meeting with the Director-General of the City and Guilds of London Institute. Virtually all the Livery Companies support the City and Guilds but the Company had ceased paying a subscription some years earlier. It was agreed that the Company should recommence the payment of an annual subscription of £50.

The gift from the Institute to the Company of a reproduction of the Institute's Armorial Bearings had been framed and was presented to the

Court. This is now hanging in the Institute's offices in Park Crescent due to a lack of wall space in the Company's office.

The Master reported that he had discussed with Admiral Allen the Company's award of two silver medals to the Royal Navy. The Court agreed with the proposals to award medals annually to the officers on the Junior Supply Officers' Courses who achieve the highest marks in Secretarial and Naval Legal Studies and to the top students on the Petty Officers' Courses.

On 12 October 1989, the Hon. Assistant Clerk presented draft unaudited accounts for 1988/89. The growth in expenditure on the Company's functions was considered unsatisfactory. It was agreed that future Court Lunches should be self-financing with only the costs of official guests being charged to revenue. The maximum cost should be set at £18 per head and efforts made to improve the level of comfort. It was agreed to transfer the remainder of the stock of ties purchased to the General Charitable Trust as a gift. After a discussion it was agreed that £1,000 per annum be transferred to a Reserve Fund to meet any contingent expenditure which might arise out of the occupation by the Company of its room in the Irish Chamber.

The Hon. Clerk reported that only one Past Master's badge was in stock. There was a discrepancy between the number originally ordered and the actual stock. Having resolved to purchase a new stock, the original jeweller could not be traced. A firm called Watkinson was instructed to prepare a new die at an estimated cost of £300 although it was not until July 1992 that the new badges were received.

Mr Hammond enquired if members of the Court could have their own gowns to wear on formal occasions. The Hon. Clerk indicated that the Company could not bear the cost of the gowns, with prices varying from £75 to £500.

The Court adjourned and reconvened at 5pm for the Livery Assembly. The retiring Master, Mr Dennis Roberts, addressed the Court and invested Mr Kenneth Parry as the new Master. Mr Parry then invested Mr Donald Durban as Senior Warden and Dr Roy Harris as Junior Warden.

Mr Kenneth Parry (1989/90)

The Master admitted Mr David Wright as a Court Assistant, reported the recent death of Past Master Mason and informed the Court that the Hon. Clerk, Mr Challis, had been elected as Chief Commoner in the City of London for the year. Mr Challis hoped to continue with his existing duties in addition to those of the Chief Commoner.

At the April Court meeting the Hon. Clerk reported the resignation of founder member Mr. Geoffrey Gardiner. The Master wished the Hon. Clerk to convey to Mr Gardiner the Court's very best wishes for the future.

The Charitable Trust's report was made by Past Master Jacques who confirmed that Mr Gardiner had also resigned as Trustee of both Trusts and as Chairman of the Charitable Trust Fund. The possibility of a common body of trustees was under consideration. The Master's appeal for more financial support for the Charitable Trusts had resulted in additional income of £1,000 p.a.

The Mansion House Dinner on 30 March 1990 had an attendance of 265, which was an increase of 43 over the 1989 attendance.

The Junior Warden circulated an analysis of the Company's functions over the past 10 years, showing the number of Liverymen attending functions. The members' attendances appeared to be declining but this was counter-balanced by an increasing number of guests.

At the October 1990 meeting the Hon. Clerk showed the Court the neck ribbons for Assistants which were available at £10 each.

Mr Donald Durban (1990/91)

At the January 1991 meeting the Master advised the Court that the Hon. Clerk Emeritus, Mr Robert Simmonds, had died suddenly just before Christmas. The Founder Master was asked to pay a tribute to the late Robert Simmonds and this has been reproduced in full earlier in this chapter.

ABOVE: *The bench in Guildhall Yard in memory of the late Mr Robert Simmonds (occupied by Colonel Dudding, Clerk).*

The Hon. Clerk reported that progress had been made on the proposal to place a seat outside the Irish Chamber in Guildhall Yard in memory of Bob Simmonds. Mrs. Simmonds approved the wording of the inscription to be carved on the upper bar of the back of the seat, "In memory of Robert Simmonds, FCIS, 1912-1990". The seat is still very much in use today, and thanks to the good offices of Past Master and Deputy Robin Eve, is now firmly bolted to the paving stones on which it stands.

The Master reported on a meeting with the LLG at which the question of a Hall for the Company was discussed. Although there was no opposition to the proposal in principle, a number of members had voiced doubts, particularly on the financing of any project. The Junior Warden summed up the discussion. In order to proceed, an in-depth study by a firm of Chartered Surveyors would be required. The fee was likely to be about £10,000. Some loan facilities would be required and other Livery Companies would be approached with a view to sharing costs. One estimate of the annual running costs was £300,000. It was felt that there was little point in pursuing the matter but the work of the Group and the Junior Warden was appreciated.

The Master reported receiving favourable comments about the Mansion House Dinner on 25 March 1991. Sadly, the attendance was only 212 and the charge to the Company was estimated at £1,350.

Estimates of expenditure for the financial year to 31 July 1992 were presented which resulted in a discussion on the level of quarterage for the following year. The Court resolved to increase the quarterage from £70, which had been unchanged for 3 years, to £80 and the Livery fine to £300.

An offer to produce Past Masters' badges by Watkinsons was accepted. The cost of the die was likely to be about £90 but would remain the property of the Company. It was agreed to place an initial order for 12 badges. The badges were due to be delivered at the end of April 1992. It was agreed that in future the die and the unissued badges should be kept in the strong room and covered under the insurance policy. Past Master Roberts offered to review the current policy and to determine what could be done about the missing medals from the earlier batch. Past Masters Wedgwood and Phillips agreed to gift their Past Masters' badges to the Company in line with other Past Masters.

At the October 1991 meeting the Court extended its congratulations to the Hon. Clerk, Mr George Challis, on becoming Chief Commoner for the second time and to Court Assistant Mr Edward Clements on being elected Master of the Scriveners' Company. Court Assistant Geoffrey Gardiner recalls that Ted Clements may have been the quietest member of the Court but was also the most eminent being a City Deputy and Chairman of the Property Committee of the Court of Common Council. Ted had also been a Director of Zurich Assurance and practised as a barrister. "He was our cleverest member and the shrewdest financial operator by a long measure".

Dr Roy Harris (1991/92)

The sixth Annual Lecture held on 18 March 1992 had been well received but the attendance was lower than in previous years. The earlier lectures had been held at City University and were sponsored by Rank Xerox up to and including 1991. The Mansion House had been closed for refurbishment and the Ladies' Banquet had been held at Stationers' Hall on 3 April 1992. It was felt that the Banquet had been a success and the Master was congratulated, particularly for the standing and eloquence of the speakers. It was reported later that the cost to the Company was £1,684.

ABOVE: *The Livery Hall of the Stationers and Newspaper Makers' Company.*

The new supply of Past Masters' badges had been received by July 1992 and the Master formally presented Past Masters' badges to Past Master Parry and Past Master Durban.

The Hon. Clerk had produced a memorandum on the future of the Company and a further memorandum was circulated with the agenda for the July 1992 meeting. After discussion it was agreed that:

(a) the Company's capital and income should be increased by the formation of The Master's Endowment Fund;

(b) a target of 250 Liverymen in the short term to be set. Members of the Court would endeavour to recruit suitable members;

(c) the fines for Freedom to be increased to £100 and for Livery to £500;

(d) the fines for Assistants to be increased to £50, for Wardens to £100 and Master £150;

(e) there was no support for a levy on members;

(f) Liverymen should be encouraged to remember the Company in their wills;

(g) there was little support for the idea of loans;

(h) members of the Court who wished to make gifts to the Company should be encouraged to contribute to the Master's Endowment Fund instead of adding to the Company's treasures.

Dr Roy Harris was the last of the Founder Members to be installed as Master of the Company. He was succeeded by Mr Eric Kirk who had become a Liveryman in July 1978 and was admitted to the Court of Assistants in January 1985. Promotion was rapid and within seven years he was installed as Master of the Company.

Mr Eric Kirk (1992/93)

The question of including the value of the Company's treasures in the balance sheet was discussed at the January 1993 meeting but it was felt preferable to exclude them. The next Livery Exhibition was due to be held in mid July 1994. It was agreed that the Company should participate and pay the sum of £300 required.

Prior to the Livery Dinner at Armourers' Hall on 3 November 1992 Letters of Association had been signed with the Adjutant General's Corps which had subsumed the Royal Army Pay Corps in a recent reorganisation of the Army. The capacity of the Hall was 81 and some members were unable to obtain tickets. The limitation on numbers had been detailed in the notice but in spite of this some Liverymen brought their wives, which caused problems and complaints.

Some Court members attended the Advent Carol Service of the Clockmakers' Company at St Lawrence Jewry on 9 December 1992. It was suggested that in future there should be a joint Carol Service with the Clockmakers and the Fan Makers.

Some thought was being given to the recording of the history of the Company. Past Master Phillips prepared a memorandum on the origins of the Company which he had had printed and circulated. The LLG members had also given the matter some thought and the Junior Warden reported that Liveryman Mollie Harris had started research into a year-by-year history of the Company. She submitted Chapters 1 and 2 to the Junior Warden and was discussing with him how to proceed.

The quarterage for 1993/4 was increased to £100.

The Master reminded the Court of the sad loss the Company had sustained through the death of the Immediate Past Master, Dr Roy Harris and the Court stood in silent tribute.

The Hon. Clerk reported that the Guildhall Club had agreed to exhibit the Company's silver and would take responsibility for insurance and cleaning etc. The Court accepted this.

THE CLERK AND OTHER HONORARY OFFICERS

The Clerk

The Clerk is the Chief Executive of the Company working under the directives of the Court. The Secretary of the Institute, Mr Barry Barker, was appointed the first Clerk to the Company on 19 January 1977, but, due to pressure of work, stood down on 3 May 1978. Mr Robert Simmonds succeeded as Hon. Clerk and was aided by two Hon. Assistant Clerks, Mr Phillip Guilford, January 1980 to September 1981, and then Mr Albert Hamilton-Hopkins. Mr Robert Simmonds recruited Mrs Sandra Tyre as a secretary, a position she filled successfully for many years, until her appointment as Assistant Clerk, with responsibilities for the preparation of candidates for the Freedom of the Company and the organisation of public functions.

The Clerk displaying the Founder Master's medals and some of the Company's silver treasures.

Mr George Challis had retired from a senior position in Lloyds Bank and was Deputy Governor of the Irish Society and a member of the Court of Common Council, sitting on various committees. Liveryman Sir Lindsay Ring, Governor of the Irish Society, approached Mr George Challis to act as Hon. Clerk, for 2 days per week. In view of the fact that the Company had its office within the premises of the Irish Society, close to the Guildhall, he was persuaded to take up the position. He considered that he was supported well by his Hon. Assistant Clerks, Mr Albert Hamilton-Hopkins, until July 1985 and then by Mr John Jones. Mr George Challis remained as Hon. Clerk for 10 years and in appreciation of his work the Court enrolled him as the Company's first Hon. Liveryman on 19 October 1994.

Other Officers

Other Honorary Officers of the Company include the Beadle, the Chaplain and the Archivist. The Beadle's original duty, dating back at least 600 years, was to act as the Law Officer of the Company. Today the Beadle continues to play an active role in Company affairs as Master of Ceremonies on formal occasions and ensuring that the Company treasures are kept securely. Brian Abethell BEM, a member of the staff at Mansion House, was the Beadle for 20 years from October 1977 to October 1997. On his retirement Mr Paul Grant, Beadle of the Saddlers' Company, took over as part-time Beadle until the appointment of Mr Terence Young BEM, in April 2000.

The Company holds a Summer Church Service and at Christmas time, a Carol service, with participation by other Livery Companies, usually followed by a supper. The first Hon. Chaplain was The Reverend Dr Newell Wallbank of the Priory Church of St Bartholomew the Great. The Reverend Arthur Brown, succeeded him from October 1979 until July 1991.

Liveryman David Coward was the first to hold the office of Hon. Archivist. He provided a display of a number of the Company's treasures at the Livery Assembly in 2001 and wrote about his activities in Newsletter No 85, Winter 2001.

THE NEXT STAGE

By 1994 a regular programme of functions had been established, a committee structure was beginning to take shape and the initial contacts with sections of the Armed Forces were successful. The Company had been very fortunate in their choice of Hon. Clerks, Messrs Simmonds and Challis both having a broad knowledge of how the City worked and who were widely respected in the City. However, there was a growing need to introduce a more robust system of budgeting and control of expenditure. The Company had been well served by the enthusiasm and professionalism of the first few Masters, but by 1994 there were one or two clouds on the horizon leading to a period of some uncertainty which is described in the next chapter.

CHAPTER TWO

THE UNCERTAIN YEARS

1994-2001

By Past Master Michael Dudding

INTRODUCTION

I have called the years 1994–2001 "the uncertain years" because they reflect a time, around twenty years after its foundation, when the impact of the founding members was fading as a result of age, illness or death, when membership was roughly static, when the Company's finances were under pressure, when it was seeking to increase its activities and civic involvement in the City of London, yet when the constraints of staff resources led, often with some reluctance, to increased delegation of activity to Liverymen and in particular to Liverymen not members of the Court.

THE NEED FOR CHANGE

The period started, appropriately, with the report of the Long Term Planning Committee, chaired by Past Master Croydon, presented to the Court in September 1994. The Committee's remit had been to look at, and make recommendations for, the future of the Company, with the widest remit. The main recommendations, the essence of which would be encountered again in later years, were that: the main objectives in the Company's future strategy should be to give maximum priority to the rapid establishment of additional funds, and to take steps that would increase the Company's prestige:

(a) there should be a recruitment drive to increase the number of Liverymen to the maximum permitted of 300 by the end of 1997, with a Recruitment Committee being established;

(b) it was quite unrealistic to pursue any project involving single or shared occupancy of a Livery Hall;

(c) additional revenue should not be raised by increasing fines and quarterage, but the rates should be reviewed regularly and an age-related grading scheme be introduced when the quarterage was increased beyond £100;

(d) the Annual Lecture should be run by the Company rather than by the Charitable Trustees, and that it should be principally aimed at enhancing the prestige of the Company in the City;

(e) the Chairman of the LLG should be elected by the Group rather than be the Junior Warden ex-officio and that the Court should from time to time review the contribution made by the Group towards the greater involvement of Liverymen in the Company's various activities;

(f) a formal committee structure be established, starting with a Finance and General Purposes Committee and an Investment Committee;

(g) it would be desirable, in due course, to recruit a salaried part-time Clerk;

(h) in view of the falling attendance by Liverymen at formal functions, the LLG should be asked to study the possibility of arranging one or two functions in the price range of £15 to £20 per head.

The Court accepted these recommendations, but two others were the subject of lively debate, eight Past Masters being present, and were only accepted at later meetings of the Court. The first was that for a few years income should as far as possible, be channelled to the Company rather than to the Charitable Trust. But fifteen months later, at the instigation of the Master, Mr. Clifford Grinsted, the Court was asked to address the considerable confusion that had occurred as the result of an appeal for funds issued by the Charitable Trustees.

The second contentious issue was that Past Masters should continue as Court Assistants with full voting rights for a period of seven years after leaving office. In the final version the Court resolved that Past Masters should remain members of the Court for only five years after leaving office, but be Honorary Court Assistants until death, resignation or removal, entitled to attend and speak at Court meetings but not vote, not counting as filling any of the twenty-four prescribed places on the Court, nor being counted in a quorum. Although these arrangements had been practised since April 1979, they had not been enshrined in the Ordinances then in force.

At the October 1994 meeting of the Court, the Master, Mr Francis Bergin, offered to be the first Master to retire from the Court after five years. His suggestion that the Court should have a similar general review every five years was accepted. It was agreed that the next review should focus on the Company's constitution. In January 1995, however, the new Hon. Clerk, Mr Wilfred Hammond, was asked to investigate the modifications that were needed to the Ordinances and the likely cost of changing them.

Work proceeded slowly until eventually, in January 1998 a working party formed by Past Masters Bergin, Croydon and Grinsted presented a draft revision of the Constitution, Ordinances and Standing Orders to the Court. In a reversion to times past, the word "Chair" had been replaced by "Chairman", but the desire of Past Masters Bergin and Grinsted to see "and Administrators" deleted from the Company's name was not pursued in order to avoid delay in submitting the revised documents to the Court of Aldermen. That Court required four amendments to be made, of which the most significant was that Past Masters would henceforth remain Court members with a vote for five years after their year as Master, and for a further five years after that without a vote, thereafter they would stand down from the Court.

In July 1999 the Master, Group Captain John Constable, was able to report that the documents had been approved. Minor recommendations, not for inclusion in the draft Constitution, were that "equal opportunity for appointment to the Court be given to members of the Livery irrespective of gender" and that "the concept of an Optimum membership of the Court be practised". The optimum, from an authorised figure of 24 Court members was set at 20 in July 2000. This very significant revision of the Company's constitutional documents, largely the work of Past Master Grinsted, formed the basis for the further constitutional revision which was required in support of the grant of the Company's Royal Charter in 2008.

COMMITTEES

Court committees were first set up in January 1995, when Colonel George Cauchi was Master. All committee members were to be members of the Court although this was changed in 2001. Provisions were made for rotation by members, no one being expected to serve continuously for more than five years. However, the retirement by rotation after not more than five years presented some problems in its early years as was pointed out to the Court by the then Hon. Treasurer, Mr Francis Spencer-Cotton, in July 2000. A Working Party, consisting of the Master, Wardens and Hon. Clerk, was set up to consider the structure and membership of all committees, with particular reference to constructive use of the services of all members of the Court, and to ensure that committees did not become self-perpetuating.

The Working Party's proposals were presented to the Court in April 2001, recommending, inter alia, the preparation of draft terms of reference for all three main committees and the Investment Sub-committee, and a review of committee membership to take place annually at the Election meeting of the Court. The subsequent draft terms of reference contained the provision for committees and sub-committees other than the Finance and General Purpose Committee to include a maximum of two non-Court members per committee. Whether such members should be counted for purposes of quorum and vote was a particularly contentious issue. The October Court meeting heard heated debate about this, but the Court accepted a majority recommendation from the Working Party that non-Court members should be granted these rights. Any casting vote by a committee Chairman was, however, to be reported to the Court. Thus did the Company gradually adopt a less "top down" approach in its governance!

FINANCE AND GENERAL PURPOSES COMMITTEE

The introduction of a Finance and General Purposes Committee and an Investment Sub-committee was approved in January 1995. Membership of the main Committee was set at nine, three of whom, to be selected for their acknowledged investment expertise, were to form the Investment Sub-committee. At the Court meeting in July 1995 the Master reported that he had appointed Past Masters Croydon, Jacques, Parry and Tutt; Junior Warden Geoffrey Finn; and Court Assistants Gordon Bristow, Donald Kirkham, Philip Marcell and Richard Sermon as the first members, with Messrs Marcell (Chairman), Finn and Parry forming the Investment Sub-committee. Court Assistant Kirkham was nominated as Chairman, although he stood down in favour of Past Master Croydon between April and July 1996 on being recalled, temporarily, as Chief Executive of The Woolwich Building Society.

The main committee was to meet at least quarterly and circulate copies of its minutes to Court members. With the exception of the Investment Sub-committee, powers of the Committee were to be advisory only. The first main test of the new Committee came in October 1995 when the Court was not content with the format and timing of the presentation of the accounts for the previous year, the absence of a budget for 1995/96 and arrangements for monitoring expenditure. The Committee was requested to convene an early meeting to remedy these issues.

The formation of the Finance and General Purposes Committee proved to be major innovation which has served the Company well ever since. In April 1996 the Committee reported that it would establish a Development Sub-committee to re-examine the concept of the Master's

Endowment Fund and develop a strategy for further fund-raising activities. The Sub-committee consisted of Court Assistants Constable (Chairman), Bristow, Hammond and Marcell, and Liveryman David Lee. However, in July 1996 its remit was increased to cover all Company activities. Court Assistant Bristow submitted a trenchant note which identified three issues:

(a) a totally inadequate capital base due to failure in the past to build one;
(b) a serious shortage of revenue income to meet present and future needs;
(c) an almost total failure to educate the membership about the financial commitment in becoming a Liveryman.

He said that "anyone who does not see the situation as serious has got to be mad!"

He went on to propose a scheme whereby Freemen under the age of 40 would, if they wished, pay only 25% of the quarterage but contribute, if they wished, to a savings scheme earning interest in order to finance their admission to the Livery at age 40. Payment of quarterage in four instalments was also proposed; but it was recognised that schemes of this kind would require greater staff resources. The Sub-committee submitted four very detailed reports to the Court during the course of 1997.

The First Report covered the main elements of income and expenditure, and concluded that "the Company could not support its present activities on its present range of income". The Second Report dealt with quarterage, recommending an increase from £160 per annum to £175 in 1997/98 and to £215 in 1998/99; in the event, the Court only agreed to a figure of £165 for 1997/98. The Third Report dealt with fines, with alternative proposals that would bring in additional capital each year of either £5,200 or £5,900.

The Fourth Report included draft budgets for 1997/98 and 1998/99. Key elements of expenditure were £20,000 for staff costs, £2,148 for the lease of a photocopier (cancellation of the contract at a later date proved extremely difficult and the total leasing, operating and legal costs over about three years amounted to £8,414), and £1,050 to the ICSA for the Company's postal costs. In the first year the draft showed a deficit of £5,830 rather than the surplus of £545 had the Sub-committee's recommendations been accepted in their entirety. This report concluded that "it is difficult to see how in the short term we shall be able to avoid increasing quarterage to bring the Company finally into balance".

Not surprisingly, given the Court's failure to opt for radical measures in 1997, another review of the future administration of the Company and its financial affairs was commissioned in April 1999 under the chairmanship of Past Master Carine. Court Assistants Bristow, Greenwell and Marcell worked with him. This Strategic Planning Sub-committee canvassed opinion from 15% of the Livery. The report presented to the Court in November 1999 noted that:

(a) given the Company's age profile, it would be difficult to maintain the current membership numbers;
(b) the Company had a high level of quarterage compared with other comparable companies; and that
(c) most of the income was taken up by staff costs and the only source of major economies would be staff reductions.

Recommendations were made concerning the use of investment profits (to go to capital rather than fund revenue commitments), staging of the initial fine, the creation of a Corps of Junior Freemen, reductions in the level of entertainment of Company guests, and for professional management of the Newsletter. This time the Court grasped the nettle. Within two years the various recommendations had been implemented and recruitment had increased significantly. The Company therefore found itself in a much better position to face the future. A change of bankers from Lloyds to Barclays was authorised. Furthermore, in 2001 it was decided to transfer the Company's small investment portfolio from individual shareholdings to a collective investment scheme managed on a discretionary basis. In mid-2003 the Court further decided that, in view of these changes, the Investment Sub-committee could be placed in suspension for the time being.

RECRUITMENT COMMITTEE

A Recruitment Committee was also established in January 1995 under the chairmanship of the Junior Warden Geoffrey Finn. The Chief Executive of ICSA, Mr John Ainsworth, although not at that time a Liveryman, kindly agreed to be co-opted in order to identify potential members of the Company. In 1997 Past Master Bergin assumed the chairmanship, until being succeeded by Court Assistant David Wright in January 2000.

The name of the Committee was changed to Membership Committee in July 1998 to reflect the continuing improvement in membership numbers. In April 1999 the Court agreed that the Chairman of London Branch ICSA might be co-opted to the Committee provided he *(sic)* was a Liveryman. Liveryman Graham Oxenham joined the Committee

ABOVE: *Liveryman Annika Goodwille.*

in this capacity. Another change came in 2001 when the Court agreed that, the Corporation of London having changed its rules, non-British nationals could be admitted to the Freedom and Livery of the Company. In July 2001 Mrs Annika Aman Goodwille, a Swedish national, was the first beneficiary of this change to become a Liveryman. Appendix One shows the Company Roll including Hon. Freemen and Liverymen.

EDUCATION COMMITTEE

In January 1997 the Court approved a proposal from the Master, Mr Geoffrey Finn, that an Education Committee be established, with Mr. Finn as Chairman. At the following Court meeting, it was reported that committee members would be the Master, Past Masters Jacques and Marwood, Senior Warden James Carine, and Messrs. Bristow and

Hammond (as Hon. Clerk). The role of this committee was somewhat uncertain in its early years. In April 1998 the new Chairman, Junior Warden Wilfred Hammond, proposed that its name be amended to "Education (Liaison and Advisory) Committee" and the Court agreed. The Master, Rear Admiral Carine, reflecting on the risk of creating committees which might generate lives of their own, suggested that the Court should review the Committee's role after one year, and that was also agreed. In October 1999 Court Assistant Adèle Thorpe succeeded Mr. Hammond as Chairman and Freeman David Lilley, Director of Education at the ICSA, became a co-opted member.

ABOVE: *Cartoon of Rear Admiral James Carine as Master.*

MASTER'S (ADVISORY) COMMITTEE

Although a Master's Committee, consisting of the Wardens and all Past Masters, had been established in 1980, as a sub-committee of the Court, to consider various aspects of the Company's affairs, its existence and role were not mentioned in the Company's Constitution at that time, when a Finance and General Purposes Committee had not been thought necessary. This situation led, as might be supposed, to some divergence of opinion as to where power and influence really lay. In January 1998, however, the Past Masters Committee was formally constituted as the Master's Advisory Committee, and its powers were defined in the Constitution of 1999 as rendering advice only on questions remitted to it from time to time by the Master or the Court. In particular its duties include:

(a) the appraisal and recommendation of candidates for election to the Freedom and Livery of the Company;

(b) the appraisal and recommendation of candidates for election to the Court and;

(c) generally, advice on the conduct and management of the Company's affairs.

To this day, however, the minutes or notes of this Committee's meetings are not put before the Court because of the confidential nature of its discussions about candidates for election to the Court or higher office. It is for the Master to report on any advice he has received which he considers appropriate to divulge.

One unusual issue for the Committee in 2001 was a disciplinary hearing. A Liveryman was reported as having engaged in conduct likely to be injurious to the character and interests of the Company. This was occasioned by excessively loud talking at a number of Company functions, including during formal speeches. In compliance with Ordinance 3.01, he was summoned to meet the Master and Past Master Marwood. They concluded that since the Liveryman concerned had not deliberately intended to be disruptive and had apologised, no further action should be taken.

MEMBERSHIP LEVELS

The task faced by the Recruitment Committee cannot be underestimated. In the period January 1995 - January 1997 13 Liverymen died and in 1997 a further 13 reverted to Freeman status against the ceiling of 300 Liverymen authorised by the Company's Constitution. The records show strengths during the period 1994 - 2001 as follows:

October 1994	224	January 1998	224
January 1995	229	December 1999	211
July 1996	226	July 2000	214
March 1997	210	March 2001	203

The make-up of these figures is often unclear in the Company records, and sometimes the figures shown in the Court minutes are not the same as those in minutes of the Membership Committee. They obscure the vital figure of Liverymen (excluding Freemen) paying Quarterage. For example, the make-up is given as follows:

	January 1996	January 1998
Membership	209	211
Freemen	3	6
Freeman in attendance that day	-	3
Honorary Liverymen	2	2
Honorary Freemen	3	2
	-----	-----
Total:	217	224

It seems that the Court was so focused on the magic figure of 300, the number of Liverymen authorised under the Constitution, that there was a considerable degree of wishful thinking about the size of the Company. This was brought out very clearly in March 2001 when the stated number of 203 Liverymen was analysed as: 183 paying full Quarterage, 17 paying the age-discounted figure and three having had payment waived by the Master in view of their financial problems.

Difficulties in maintaining membership records were specifically mentioned on several occasions. For example, in October 1996 the Hon. Clerk said that "a thorough reappraisal of the membership was about to be made to verify or modify the data held". Again, in January 1998 "The Hon. Clerk gave the Court a breakdown of membership but was unsure of the accuracy of the records." In April 1998 "The number of Liverymen had been confused over the period, and was now confirmed as 198 paying members." In January 2000 "for some time the Company's list of members and their addresses had not tallied with the membership statements that had from time to time been submitted to the Court". It was not until 2000 when the then Court Assistant Wright devoted a great deal of time to a reconciliation of the figures that the true situation was confirmed.

THE STAFF AND OFFICE PRACTICES

While the Company is governed by the Master, Wardens and Court of Assistants, the execution of their policies and the organisation of functions are left to the employed staff. At the beginning of this period, the Company was fortunate to have Mr. George Challis CBE, a member of Common Council, as its Hon. Clerk. A banker by background, with a sound war record with the Gurkhas, he was well versed in City matters. Although a member of the ICSA, he never became a Liverymen of the Company. However, in recognition of his services over the previous ten years, he was made an Hon. Liveryman in October 1994 on standing down as Hon. Clerk and given a parting gift of £1,000; his wife Margaret was presented with some crystal glassware. The Long Term Planning Committee had recommended that it would be desirable when George Challis retired, to recruit a salaried part-time Clerk with defined responsibilities. But the Master, Mr Francis Bergin, and Court Assistant Kirkham managed to persuade Court Assistant Hammond MBE JP, who had been Managing Director of the Gravesend Building Society, to offer his services in an honorary capacity. He too was well versed in City matters, being for a number of years Secretary of the City Livery Club.

From 1 January 1995 the honorarium paid to the Hon. Clerk was increased to £2,500 per annum, which reflected the fact that he was not required to attend the Company office on a daily basis, increased again to £2,625 in January 1996. In January 1997 the financial position of the Company was such that the Court resolved, following proposals from Past Masters Jacques and Cauchi, that the idea of a salaried Clerk should be abandoned for the foreseeable future. But only nine months later, when Mr. Hammond relinquished office on becoming Junior Warden, it was conceded that a salaried appointment, albeit at a very modest salary (£7,800 in 1998/99), would have to be introduced.

Mr. Hammond was succeeded by Major Iain Stewart, recruited by means of an advertisement in national newspapers, who was to work in the Company office on three days per week and also to act as Secretary to the Charitable Trustees. In what has been a constant refrain in this and other Livery Companies over the years, a report from the Development Sub-committee in 1997 said of the Clerk's workload: "although he is paid for three days work per week, his hours at present represent a five-day working week". Following discussions with Major Stewart, it was agreed that he would retire on 29 February 2000 and that an ex-gratia tax-free payment would be made to him by the Company. The Court passed a resolution recording its appreciation of his dedicated service and commitment to the Company.

Past Master Grinsted volunteered to act as Hon. Clerk pending the appointment of a successor, and Past Master Jacques similarly undertook to act as Hon. Secretary to the Charitable Trust. Past Master Grinsted gave an undertaking to serve until October 2000, and the Court approved a draft notice to be sent to all Liverymen seeking candidates for the post. This elicited two enquiries, neither of whom was thought appropriate by the Master and Hon. Clerk. However, before the Court meeting on 1 February 2001 Court members were able to meet two other candidates and it was resolved that one of them, Liveryman Gaynor Lintott, should be offered the appointment on an initial salary of £10,000 per annum which she accepted, starting her probationary period working with Past Master Grinsted until her installation as Clerk on 19 July 2001.

Mrs Lintott brought to the appointment as Clerk her skill and previous career experience as a computer programmer. In the space of just one year, besides carrying out the routine functions of the office, she took it upon herself to install the first computer database of members and a Sage accounting system. She also designed the Company's first web-site at no significant cost to the Company and acted as webmaster for a number of years. These developments were to prove of immense benefit to the Company in the next decade as the revolution in electronic communications took hold.

In the meantime Past Master Grinsted had, at the Court's request, drafted a Loyal Address to Her Majesty The Queen Mother on the occasion of her 100th birthday. He delivered it in person to Buckingham Palace in his Rolls-Royce car. The Court expressed its warmest thanks to Past Master Grinsted for his eighteen months service as Hon. Clerk and presented him with a gift which was used to take himself and his wife, Patricia, on a short holiday in the United States of America.

Successive Hon. Clerks were supported by an Assistant Clerk for some of the time. These were paid honoraria, the rate in 1996 being just £1,050 per annum. Liveryman John Jones filled this role very efficiently, with particular reference to the financial affairs of the Company, for many years until standing down in July 1996. He was succeeded by Liveryman David Lee until December 1997, and from July 1999 until October 2000 by Mrs Sandra Tyre who had been a tower of strength as the secretary in the office since the very early days of the Company's existence. In October 2000, however, the Court decided to withdraw the post of Assistant Clerk and not to make a new appointment. As a result, Mrs. Tyre was offered retirement and the Honorary Freedom of the Company, both of which she accepted.

In 1997 Mrs Lillian Pridham had been employed as an additional secretary on an initial salary of £2,775 per annum, later increased significantly. She retired in January 2002 when she accepted an immediate payment of salary in lieu of notice and an ex-gratia tax-free payment of £500.

That the office practices during the early part of the period were a little less than perfect was illustrated in 1995 by the absence of a statutory display of an certificate of employer's liability insurance and by a report from the Hon. Assistant Clerk that insurance cover for the Company could be obtained at about one third of the premium paid in the previous year. In 1999 the numbering of Court minutes jumped from 810 to 1007 without any explanation which illustrated some of the concerns.

THE COURT

Court members obviously took a keen interest in all aspects of the Company's affairs. The size of the Court and selection processed caused some debate in 1997 and a small working party was set up under Past Master Bergin to consider the matter. Thus in April 1998 it was decided that candidates would be only nominated twice, after which unsuccessful candidates could not be re-nominated for at least two years. In 2000 the optimum size of the voting membership was set at twenty.

It is not proposed to name all those Liverymen who served as Court Assistants during the years 1994-2001, but it is thought right to name those who did not, for one reason or another, normally on grounds of ill health or death, proceed to the office of Warden. They are Court Assistants Gordon Bristow, Denis Child CBE, Deputy Edward Clements, Alderman Sir Roger Cork, Sidney Donald, Ronald Gardner, Susan Hughes, David Probert CBE and Richard Pugh DL. The pre-nominal titles and post-nominal letters indicate the wealth of talent that we lost in these eight Court Assistants, but Susan Hughes did become Master World Trader in 2000/01.

Three of them were endowed with the distinction of Hon. Assistant. Gordon Bristow had fulfilled the role of Hon. Treasurer with both diligence and distinction. By early 2001 he was very ill and housebound, he accepted the honour just days before he died.

Sir Roger Cork had been admitted as an Hon. Freeman of the Company whilst Lord Mayor, after admission to the ICSA as a Fellow which the Institute's constitution permits. An unusual situation arose when it was suggested that he be elected to the Court. Sir Roger treasured his appointment as an Hon. Liveryman and did not want to lose it although he was prepared to pay his way. Did this render him ineligible for Court membership? This was one of the relatively rare occasions on which a formal vote was necessary. In July 2001 it was resolved, by seven votes to four with two abstentions, that he was eligible; and by nine votes to four that he should, if elected, retain the title of Hon. Liveryman. He was, of course, then elected but, sadly, he died in October 2002. Richard Pugh was appointed Hon. Assistant for five years in October 2003.

HONORARY FREEMEN AND LIVERYMEN

In January 1996 the then Master, Mr Clifford Grinsted, tabled a paper proposing two possible additions as Hon. Freemen. In discussion there

ABOVE LEFT: *Hon. Freeman Sir Robert Fellowes (now Hon. Liveryman The Lord Fellowes of Shotsam).* ABOVE RIGHT: *Mrs Sandra Tyre.*

was a general consensus in favour, with two dissenting voices. The Court emphasised that it wished to use the power of appointing Hon. Freemen sparingly, with the object of raising the prestige of the Company. One of the nominees, declined because he felt unable to fulfil the obligations to the Company. However Sir Robert Fellowes GCVO KCB, Private Secretary to Her Majesty The Queen, was pleased to accept. He was admitted at a private luncheon, hosted by the Master and attended by some Court members, at the Royal Air Force Club.

In 1997 Alderman Sir Roger Cork, the Lord Mayor, had been admitted as an Hon. Liveryman. In 1999 the Master, Group Captain John Constable, advised the Court that Sir Richard Wilson KCB, who was then Head of the Home Civil Service and with whom the Master had had dealings in the past, had accepted with pleasure an invitation to become an Hon. Freeman, and Sir Richard was admitted at a Court meeting held on 20 January 2000. The Court's perspicacity in inviting Sir Robert and Sir Richard to honour the Company in this way was subsequently confirmed when both were made Peers of the Realm!

As already mentioned Mrs Sandra Tyre accepted an invitation to become an Hon. Freeman in recognition of her long and faithful service and was admitted at the Livery Assembly on 19 October 2000.

HONORARY TREASURER AND HONORARY ARCHIVIST

Honorary Officers, in addition to the Master and Wardens, developed significant roles during the 1990s. In particular, Court Assistant Bristow was appointed the Company's first Hon. Treasurer in April 1998. As has already been recorded he had already been involved in the Company's financial affairs for three years. He served with great diligence until ill health forced his resignation in April 2001. He was succeeded by Court Assistant Spencer-Cotton. The post of Hon. Archivist was first mooted by Senior Warden Clifford Grinsted in January 1995, and Liveryman David Coward CMG OBE was appointed. He was unable to make much progress in assembling material in the first few years due to lack of storage space, but this was overcome when the Company office moved to Saddlers' House and storage

ABOVE: *Hon. Archivist Liveryman David Coward.*

space in the basement was made available. Papers and photographs going back to the early days of the Company were gradually assembled and histories of other Livery Companies obtained. Liveryman Coward made a presentation about his work to the Livery Assembly in 2000 and gave occasional reports to the Court.

HONORARY ALMONER

The idea of having an Hon. Almoner, to maintain contact with the widows of Liverymen was also first mooted by Mr Spencer-Cotton, as Chairman of the LLG in 1995 but no appointment was made for many years as it was thought that the role was adequately filled by the Chairman of the Membership Committee, the Hon. Chaplain and the Clerk. The issue was raised again in April 2001, but again no appointment was made.

HONORARY CHAPLAIN

The Company had been associated with the Priory Church of St Bartholomew the Great since the early days of the Company and the Rector had served as Hon. Chaplain to the Company. In 1995 The Reverend Dr Martin Dudley was appointed Rector, and became Hon. Chaplain in January 1996. By fortunate chance, the Master in 1996/97, Mr Geoffrey Finn, and his wife Miriam, were regular worshippers at this church and therefore relations looked to be set fair.

However in 1998/99, when the Master was Group Captain Constable, the relationship became a little strained. At the beginning of 2000 the Hon. Chaplain expressed, through Court Assistant Thorpe, his regret that the date for the Rivers Lecture that year fell on Ash Wednesday. The Court agreed that, when dates of functions were being set, dates of major festivals of each faith recognised by the Company should be avoided, if possible.

The then Junior Warden (Colonel Michael Dudding) resolved to improve things were he to be elected Master and, to that end, had a meeting with the Rector when he became Master Elect. One of the issues discussed was the identity of the preacher at the Annual Service in June 2001. Colonel Dudding had in mind inviting a Rabbi (Reverend Jonathan Romain) to preach, taking account of the number of Jewish Liverymen in the Company. Whilst he came away from the meeting with the impression that that would be acceptable, it became clear later that was not the case and Rector offered his resignation as Hon. Chaplain, which the Master accepted.

This was obviously a matter of considerable concern to Past Masters and the Court, and the Master therefore presented a written brief on these events to the Court meeting on 1 February 2001. In the light of this brief, the Court approved the Master's action. The venue for the service itself was changed to the nearby Church of St Sepulchre-without-Newgate, which by a happy coincidence was the Regimental Chapel of the Master's former regiment (Royal Fusiliers). The Priest-in-Charge, The Reverend Dr. Peter Mullen, was pleased to welcome Rabbi Romain as preacher. Thus began a long relationship with Peter

Mullen, who was installed as Hon. Chaplain to the Company at the Court meeting on 10 October 2001.

THE BEADLE

The post of Beadle to the Company is one which is very much in the public eye at the Company's formal functions. The appointment had been filled with great distinction from October 1977 by Mr Brian Abethell BEM, a former non-commissioned officer of the Scots Guards, who worked at Mansion House. He was paid a small honorarium (£945 in 1996). He resigned in October 1997 after retiring from the Mansion House staff. Mr Paul Grant, Beadle of the Saddlers' Company, agreed, with the permission of the Clerk of that Company, to replace him. But the workload of the Saddlers' Company increased so that Mr Grant offered his resignation as our Beadle after just two years in post. At that point the Senior Warden (Colonel Dudding) introduced Mr. Terence Young BEM, a former Territorial Army soldier, to the Master. After an interview by the Master and Wardens, Mr Young was recommended to the Court and took up the appointment in July 2000.

ABOVE: *Mr Brian Abethell.*　　ABOVE: *Mr Terence Young.*

THE AUDITOR

The final appointment to be mentioned is that of Auditor to the Company. Until the mid-1990s a small firm of accountants had examined and signed off the accounts. But after nearly 20 years in existence, the size of the Company's funds, the complexity of its accounts and the workload of the Hon. Treasurer had reached the stage at which it was considered appropriate to appoint someone from a more substantial firm. Through the good offices of the Hon. Clerk, Mr. Hammond, the Master (Mr Finn) appointed Mr Kevin Hayman of chartered accountants King & Taylor in Gravesend. The appointment was ratified by the Court in July 1997, and an excellent working relationship was built up with Mr Hayman over the following 13 years. Although he was always referred to as "the Auditor", he did in fact act as an independent examiner, a role which was less onerous than that of an auditor and less expensive for the Company.

SOME INDIVIDUAL LIVERYMEN

Finally, word should be mentioned of a few individuals who contributed, sometimes indirectly, to building up the standing of the Company. Those who were members of the Court when it first met were entitled to remain members for life. None were more conscious of this honour and responsibility than Founder Master Wedgwood and Past Masters Jacques, Marwood and Tutt. The Founder Master eventually decided that he would stand down from the Court in mid-1998. That decision was accepted by the Court with great regret; he had been a tower of strength to successive Masters when a seemingly intractable problem arose. His quiet, and often private, advice was valued by them all.

In similar fashion Past Master Phillips had been another tower of strength in the Company's early days, serving as Master in 1978/79 and again in 1986/87; he died in February 1998. Past Master Jacques stood down from the Court in 2011 due to ill health. His lengthy service, 13 years, as Chairman of the Charitable Trustees, provided a sound foundation for the growing financial strength of the Trust.

Past Master Tutt died in December 2011. She decried what she saw as a proliferation of committees, but nevertheless was not to be shifted easily from her place on the Finance and General Purposes Committee, nor as a Charitable Trustee. In July 2001, when the Court was considering committee membership for the year ahead, she "expressed surprise that she had not been included on the list" [for the Finance and General Purposes Committee]. It was pointed out that it had been the intention to provide some movement in the Committee structure to enable younger Liverymen to gain experience in the Company. Past Master Carine agreed to stand down from the Committee in favour of Past Master Tutt.

Liveryman Freddy Mead reached the age of 100 in 1998 and the Court sent him an illuminated Resolution of Congratulations, for which he was able to write a letter of thanks. It was also realised that as a veteran of the First World War, he was eligible to be appointed to the Legion d'Honneur, a distinction which the French government was granting to all surviving veterans to mark the 80th anniversary of the end of that war. An application was submitted to the French Embassy in London and the award was granted but, sadly, Mr. Mead died before it could be presented.

Another war veteran, of the Second World War, was Liveryman The Reverend George Gerrard, whose autobiography *By George* was published in 1998; it is a fascinating story of life as a hospital administrator before and after the war, and of his service in the wartime Army (evacuation through Dunkirk in particular).

Liveryman Keith Lawrey was appointed Honorary Foundation Clerk to the Guild of Educators in 1977 and has steered its progress to Company status since.

The following were granted British honours during the period:

Liveryman Donald Fleet	OBE	July 1995
Court Assistant Donald Kirkham	CBE	January 1996
Court Assistant Michael Dudding	OBE	January 1996
Court Assistant David Probert	CBE	July 1996

Hon. Freeman The Rt. Hon. Sir Robert Fellowes	GCVO	July 1996
Hon. Freeman The Rt. Hon. Sir Robert Fellowes	GCB	January 1998
Court Assistant David Wright	MBE	January 2000
Court Assistant Alderman Clive Martin	Knight Bachelor	January 2001
Hon. Freeman Sir Richard Wilson	GCB	July 2001

Sadly, in 1998/99 and 1999/2000 the Masters were either unable to devote sufficient attention to Company affairs as they would have liked. Group Captain Constable had an arduous job as head of administration in the complex building that is the Central Criminal Court. His death on 18 November 1999, just one month after standing down as Master, came as a shock, but was not a surprise. Mr. Hammond was hit hard by the death of his wife, Audrey, in May 1999 and those who knew him well recognised that he might be in the very early stages of the dementia that claimed his final years of life. But the Wardens, Clerk and Court members, conscious of his great service to the Company in the past, did their best to ensure that he had their full support in enjoying the reward of serving as Master of the Company he loved.

No record of these years could omit mention of Liverymen Mollie Harris and Thelma Wilson. They have more mentions in Court minutes than any other non-Court members of the Company, except Mrs Sylvia Moys. For a number of years they were respectively Secretary and Chairman of the LLG. Mollie master-minded the organisation of LLG events, and operated the Group's bank account. Her type-written minutes stood out as the last of an era. She also later served as Secretary of the Education Committee.

Other regular supporters of Company functions were Liverymen Mary Phillips and Betty Rees, who both travelled up from South Wales, Peter Hawley and his wife Doreen, Leslie Needham and his wife Vera and George Pannett and his wife Marjory.

Mention should also be made of the Masters' ladies in these years – Madeleine Cauchi, Patricia Grinsted, Miriam Finn, Sally Carine, Karin Constable, Mary Cornick (Mr. Hammond's daughter) and Jan Dudding. A Master's Lady's badge had been presented to the Company in 1982

FAR LEFT: *Liveryman Mollie Harris.*

LEFT: *Liveryman Thelma Wilson.*

by Past Master Marwood and was thereafter presented by the outgoing Master's Lady to the incoming Master's Lady at the Installation Court meeting or at the Livery Assembly. There was a tense moment in 2000 when the badge slipped from Mary Cornick's hand and fell into Jan Dudding's bosom. The ladies formed welcome additions to the receiving line of Master and Wardens at formal Company functions, and were most gracious supporters of their husbands throughout their years in office as a Warden and as Master. In addition, it gave members of the Company great pleasure to see the Lady Mayoress in 1999/2000, Lindy Martin, working tirelessly in support of Court Assistant Alderman Clive Martin as Lord Mayor.

THE CHARITABLE TRUSTEES

The Chairman of the Charitable Trustees throughout the period 1994 – 2001 was Past Master Jacques. He resolutely protected the independence of the Trustees whenever Court members, including Masters and Wardens, made suggestions about the way in which the Trustees should allocate grants. The range of activities of the Trust is dealt with in Chapter Four.

POLICIES

The Company Office

At the beginning of this period the Company shared an office with the Clockmakers' Company, in St. Dunstan's House in Carey Lane which was due to be redeveloped. Before handing over as Hon. Clerk to Mr Hammond, Mr Challis secured the agreement, in 1994, of the City of London Corporation for display of the major items of the Company's treasures in the Members' Bar in Guildhall. Mr Hammond and the Clockmakers' Clerk, Group Captain Peter Gibson, got on well with each other and this led to the introduction of a very successful and enjoyable Joint Carol Service.

But by April 1996 the need to find new accommodation was becoming urgent, with an annual cost not exceeding £7,500 being stipulated. In October 1996 the Master, Mr Grinsted, and Hon. Clerk, Mr Hammond,

were able to report to the Court that new accommodation had been secured on the third floor of Saddlers' House, Gutter Lane EC2 within the financial parameters set by the Finance and General Purposes Committee. A lease of 20 years would be granted, with a break clause at the end of the first 5 years and rent reviews in June 2002, 2007 and 2012. Access would be easier than at St. Dunstan's House; space for the storage of gowns, wine and other paraphernalia would be available and, if necessary, secure storage of the Company's treasures then displayed in the Guildhall Club. In order to make the office self-sufficient, £7,700 was allocated from a Relocation Reserve for the purchase of office furniture, word processing equipment and a photocopier. An informal arrangement would provide use of meeting rooms on the fifth floor free of charge (subsequently revoked some years later by the lessees of that floor). In all, the total costs of the move, which took place on 1 November 1996, amounted to £11,714. The legal work regarding the lease, of 20 years to 23 June 2017, was undertaken by solicitors Brown Cooper (later Brown Cooper Monier-Williams).

Court Meetings

Court meetings were normally held in conjunction with a Court or Livery luncheon in January, April, July and October each year. Venues for meetings, excluding meetings adjourned to the dates of Livery Assemblies, were St. Dunstan's House (3), Haberdashers' Hall (then in Staining Lane) (2), Saddlers' Hall (15), Wax Chandlers' Hall (1), Barber Surgeons' Hall (4), Aldermen's Court Room, Guildhall (1), Drapers' Hall (1), Tallow Chandlers' Hall (1) and Armourers' Hall (1). The cost of using Livery Halls was not insubstantial, but in 1996 the Court accepted the cost as a proper expense.

Recruitment

Recruitment became a serious issue in 1995. At first prospective candidates were entertained at private lunches with around six hosts and six guests, but this was soon found not to be cost-effective. A joining rate of about 50% had been achieved, but at a cost of some £2,500. In 1998 invitations were issued to 38 members of the ICSA to attend a lunch, but only four accepted. Later that year it was decided to maintain a list of all approaches made and record progress in following them up. The publicity to be gained by the attendance of the Master and Clerk at the Institute's annual Convocation was also recognised.

In April 1999 the Chairman wrote to various chairmen of branches of the ICSA extolling the virtues of the Company. The Committee minutes of June 1999, noting that 10 Liverymen had joined in the last (Company) year added: "Interestingly, four of them have been women members". This would not have been commented upon in the following year when Court Assistant Adèle Thorpe joined the Committee and Liveryman Sylvia Moys, an active member of London Branch, was co-opted.

The Committee set itself the target of recruiting 10 Freemen per year, and by 2000 the list of potential applicants consisted of 57 names. The Committee began to meet quarterly instead of six-monthly. Shorter evening briefings, organised by the successive Committee chairmen, were found to be more cost-effective. In May 2000 an informal reception at Marshall House SE1, attended by 9 out of the 10 applicants invited, resulted in 5 applications to join. In 2001 a leaflet entitled *"An Outline for Potential Liverymen"* was prepared by Liveryman Moys, and the Master, Colonel Dudding, published an article in "ICSA Matters" which attracted a good response. The results of these various efforts are reflected in the numbers admitted to the Freedom of the Company by calendar year over the period:

1994 - 4	1997 - 12	2000 - 13
1995 - 5	1998 - 12	2001 - 11.
1996 - 8	1999 - 13	

One other possible recruitment method was identified in the 1990s – a Junior Corpus, or Apprenticeships as it was later called. This is described in detail in Chapter Five.

THE INSTITUTE OF CHARTERED SECRETARIES AND ADMINISTRATORS

The Company wanted to maintain cordial relations with the Institute, although not wanting to appear to be the creature of the Institute and beholden to it in any way. The report of the Long Term Planning Committee in 1994 commended a strengthening of the link, and to that end requested successive Masters to contribute annually a brief report about the Livery for publication in "Administrator", the Institute's magazine. Past Master Jacques had been appointed the Company's "link man" and his role was confirmed, under the auspices of the Finance and General Purposes Committee when that Committee was established.

In 1997 the Master, Mr Finn, held the first of what were to become annual liaison meetings between the Master, Wardens and Clerk from the Company and the President, Chief Executive and some senior officers from the Institute. In early 1999 Past Master Jacques was succeeded by Court Assistant Wright. Of particular benefit to the Company were the contacts between the Company's Membership Committee and the Institute's membership department, which resulted in potential Liverymen being identified. That relationship was made even stronger when the Institute's Chief Executive, Mr John Ainsworth, became a co-opted member of the Membership Committee in 1997 and by the co-option to the Education Committee of Freeman David Lilley, the Institute's Director of Education, from mid-1999.

In late 1999 the Court was pleased to receive a message from the United Kingdom President of the Institute, Mr Peter Hammonds, saying: "The Council wishes to place on record its congratulations to the Livery for the wonderful efforts made, and the generous response from the Worshipful Company and its Liverymen in support of the Lord Mayor as a fellow Liveryman of the Company and as a member of the Institute".

PUBLIC RELATIONS

Public relations was an issue that the Livery Liaison Group considered as early as 1995, when the Group asked the Finance and General Purposes Committee to consider the most appropriate method of publicising the Company to the media and general public. No significant initiatives appear to have resulted from this and three years later Founder Master Wedgwood expressed disappointment that publicity for the Company was in the hands of the Education Committee. The only regular internal communication/publicity was in the form of Newsletters prepared by the Clerk; a new format was adopted for Edition No. 84 in 2000. The constraint in doing more was that of lack of staff resources.

In 2000 the Livery Consultative Committee, a body run from Guildhall, stressed the need for proper internal communications within Companies and external publicity. At about that time 16 Livery Companies (not including ours) had come together to draft what became known as the

"Livery 2000 Initiative", aimed at disseminating best practice and making recommendations about recruitment and retention of Liverymen, and the future role of Livery Companies. The report included 38 examples of best practice. The Court noted them and concluded that the Company either had steps in hand to implement them, or did not have the resources to do so. The Court did, however, agree to consider the selection of an experienced Liveryman as Editor of a Company Newsletter, but the vacancy had not been filled by 2001.

FUNCTIONS AND OTHER ACTIVITIES

Formal Events

This is not the place for descriptions of the Company's formal functions over the years. They are listed in Appendix Five. What can be given is a brief overview and comments on significant changes. The story starts in 1994 when the then Master, Mr Bergin, introduced the first very successful formal lunch for Liverymen and their guests at Barber-Surgeons' Hall. The established pattern was for a Livery Dinner in November, a Ladies Banquet (if possible in the Mansion House) in about April, a Livery Luncheon in July and simple refreshments after the Livery Assembly in October. While it was custom to invite guests other than spouses/partners to the dinner in November, Court minute 584/1995 asked that "Liverymen again be reminded tactfully that the dinner was not the occasion to invite spouses/partners". Cost was of course a factor and in 1995 Court Assistant Bristow argued that the refreshments after the Assembly should not be subsidised (by £10 per head), but the Court did not support him. In January 1996 the Court did, however, consider guidance about responsibilities for payment for important guests. Less formal lunches were held in the Guildhall Club in conjunction with some Court meetings. A precedent was set in 1997 for joint functions: a musical evening with the Masons' Company at the Guildhall School of Music and Drama and a historical and musical presentation with Broad Street Ward Club, both of which were deemed to have been very successful.

In 1998 the Master, Rear Admiral Carine, proposed that, as a trial, the formal Luncheon in July should be replaced by a reception, lecture and buffet supper; and the establishment of a Company Common Hall (Assembly) associated with an Installation Dinner to be held in October, replacing the customary dinner in November. Whilst it was not customary for spouses/partners to attend the Installation Dinner, it was agreed that in view of the important support given by the wives of the incoming and outgoing Masters the Company they should be allowed to attend. These trial changes were approved, albeit with some regret at the loss of the luncheon in July.

In April 2000 the Court's attention was drawn to the financial losses being suffered from social functions and future Masters were asked to consider limiting prestigious, formal luncheons to one per year. However, by 2001 not only had the Livery Luncheon in July been reinstated, but a "Family Lunch", with spouses/partners, was held in April to mark the service of the Immediate Past Master, Mr Hammond, Court Assistant Sir Clive Martin (Millennium Lord Mayor) and Court Assistant Robin Eve (Millennium Chief Commoner). That lunch proved to be a great success and so became a standing feature of the annual programme thereafter, albeit in place of the Livery Luncheon in July. In 2001 the Mansion House was unavailable for our Livery Banquet and Carpenters' Hall was used instead. A similar situation was to occur in 2005 when Haberdashers' Hall was used.

RIGHT: *Carpenters' Hall.*

The Livery Assembly

The Livery Assembly has been a continuing part of the Company's annual programme since before 1994. Traditionally, the outgoing Master presents a review of his year in office. Chairmen of committees and of the LLG present reports on their activities and a ballot for places in the Group is held. Prior to 1995 the Assembly followed immediately after a Court meeting and was held at various locations including the Institute's headquarters at 16 Park Crescent, or the Court Room at Carey Lane. In 1995 Haberdashers' Hall was the venue and Livery Halls were used

LEFT: *Pikemen of The Honourable Artillery Company at Haberdashers Hall, 2005.*

thereafter because their surroundings were more conducive to the occasion. In 1996 the installation of the new Master and Wardens took place at the Assembly and supper followed. In 1996 an Annual Report and Accounts were issued to Liverymen for the first time in fulfilment of the thinking that Livery Companies generally should be more open with their members. In 1998 the arrangements were changed again, as already described and have so remained until the present day.

Church Services

A church service also formed a regular part of the Company's year, normally in June on the evening of Common Hall for the election of Sheriffs, and initially followed by a buffet supper. Selection of the preacher, if not the Company's Hon. Chaplain, is the responsibility of the Master. Before 2001, services were held in the Priory Church of St Bartholomew the Great by kind permission of the Rector. In 1995 the preacher was Reverend Stephen Green, then General Manager and Group Treasurer of the Hong Kong & Shanghai Bank, of whom we were to hear more some 15 years later in his business capacity. The meal afterwards had been upgraded to a formal dinner, attended by 81 people. In 1996, under Master Clifford Grinsted, the service was preceded by a concert of sacred music performed by the London Salvation Army Band and the Company's thanksgiving hymn was performed for the first time. Afterwards 105 people dined in Ironmongers' Hall.

Joint Carol Services, based on the Company's relationship with the Clockmakers' Company, were held each December since the mid nineties, with retiring collections being given to charities concerned with the homeless. The two Companies alternated in making the arrangements for venue and supper afterwards, although a number of other Companies participated as well.

Inter-Livery Sport and Pastimes

Sport has played a small part in the Company's life, in particular swimming and golf. In 1995 Past Master Marwood raised a team for "City Dip", an event in the Lord Mayor's Appeal; the team raised £1,689, more than any other Livery Company. Another good result was achieved in 1999 when 16 swimmers raised £6,200, of which Immediate Past Master Carine raised £1,800 in sponsorship on his own. In 2001 Freeman Alastair Friend took over as organiser. Others who swam during these years included Sir Alexander Graham, Michael and Jan Dudding, Donald Kirkham, Paul Phelps, David Wright and Adèle Thorpe's daughter, Katy.

Golf was taken up in 1997 when Court Assistant Wright was appointed Golf Captain. A three-sided tournament against the City Livery Club and the Chartered Accountants' Company saw our team come second to the City Livery Club. In 1998 a Company team came 20th out of 54 teams in the inter-Livery Prince Arthur Cup, but a match against the Chartered Accountants' Company was lost. In 1999 the Company moved up the table, coming 11th out of 55 teams. In 2001, under the Master Elect, Mr Philip Marcell, a match was played against the Adjutant General's Corps. Others who played over this period included Liverymen Michael Foulkes, Ian Newton and Geoffrey Shepheard.

In the mid-1990s the Company entered a pair in the Inter-Livery Bridge Competition. Past Master Marwood and Court Assistant (later Master) Finn were the main protagonists, usually coming about halfway up the table of rankings at the end of the evenings.

Regional Lunches

Regional lunches have been held at intervals as a way of maintaining contact with Liverymen who find travel to London onerous, being held in Hathersage, Derbyshire (1995), Bath and Birmingham (1996), and Leeds (2001). But the wide geographical spread of Liverymen outside London and the South East has always meant that numbers have not exceeded 30 at any one lunch. "Master's Weekends" were initiated at some time during the period. Since they were organised by the Master of the year, possibly with some support from the LLG, they are not recorded in the Court minutes; but Mr. Hammond's weekend in Bruges in September 2000 was well supported by 26 participants.

The City Civic

Support for the Lord Mayor and Corporation has always played a strong part in the Company's activities. Hon. Liveryman Sir Alexander Graham, Hon. Freeman Sir Roger Cork and Court Assistant Alderman Clive Martin gave us good links into the Court of Aldermen; Liverymen have been encouraged to attend Common Hall for the elections of Lord Mayor and Sheriffs; standing for election to Common Council has also been encouraged (with Hon. Liveryman George Challis, Court Assistants Edward Clements and Robin Eve, and Liveryman Sylvia Moys (elected in 2001) all serving for many years, with two (Messrs Challis and Eve) being appointed Chief Commoner.

In 1996 the Company made a presentation at the usual ceremony in Guildhall to Alderman Martin following his taking office as a Sheriff. In September 1999 Group Captain Constable (Master) was succeeded as Secondary of London and Under Sheriff, responsible for the administration of the Central Criminal Court, by Past Master Cauchi.

A real highlight was the election of Alderman Martin to be Lord Mayor in

RIGHT: *Past Master Cauchi as Secondary of London and Under Sheriff.*

Master John Constable as Secondary and Under Sheriff.

ABOVE: *The Master, Mr Wilfred Hammond, presenting the silver secretary bird to Sir Clive Martin, Lord Mayor.*

1999/2000. On the day of his accession, the many gifts presented to him included a solid silver paperweight in the form of a secretary bird from the Company. A joint Company/ Institute float took part in the Lord Mayor's Show on 13 November 1999 – a good advertisement for the Company and profession. A cheque for £2,000 was presented towards his mayoral Appeal, and Senior Warden Dudding played a leading role in the organisation of a very successful and challenging fund-raising event involving some 400 Liverymen of many Companies exercising their right as Freemen of the City of London to drive sheep to market in the City over London Bridge without paying tax. Liveryman Ron Hancock, dressed as "Little Bo Peep" and his wife, Clare, came from Yorkshire to take part, and raised £600 for Barnardo's,

ABOVE: *Terence Young, Beadle, herding sheep across London Bridge.*

the Lord Mayor's charity. In all, members of the Company raised over £12,000 for that charity during the year, of which the biggest contribution came from "City Dip".

In 2001 Liveryman Sylvia Moys was elected as member of Common Council for the Ward of Aldgate. This was followed later in that year by the first award of the Sir Edward Howard Memorial Prize, named after our sponsoring Alderman (see Chapter One) to a student at the Business School of the University of East London, presented by Sir Edward's son, Sir David Howard Bt., during his tenure as Lord Mayor. The Master and Chairman of the Charitable Trustees, the University's Vice-Chancellor and School Dean and the student, from Finland, were given half an hour of the Lord Mayor's time in Mansion House before leaving for a celebratory lunch.

The Armed Forces

Visits to units of the Armed Forces, arranged through the Company's affiliated branches of the three Services have also played a prominent part in the Company's programme. They are described in more detail in Chapter Six.

FINANCE

The Broad Picture

A picture of the general state of the Company's finances over the period has already been given. In 1996 the accounting year changed from 31 July to 30 June to allow more time for production of the accounts before the October Court meeting and Assembly. In January 1997 collection of quarterage by Direct Debit was considered as a means of easing the office workload, but our then bankers would not agree to operate such a system for us.

In 1997 not only were the accounts forecasting yet another deficit, but they were in a muddle. In January 1998 the Finance and General Purposes Committee asked Court Assistant Bristow to assist the Clerk in unravelling the tangled set of accounts so that a true position could be established. Very high hospitality costs were part of the problem, but Mr. Bristow also said that the deficit was due mainly to "the Grace and Favour existence that the Company had enjoyed in the past. Times had changed and the Company was having to operate as a commercial entity, which in turn generated new costs". He concluded his report on the state of the accounts by saying: "If I state that I have not been happy with what I have discovered during the past month, this has to be a massive understatement. The simple truth is that what I have found reflects badly on all of us. This is not in any way intended to be a reflection on the Clerk, who is not professionally qualified in this discipline and, thankfully, recognises his own limitations."

Mr Bristow later confirmed the Company's true position as having a likely revenue deficit in excess of £10,000 in the year. In May 1998 the Master took the unusual step of writing a personal letter to every

Liveryman explaining the need for an exceptional increase in Quarterage for 1998/99 and asking for improved attendance at the Company's major functions so that they did not make a loss. An ad hoc sub-committee consisting of Messrs Carine (Master), Hammond (Junior Warden), Kirkham (as chairman) and Bristow was formed to review the accounts and ensure that the Company lived within its means in future.

When considering the budget for 1998/99 the Court was told that "the Company should for the first time in five years be showing an operating surplus". The work of the Strategic Planning Sub-committee in 1999 marked the beginning of a significant improvement. But it was a slow process. In April 2000 the Chairman of the Finance and General Purposes Committee (Court Assistant Kirkham) reported that "while the Company's basic costs had been well controlled, the greatest losses were to be found in optional expenditure (mainly for Court luncheons, dinner, meetings etc)"; and confirmed that as soon as a proper accounting system had been introduced into the office, the Court would thereafter receive regular financial reports. Quarterly management accounts were introduced in October 2000 following the installation of a SAGE accounting system. Finally, financial authorities were set out for the first time, April 2001. Thus was order brought out of chaos! All that remains here is to flesh out some of the numerical details.

Fines

(Payments made on admission to the Court and on promotion)

	1994	1997	1999	2000
Admission to the Freedom	£100	£100	£370	£390
Admission to the Livery	£500	£500	£685	£720
Election to Court/Warden	£50/100	£100		£200
Election as Master	£150	£150		£300

In 2000 the Court agreed that the charge to Liverymen under 40 might be 50% on admission, with the balance to be paid within 12 months of admission.

Quarterage
(A subscription but actually paid annually)

1994/95	£100
1995/96	£100
1996/97	£135
1997/98	£165
1998/99	£200
1999/2000	£210, with an over-70 discount at £173, if desired
2000/01	£220, with an over-70 discount at £180, if desired
2001/02	No change from the previous year

In October 2000 the Court agreed that Freemen might be charged 50% of the amount paid by Liverymen.

Master's Endowment Fund
(renamed Capital Reserve Fund, April 1997)

This fund was set up by Dr Roy Harris (Master 1991/1992) who was particularly concerned about the small capital base of the Company. Court Minute 695 records that "The object of this Fund shall be to establish the capital base required by the Court of Mayor and Aldermen in the City to sustain a Livery Company, and that until this Fund reaches that state and is in a position to match the Court's ongoing requirements in this respect no use of either income or capital shall either be contemplated or permitted save in exceptional circumstances with the specific resolution of the Court".

In 1997 a one-off appeal for a voluntary contribution of £500 per Liveryman, and legacies was approved. This in large measure accounted for an increase of £21,578 by mid-1998. In July 1997 the Court agreed that all fines were to be credited to the Capital Reserve Fund, but this was amended one year later when it was decided to regard realised profits on the sale of investments, and fines on election to the Court and on promotion to Warden and Master, as revenue items.

Investment Performance

Value of the Portfolio managed by Cazenove Ltd. and overseen by the Investment Sub-Committee

	At cost	Market value
31 July 1994		£107,000
31 July 1995	£70,992	£91,576
30 June 1996	£70,867	£100,082
30 June 1997	£62,147	£84,601
30 June 1998	£74,293	£121,037
30 June 1999	£84,314	£134,056
30 June 2000	£84,669	£112,129
30 June 2001	£99,838	£102,588

In April 2000 Liveryman Derek Bartlett was appointed a member of the Sub-committee to review the performance of the asset managers. As a result, in October 2000 the Court authorised the Sub-committee to negotiate a change from a segregated portfolio to a collective investment scheme. Between 30 June and 19 September 2001, the value of our portfolio declined by over £8,000 (partly due to the effect on stock markets caused by the attacks on the World Trade Center and the Pentagon in the USA).

Budgets

1995/96	£28,410
1996/97	£37,010
1997/98	£38,100
1998/99	£48,950 of which salaries, National Insurance and honoraria amounted to almost 50%.
1999/2000	£49,850
2000/01	£48,700
2001/02	£46,564, of which salaries etc amount to 44%

Revenue Account - Surpluses and Deficits

1993/94	+ £4,617
1994/95	– £9,441
1995/96	– £8,752
1996/97	– £9,803
1997/98	– £1,812
1998/99	+ £711
1999/2000	– £5,778 of which £5,626 was tax on investment gains over the previous four years
2000/01	+ £5,848

Net Assets
(including Master's Endowment/Capital Reserve Fund)

1994	£87,186
1995	£81,799
1996	£80,724
1997	£79,654
1998	£101,232
1999	£113,715
2000	£118,815
2001	£131,318

AN OVERVIEW OF THE PERIOD AND THE CONTRIBUTIONS OF THE MASTERS

By 1994 the Company was well established, but facing the need to move out of the temporary office accommodation at Carey Lane. The level of quarterage income did not reflect the Company's real needs and recruiting of new members was at a low level. As a result, by the mid 1990s the Company faced severe financial difficulties, which perhaps the Court was slow to address. The problems were compounded by a rapid turn over of Clerks (five in eight years) and inadequate financial accounting records, both reflecting the lack of income to the Company. By the end of the decade, however, measures had been put in hand to overcome these problems, not least the appointment for the first time of a paid Clerk and an Hon. Treasurer. By 2000/01 the annual accounts showed a respectable surplus, in stark contrast to the deficits of earlier years, and recruiting was greatly improved. Many members of the Company helped in this transformation. Every single Master made a significant contribution before, whilst in that office, or shortly afterwards and it is worth ending this perhaps troubled chapter by highlighting their most significant achievements. Thus:

Mr Francis Bergin 1993/94

Launched the wide-ranging and influential Long Term Planning Committee; master minded a change of Hon. Clerk; initiated private lunches for potential applicants; held the first Livery Luncheon with a speaker (the Chairman of Barclays's Bank); and later, as Chairman of the Recruitment Committee paved the way for a significant increase in Liverymen.

Colonel George Cauchi 1994/95

Established the Finance and General Purpose and Recruitment Committees; appointed the first Hon. Archivist; oversaw the first election for chairmanship of the LLG by its own members and as Secondary and Under Sheriff at the Central Criminal Court, enhanced the standing of the Company in the City of London.

Mr Clifford Grinsted 1995/96

Supported the establishment and work of a Development sub-committee: composed the Company's hymn; was instrumental in the admission of Sir Robert (later Lord) Fellowes as an Hon. Freeman; drafted a revised Constitution and Ordinances and secured the approval of the Court of Aldermen thereto; introduced the publication to the Livery of an Annual Report and Accounts and, as an emergency measure, served as Hon. Clerk from March 2000 to July 2001.

Mr Geoffrey Finn 1996/97

Oversaw a 20% increase in quarterage; increased fines significantly; set clear objectives for the Capital Reserve Fund; was instrumental in the establishment of an Education Committee; appointed the first salaried Clerk, initiated a most fruitful link with the London Chamber of Commerce and Industry – Commercial Educational Trust; admitted Sir Roger Cork, Lord Mayor, as an Hon. Liveryman and initiated annual meetings between the Master and Wardens and the President and officers of the Institute.

Rear Admiral James Carine 1997/98

Made a major contribution to the financial stability of the Company, by explaining to individual Liverymen the need for a further 20% increase in quarterage: saw the appointment of the Company's first Hon. Treasurer; chaired the important Strategic Planning Sub-committee in 1999 which set the Company on the road to financial viability and presided over a significant increase in the numbers being admitted to the Freedom of the Company.

Group Captain John Constable 1998/99

Chaired the Development Sub-committee in 1996; was instrumental in the admission of Sir Richard (later Lord) Wilson as an Hon. Freeman and, as Secondary and Under Sheriff at the Central Criminal Court, further enhanced the standing of the Company in the City of London.

Mr Wilfred Hammond 1999/2000

Served as Hon. Clerk from 1994 to 1997; negotiated the lease for the occupation of an office in Saddlers' House and master minded the move from Carey Lane; served as President of the United Wards Club in 1996/97; introduced King & Taylor as auditors; had the unenviable task of reducing staff numbers; had the privilege of supporting members of the Company in the offices of Lord Mayor and Chief Commoner and enhanced the image of the Company in the City by his inspired choice of a speaker at the Rivers Lecture, more details of which are given in Chapter Five.

Colonel Michael Dudding 2000/01

Appointed the second salaried Clerk; managed an unplanned change of Hon. Chaplain; introduced an Apprentice scheme; instituted the first "Family Luncheon" for greater involvement of spouses of Liverymen; chaired a working party to review the structure and membership of all committees; initiated regular co-ordination meetings of Master, Wardens, Hon. Treasurer and Clerk and invited the Court to consider how to celebrate the Company's 25th anniversary in 2003.

In addition to these achievements, all the Masters had a significant time commitment representing the Company and the profession in the City of London and elsewhere. In 1995/96 Mr Grinsted reported over 90 external engagements as Master and this number tended to rise in subsequent years.

It would be fair to say that these Masters laid down the foundations for the success of the Company from 2002 onwards described in the next Chapter.

CHAPTER THREE

INTO THE TWENTY-FIRST CENTURY

2001–2012

By Court Assistant Christina Parry

From its inauguration, the Company has taken pride in its status as a modern livery company, and as the Millennium turned, new ways were found to establish its authority and confidence.

LOYAL ALLEGIANCE

The Livery treats seriously its duties to the Crown, the City and to society. Each member, in becoming a Freeman of the Company, and then of the City, takes the oath of allegiance, loyally pledging to honour and promote all that is honourable in civic duty. These promises are re-affirmed on being admitted to the Livery, and when taking senior office in the Company.

As a mark of respect the Company has been delighted to submit Loyal Addresses on significant occasions, such as recent ones listed. These give chance to pay tribute to the service given to the nation by members of the Royal Family, and have received generous royal acknowledgements, always greatly encouraging to the Master and the Court. Some of the significant Loyal Addresses submitted by the Company have been to:

Her Majesty Queen Elizabeth the Queen Mother on her 100th birthday (2000)

Her Majesty Queen Elizabeth II on the Company's Silver Jubilee (2003)

Her Majesty Queen Elizabeth II on her 80th birthday (2006)

Her Majesty Queen Elizabeth II on her Golden Jubilee (2002) and on her Diamond Jubilee (2012).

Past Master Clifford Grinsted drove in his Rolls Royce to Buckingham Palace to deliver two of the Loyal Addresses. He had also used this car when he attended on Lord Fellowes (then Sir Robert and Private Secretary to HM The Queen) in a private ceremony when Lord Fellowes was enrolled as an Honorary Freeman and signed the Company's Freedom Roll in 1996.

The nation celebrated the Queen's Diamond Jubilee in 2012 and Livery Companies joined together to honour this remarkable event. They were granted the distinction of hosting the receptions at Guildhall and Mansion House which followed the solemn service of thanksgiving at St Paul's Cathedral, as well as hosting the grand luncheon in Westminster Hall on 5 June 2012. The Company was honoured to be part of the livery movement's tribute to Her Majesty. At the Master's table were the Company's guests: Squadron Leader Beverley Gill, who performed exceptional work in supporting Service personnel in Afghanistan and Libya and won the Company's prize for the best performance in the field by a member of the RAF's Personnel Branch in 2011, Mustafizur Rahman, the 16-year old Head Boy of Rokeby School, who has shown exceptional leadership in the school, Joe Woodward, from Guernsey, winner of the Company's prize for the best results in the Institute's 2011 examinations (and recently admitted ACIS) and Anneka Kingan, an Apprentice of the Company (and a recent Graduate ICSA).

THE ROYAL CHARTER

In 2008 the Company received the ultimate recognition of its status and maturity. A petition for a Royal Charter had been submitted in 2007 to The Queen in Council. Approval, and grant of the Royal Charter, was a distinction worthy of great celebration. Commemorative functions ranged from the solemn presentation of the Royal Charter at St Michael's Church, Cornhill, to the truly sumptuous banquet at Drapers' Hall, and also included a number of fun events to raise money for charity.

In accepting the accolade, the Company has interpreted the Royal Charter as offering a continuing challenge, as well as a mark of highest recognition, signalling the obligation to contribute positively to national life, to the City, and to the chartered profession. The Royal Charter now serves as the bedrock of Company governance, setting out fundamental responsibilities and duties, and providing authority and guidance when difficult judgements have to be made. This secure foundation has fostered a healthy balance between innovation and tradition, in which the Company takes pride.

This chapter merely touches on what was perhaps the most significant event for the Company in recent years. The history of the Charter grant is discussed in Chapter Nine written by Past Master Clifford Grinsted, who orchestrated the Petition and by Past Master Adèle Thorpe, who gives a personal reminiscence of the presentation itself.

As a continuing commemoration, the Court agreed that the annual July Family Luncheon should be redesignated as the Royal Charter Luncheon.

GROWING RECOGNITION

The Royal Charter was the culmination of a decade which saw the Company grow in stature, giving opportunity for some memorable events. The tradition continued of holding an annual church service, where the Livery offered thanks and re-dedicated itself to its mission and ideals, and commemorated those who had played a part in its activities. To facilitate wider attendance, it was later decided that the Annual Church Service would be held immediately before the Royal Charter Luncheon, in a combined event. As Almoner and Past Master David Wright commented one year: "the function was greatly enjoyed by everyone present particularly those widows and widowers who had been specially invited and whose husbands and wives were named in our prayers. It was very gratifying to hear that the service brought them great comfort…".

Formal dinners or luncheons have provided a platform for distinguished speakers to honour the Company's achievements. They have also enabled the Company to thank and entertain guests who have offered support and encouragement, while affirming commitment to the future as an innovative and respected modern Livery Company. A list of

ABOVE: *The scene at a Company Banquet in Mansion House.*

principal guests entertained at the Company's Banquets is at Appendix Five.

In 2003 the Company's Silver Jubilee of receiving Letters Patent was celebrated at a banquet at Mansion House in the presence of HRH The Duchess of Gloucester, Sir Richard Nichols (Lord Mayor Locum Tenens) and Lord Fellowes who replied on behalf of the guests. Some 300 Liverymen and guests heard glowing tributes. Evensong at St Paul's Cathedral became a service of thanksgiving for the Company, at which the Dean, The Very Reverend John Moses KCVO, preached the sermon.

ABOVE: *John Moses, Dean of St Paul's Cathedral, with Master David Wright.*

SERVICE TO THE CITY OF LONDON

The Lord Mayor welcomes wide representation from the City to meet delegations, make presentations and raise relevant issues for the seventy or so inward and outward visits each year. Typically in 2010–2011 outward visits included Turkey, the Gulf, Malaysia, Taiwan, Vietnam, China, Israel and the Palestinian Territories, Chile, Brazil, Russia, South Africa, Nigeria, Angola, Kenya, Egypt, Libya and Russia.

In 2006 the Financial Services Group of Livery Companies was established "to assist the Lord Mayor when providing briefing for his work as an ambassador for the City of London, when receiving foreign visitors in London, and when making visits abroad". Our company was a founder participant, together with eleven other Livery Companies with interests in financial services in the City. While Master Jeffrey Greenwell was involved in its formation, the Court asked Past Master Marcell to be the working representative of our Company, and the Group accepted Court Assistant Richardson's offer to act as its secretary.

By 2008 the Lord Mayor was calling for Livery Companies to do more: "The challenges are to recruit the best people in the financial city; to use younger liverymen more effectively, and to encourage Liverymen to stand for election to civic office." The financial services companies clearly rose to the challenge, as the Group gained recognised status from the City Corporation in 2010. The Lord Mayor commented favourably in his Mansion House speech that year on the role of Chartered Secretaries in corporate governance. Also in 2010, Master Robin Eve was appointed OBE for "services to the City of London Corporation". Michael Chitty, Liveryman and Secretary of the Financial Services Group reported in 2012: "In recognition of the changes in the City the FSG is reviewing what the future strategy of the group should be over the next three years. We must move with the times".

Many members have held distinguished civic office and such appointments continue to ensure the Company punches above its weight in terms of contribution. In 2000 both the Lord Mayor, Sir Clive

Martin, and the Chief Commoner, Robin Eve, were members of our livery, each later becoming Master of the Company. In 2008 the Clerk reported that Chartered Secretaries were concurrently Masters of four Livery Companies: Mr Tony Davis (Master Mariners), Miss Sylvia Tutt (Scriveners), Mr Gerry Everitt (Master Masons), and Mrs Adèle Thorpe (Chartered Secretaries and Administrators), a situation which has been replicated to some extent, in other years. By 2010 the Clerk noted that, despite its youth, the Company had contributed three Sheriffs, three Chief Commoners and one Lord Mayor.

A full list of Company members who have been City office holders, and fuller details of civic participation are contained in Chapter Ten, contributed by Past Master Sir Clive Martin, a former Lord Mayor.

In the aftermath of the 2008 banking crisis, Livery Companies played a significant role in work to restore the City's reputation. In 2011 the Lord Mayor, Alderman Michael Bear, charged Sheriff Richard Sermon to lead work on proposals for "Restoring trust in the City", tapping his experience, both as a distinguished company chairman and director, and as a Past Master of our Company and of the Wheelwrights. He commented: "The City Values Forum, which I chair, reports to the Lord Mayor. The CVF took over the programme of work known as "Restoring Trust in the City", started in 2010/11, and aims to identify, recognise, encourage and embed best practice and ethical values in all businesses which operate in the City." This initiative generated a swathe of collaborative programmes, engaging the vast range of City organisations, in a drive to re-invigorate the City's reputation and pre-eminence.

A flowering cherry tree outside Haberdashers' Hall in West Smithfield was flourishing at the time of writing and represents the Company's contribution to a request from the City Corporation for more trees to be planted throughout the City. The Corporation advised on types of tree and possible locations and, following persuasive representations from Past Master Wright, the Court agreed to fund the planting in 2005.

SERVING THE ECONOMY

As Francis Spencer-Cotton (Master 2008/09) put it: "As Chartered Secretaries we are involved in many diverse fields, including banking, the financial services industry, commerce, local government, the Armed Forces and many others. With our background of professionalism, integrity and good governance we can make a substantial contribution wherever we operate. As always, this will go largely unsung as the profession works quietly in the background".

Many individuals are held in the highest public esteem, occupying senior and responsible positions. Members work in a vast range of jobs and organisations, deploying professional disciplines and skill to raise standards and improve efficiency. The Chartered Secretary and Administrator profession, in its widest scope, enjoys a growing reputation, an outcome delivered in no small measure by members of the Livery. This diversity is clear when glancing at members' career histories, which bring home the breadth and depth of the economic contribution made by Liverymen, usually over many decades.

ABOVE: *Notting Hill Carnival.*

OPPOSITE: *The cherry tree in West Smithfield donated to the City Corporation by the Company.*

For example Miss Claire Holder OBE, MA MSc ACIS, clothed with the livery in 2002, is a Barrister and Senior Crown Prosecutor, and was for many years the Notting Hill Carnival Organiser. In an unusual feature on her unique career, the Seychelles Tourism Board reported her visit in 2011: "Claire Holder OBE is used to organizing major events as the former Chief Executive Officer of Notting Hill Carnival. She said: "The reason I became a Chartered Secretary was to assist me in the planning and management of Carnival. Its growth and development are founded on principles of good administrative policies and controls". Taking the costume bands around the world brings with it other challenges. "When we decide on the bands we are planning to take to presentations around the world, there are a number of considerations, such as the skills and creative input of each of the bands. We also like to share the privilege of attending these international events between all of the carnival bands, so that no one band takes precedence… The logistics of taking Carnival on tour are also fairly challenging, organizing the air freight for the delicate costumes, the steel pans, and the disc jockeys' lighting and sound equipment in itself is a substantial task. But once we arrive at the destination and we start the performance, it always becomes so worthwhile…we showcase the standards and the talents we have here in London".

Presently around 30% of the Company's members have disengaged from formal working life, although such is the range of voluntary and charitable duties they shoulder that it is hardly appropriate to consider them retired. National life would be greatly impoverished without this contribution from altruistic and dedicated individuals.

Notable contributions to public life and service often go unrecognised but the Company has a number of members who have been granted formal awards. The Clerk commented in 2004, in a report of the St Paul's Cathedral service for members of the Order of the British Empire: "this year must be quite unusual, in that the Master, both Wardens, the Immediate Past Master, the Clerk and the Beadle are all members of the Order". In 2012, 20 members of the Company were eligible to attend that year's service.

ABOVE: *Order of the British Empire service, 2012 attended by (left to right: Donald Kirkham, Terence Young, Terrence English, Jeremy Elwes (in dark glasses), Rod Kenyon, Christina Parry, Jeffrey Greenwell, David Wright, John Robertson and David Prescott).*

SUPPORTING CHARITIES THROUGH DONATIONS AND VOLUNTARY EFFORT

After 30 years the Company was well into its stride and raising money for charity had become central to each year's activities. The tradition continued that virtually every event incorporated some form of charity contribution, whether donations, collections, ticket levy, or dedicated events designed for fun as well as fundraising. The proceeds regularly support the Lord Mayor of London's nominated charity, as well as a charity nominated by each Master, with numerous donations to other good causes. This forms part of the total charitable giving by City Livery Companies, estimated by the Lord Mayor at £41.85 million for the year 2010.

Some of the Charities which have benefited from the Company's fund raising include Barnardos, many of the Service Charities, Save the

ABOVE: *Presentation of a cheque to the Renewal Programme Night Shelter in Newham, 2001.*

Children, the Federation of London Youth Clubs, Royal National Institute for the Blind, Combat Stress, the Royal National Lifeboat Association as well as the Sheriff's and Recorder's Fund. Fundraising involves fellowship and fun, as well as challenge, as the following very limited selection from the archives illustrates.

In 2001, a church collection raised £900 for the Newham night shelter and the Salvation Army, for relief of those in distress at Christmas time.

The Apprentices have done much to help raise money for the Company's charities including in 2005 a team raising about £10,000 by taking part in the Three Peaks Challenge. In 2007 they took part in a sponsored walk in aid of London Youth and in 2008 a team consisting of David Taylor, Laura Jackson, John Rowland-Jones, Chris Cordrey, Steve Owen and Katy Thorpe, the daughter of the then Master, abseiled in Canary Wharf to raise £3,841 plus Gift Aid for Cancer Research UK. In 2011 Apprentice James Schirn cycled from London to Paris, 250 miles in four days raising over £1,000 for Help for Heroes and the Alzheimer's Society and Apprentice Kirstan Boynton raised over £1,000 for British Red Cross by a sponsored sky-dive: After the dive Kirstan said "I had a fantastic time and thank you to all at the Company who so generously supported me"

LEFT: *Apprentices abseiling in Canary Wharf.*

BELOW:*Apprentice Kirstan Boynton sky-diving for charity.*

CITY DIP

The City Dip is an annual swim to raise money for the Lord Mayor's Charity. In 2000, sixteen Company swimmers raised £6,200, 26% of the total pledged from the event.

In 2006 Company support for the nine boys from Rokeby School raised £1,170 plus Gift Aid.

In 2008 George Bayer, Alan Wood and Peter Young, raising money for "Orbis" (a sight charity) and "Wellbeing of Women" explained: "the five kilometre distance is shared between us , about a mile each (42 laps)". In 2009 there were six company-supported teams entered, raising £7,448 (including Gift Aid), the highest amount of sponsorship in the event. The two teams from Rokeby School managed 548 lengths in all, more than any other two teams put together. In 2010 11 boys from Rokeby raised over £500 in sponsorship from members of the Company, a memorable year as the Company's team swam with the Lord Mayor, the Aldermanic Sheriff and 3 mallard ducks. The boys and their sports teacher, Mr Martyn White, were thanked personally by the Lord Mayor, Alderman Nick Anstee, who himself swam the first 1000 metres.

ABOVE: *City Dip 1995 (left to right: Alastair Friend, Dave Marwood, Katy Thorpe and Paul Phelps).*

ABOVE: *City Dip 2009 teams from the Company and the Association of Women Chartered Secretaries.*

ABOVE: *Liveryman David Ogden (No. 103) training for the London Marathon in 2012.*

CHARITY RUNS

In 2006 Liveryman Charles Ledsam and two Apprentices ran the Silverstone half-marathon for charity. Charles Ledsam also ran his third London Marathon in 2009 shortly after his 60th birthday and raised over £2,000 for WaterAid. In 2012 Liveryman David Ogden ran the London Marathon in aid of Send a Child to Hucklow Fund. He explained: 'This year was special for two reasons: it is the 30th anniversary of my first marathon in 1982. Secondly, it is the 50th anniversary of the Send a Child to Hucklow Fund, a charity of which I have been Treasurer for about 20 years and which provides holidays in Derbyshire for under-privileged children. We had been promised matching funds for what we raised up to £50,000".

VOLUNTEERING

Like most professionals, Liverymen are always in demand by voluntary organisations for their skills and experience. The Company joined Livery Schools Link, a renewed approach by a number of Livery Companies to collaborate with schools in London. Participation was discontinued after a few years but has recently been revived in response to initiatives planned by the organisation.

Liveryman Suzanne Davison reported to members in 2006 on her experiences as a volunteer in secondary schools in her local or neighbouring boroughs. She took part in a range of initiatives, including "Enterprise Laboratory programme", "Young Enterprise Challenge", "Big School Seven", a Young Enterprise competition judging the award of the ICSA Corporate Governance trophy, "money matters" case studies, business problem solving team competitions, and sessions to help students with job-seeking, applications and interviews. Suzanne said at the time "the schools always seem extremely appreciative of the time and effort volunteers put in, and invariably report that the student feedback indicates that they have gained insights from them that they were not able to get from their teachers".

A new leaflet, "Education Initiatives" was issued, to highlight "how Liverymen can be involved in education as volunteers". The Company appealed for more members to serve as school governors, especially in Essex and Nottingham, and began to support the Young Enterprise Scheme.

The Company's Pro Bono Support for Small Charities scheme was launched by Court Assistant Rory Jackson, which has enabled such organisations to receive much needed professional help.

EDUCATION – APPRENTICES

The Company is committed to education, particularly learning which fosters high standards of public administration. Since year 2000 this has led to a number of collaborative schemes.

The Apprentice Scheme was approved by the Court in early 2001 and has been an ongoing success. John Rowland-Jones was apprenticed in 2005, admitted to the Livery in 2008, and achieved a Company first, as the first former apprentice to be appointed to the Court as an Assistant in 2010.

As scheme organisers, Patricia Day and later David Lock made great personal efforts to ensure the Apprentice scheme has been of benefit to those involved. Apprentices enjoy a programme of lectures, workshops, and events, intended to support their studies, careers and commitment.

In return they join in sponsored activities to raise money for charity, and benefit from the guidance of senior Chartered Secretaries. The Apprentice Scheme is covered in more detail in Chapter Five.

EDUCATION: PRIZES, SCHOLARSHIPS AND BURSARIES

As charitable resources built up, the Company was able to inaugurate, through its Charitable Trust, a number of awards and by 2008 the Trust was allocating £13,000 annually to educational purposes. Prizes, bursaries and scholarships have been awarded to students performing exceptionally well on university and college courses, on Armed Services Chartered Secretary programmes, and in ICSA examinations. Several of these institutions invite the Company to nominate representatives to their own governing bodies, which fosters beneficial exchanges of ideas and knowledge. In the best tradition, such contacts also invigorate the Company's contribution to civic and social well-being.

The "Sir Edward Howard Memorial Prize" was established in 2001, at the University of East London: Sir David Howard Bt, Lord Mayor 2002, agreed to name the prize in honour of his father, the Company's supporting Alderman when the Company was founded. He reminisced: "My mother and the family and I would be very honoured to approve of the "Sir Edward Howard Prize". We cherish his memory and this would be a wonderful way of marking his association with your Company. Indeed as a stockbroker and as Chairman or director of many public companies, he devoted much of his professional career to the activities which your company so ably represents. At times he would act as Company Secretary, manager, finance director, corporate broker and share registrar, and much of our business is built round a detailed knowledge of company law. He would have been very flattered at your generous suggestion."

Sir David presented the prize to the winner of the first award, Finnish born Miss Outi Isopuro and commented "that the first award goes to a student from Finland, who has decided to stay in London to work, demonstrates the cosmopolitan nature of this great City of ours". He was supported by the Lady Mayoress, the Master and Clerk, the Vice Chancellor and the Dean of the Business School of the University.

Miss Silvia Pajor, a subsequent prize-winner, who won the award for her excellent performance looking at corporate strategy in the pharmaceutical industry, expressed her delight: "I feel wonderful to have won this award – it gives me even more motivation to go on and succeed in my degree and career".

The next Chapter provides an account of the full extent of the educational funding provided through the Educational Trust.

BEYOND THE CITY

This decade saw the beginnings of a long-term relationship between the Company and organisations in the London Borough of Newham, one of the most deprived areas of the capital, not far from the City. This developed through Master Michael Dudding's appointment as Deputy Lieutenant for the Borough, and the Company's ambition to act as a positive influence in the wider community. The Company recognised it had charitable resources and valuable skills available to give help where needed.

Links with the University of East London, and the Royal Docks Business School in particular, were formalised in 2001.

In 2003 the Company agreed to pursue affiliation with Rokeby School, initially for a 5-year period. This proved tremendously successful in the long term, largely due to the personal commitment of the Liverymen involved. Richard Vardy, John Ainsworth and Ian Richardson have served as Company nominees on the school's governing body. Ian Richardson served as Vice-Chairman of Governors during an especially critical period, when the school moved to its current, state-of-art, premises.

As well as expertise, the Company provided vital funding, as Donald Kirkham, Chairman of the Trustees, explained in 2008: "Rokeby School has been granted specialist status as a mathematics and languages college. The school had to raise £50,000, which it did. Our donation, which was the first one received, effectively primed the pump". Ian Richardson was able to report in 2010: "under the inspirational leadership of the current Head Teacher, Charlotte Robinson, and her team, Rokeby School has moved from being in special measures a few years ago to being one of the most improved schools in the country".

Chapter Five provides a fuller account of the Company's involvement with the school.

Formal affiliation with West Ham Sea Cadets followed in 2006, based at Training Ship "Thunderer", was inaugurated with a plaque. The accompanying donation was gratefully acknowledged: "We have purchased a second-hand minibus using your generous donation. We could not have done this without your help and again would like to thank you". The Cadets now regularly provides the Company with an impressively smart guard of honour at formal functions.

ABOVE: *The Master, Commander Rory Jackeon RN, at the presentation of Letters of Association to the West Ham Sea Cadets.*

A pro bono effort to help the Newham Swords, an outstanding fencing club for young people, proved less successful. Mr Michael Chitty and Miss Anneka Kingan spent considerable time trying to assist Newham Swords, which had lost substantial income from Council funding cuts, to apply for charitable status. Through no fault of the two Company members, these efforts were to no avail.

SERVING OUR MEMBERS

From the outset the Company aimed to be a friend in need to its members and their families, and by 2002 the value of this service had been proven. The Almoner Scheme was duly formalised, aimed at keeping in better contact with sick and less mobile Liverymen and also their widows and widowers. Almoner, David Wright, with assistance from other members, has built up this office, so that needs are recognised and met with understanding, dignity and practical help. A Liveryman's widow explained in 2011: "I am welcomed with such courtesy and interest in my well-being. To be met and accompanied by a kindly face is so thoughtful and much appreciated…This surely is the essence of WCCSA.

The Hon. Chaplain, Reverend Dr. Peter Mullen.

We widows are always remembered at Christmastime with a greetings card and a beautiful box of chocolates…it does indeed feel like being part of an extended family". Past Master Wright, points out: "It is not always financial assistance that is needed. There are times when people seek comfort to cope with bereavement, illness or a change of circumstances, when a member may like someone with whom they can discuss their plans".

The Company chaplaincy was inaugurated to ensure that proper attention was paid to spiritual welfare. The Rev. Dr Peter Mullen was appointed as the Company's Chaplain in 2001 and became a regular preacher and guest at Company functions. Mrs Lynne Mullen gave invaluable administrative support when the Company used the Church of St Sepulchre-without-Newgate. The link with the church proved a two-way benefit, as the Company was able to support efforts to secure the Church's future through its development as the Musician's Church. For many years Liveryman Mollie Harris served Peter Mullen's other church, St Michael's, Cornhill, as Administrator.

The annual carol service similarly widened the Company's network of fellowship and friendship. It began when Mr Wilfred Hammond served as Hon. Clerk, sharing a room with the Clockmaker's Clerk. They got on well together and began a tradition of a shared service, later expanded to include, at various times, the companies of Gold and Silver Wyre Drawers, Poulterers, Security Professionals and Educators.

The Company's governance provides for the appointment of the Master and Wardens, drawn from Liverymen serving as Court Assistants. In accepting appointment Court Assistants undertake the Company's leadership and direction and, if required, the privilege of serving as Master. On occasion Court Assistants have been unable to progress to this highest office, most usually through reasons entirely beyond their control, and many rendered immense service and wisdom to the Company. Among those who fall into this group have been Derek Bartlett, Donald Campbell, Sidney Donald, Richard Vardy, Stephen Bennett, Susan Hughes and John Ainsworth.

In 2010 the Company inaugurated meritorious awards to recognise Liverymen, not on the Court, who had made an exceptional contribution. The first two recipients were Liverymen Mollie Harris, for her service to the LLG and other activities, and Liveryman David Coward, for his work as Hon. Archivist. In 2012 Liveryman Simon Jamison was awarded a meritorious service award for his work as Hon. Treasurer.

One of the most enjoyable events in the Company's calendar for socially-minded members is the Master's annual weekend. These have become an institution, usually lasting over a long June weekend. The venue and programme is entirely the responsibility of the Master, which may well be a worrying obligation. Invariably, members are touched to experience the immense personal trouble taken by the Master and consort to ensure everyone who attends is welcomed and made comfortable over the period. To give a flavour, since 2006 Master's weekends have been held in Durham, Oxford, Isle of Man, York, Chichester, Exeter, Liverpool and Birmingham. At these, guests were privileged to experience Evensong in great cathedrals, a peep behind-the-scenes at local attractions and splendid dining at a succession of historic and contemporary venues. One of the joys is that Masters bring their own enthusiasms and influence to bear, which might take the shape of a steam train experience, a river excursion, a visit to a heritage venue, a special ceremony and similar events with expert local guides in attendance to share their knowledge with the Company.

INTEGRITY AND LIVERY LIAISON EVENTS

For many years the Company had kept members in touch with events and each other through the time-honoured media of Clerk's briefings, the annual report, and members' meetings. But in the modern era there was place for a livelier format. In 2006 the Company decided on a new publication, *Integrity*, intended as a self-financing, annual publication reviewing the year. Court Assistant Donald Campbell, Liverymen John Robertson, Kerry Porritt, and Peter Young and Clerk Michael Dudding were involved in the early days. *Integrity* was an immediate and continuing success with Liverymen Jo Whiterod, Graham McVey, Peter Young, and Richard Reger taking the publication forward.

The LLG continued to organise unusual and innovative events which encouraged many members to become active livery participants. Visits have included London landmarks, museums and businesses, institutions such as the Magic Circle and Royal Albert Hall concerts. Such events are very enjoyable for all who take part, and support the Company's charitable aims and fellowship, key objectives in our Royal Charter. Chapter Seven gives fuller details.

BRIEFINGS FOR POTENTIAL MEMBERS

The Company's Ordinances prescribe a maximum number of 300 Liverymen. To promote recruitment to that number the Company continues to hold informal briefings, hosted by the chairman of the Membership Committee, for ICSA members who might be invited to join the Company. These have proved tremendously successful in boosting interest and numbers. The briefings are often a Chartered Secretary's first encounter with the Livery and give an opportunity to get a flavour of the way the Company operates. The good humoured and informative atmosphere is usually successful in dispelling any doubts about the warmth of welcome the Company offers new members. Liveryman David Turner confirms: "I felt somewhat apprehensive about the prospects of joining the Livery and was uncertain what membership would entail. The briefing session provided both an informative insight into the Livery's activities and an introduction to some of the interesting characters to be met! I concluded that membership would provide opportunities both to put something back into the company secretary profession and to enjoy some interesting social occasions; which has proven to be the case since joining."

MODERN EFFICIENCY

In the Company Office, the drive for efficiency pressed on, taking advantage of the arrival of direct debit, Gift Aid, computerisation, internet and e-mail to keep costs down. The website was launched, www.wccsa.org.uk .

Budgeting was carried out in accordance with the Financial Guidelines drawn up by Past Master Kirkham which stated:

(a) that the revenue expenditure of the Company in any year shall not exceed 90% of its revenue income comprising the aggregate of quarterage, fines on promotion, investment income, deposit interest and any such miscellaneous income;

(b) that the Company maintains a liquidity ratio of cash (in hand and at bank) to total balance sheet assets of not less than 25%;

(c) that at year end the value of quoted investments shall be marked to market that is to say written up or down in line with the market value in order that, at balance sheet date, the true worth of the Company can be readily seen and;

(d) that the proportion of assets held in quoted investments shall not exceed 60% of total assets.

The Guidelines assume that quarterage and fines will be increased broadly in line with inflation.

In May 2002 the Court approved the appointment of Tilney Asset Management to replace Cazenove to manage the Company's investments. In 2009 Tilney was taken over by Deutsche Bank Asset Management Ltd.

The banking crisis in 2008 and the pervasive atmosphere of economic gloom did not go unremarked. Stringent efforts were made to run a tight ship.

Clerk Michael Dudding worked tirelessly, long beyond his contracted hours, to ensure the Company's sound footing and expansion, despite financial pressures. The price of success was the need to register for Value Added Tax with Her Majesty's Revenue and Customs in 2008. He recalls "Registration led to a significant battle with the Revenue over the application of VAT to quarterage. We argued that VAT was not payable since membership was confined to members of ICSA, a recognised professional body. Whilst the Revenue soon accepted that we were members of one body, they then argued that "chartered secretary" was not a recognised profession, and was not what "the man on the Clapham omnibus" would consider a profession. Eventually, the company sought advice from Counsel. He pointed out that our profession was included in a European Directive on qualifications acceptable throughout the Community/Union, and the Revenue conceded the point. While Counsel's opinion cost a considerable sum, the Court considered it money well spent."

In what was to be a continuing refrain during the long years of recession and a flat economy, members were kept informed. As Master Robin Eve said "Over the last decade membership has increased by a quarter, we have registered for VAT, moved to a full audit process, been granted a Royal Charter, increased the number of affiliations and linked activities, increased our involvement in civic affairs in the City...value for money should be our watchword".

In 2010 Master Rory Jackson at his Installation said "I suspect that very few of us will be financially better off this time next year and the intention is to contain costs for Liverymen wherever possible but maintaining the high standards you have all come to expect from a leading modern Livery Company such as ours".

Periodic reviews were initiated, to invigorate strategic direction and focus in changing times. In 2009 a holistic review of the Company's affairs, was launched, chaired initially by the Junior Warden, John Murray. His premature death brought his contribution to an end and Past Master Spencer-Cotton took over. The Company was mindful of the explosion of paperwork and the ever-increasing time demands on the Clerk's office, which had to be addressed before Clerk Dudding's retirement. Detailed workload analysis and potential computer solutions were researched. This drive for cost-effectiveness will continue, as the Company looks to find its next home and to use its resources and talents wisely.

Growing demands led to the appointment in 2010 of Mrs Erica Lee FCIS, firstly as administrative assistant, later promoted to Assistant Clerk in 2012.

ABOVE: *Junior Warden John Murray.*

117

THE GALLANT AND LEARNED CLERK

In July 2002, the Court accepted with great regret the resignation of the Hon. Clerk, Mrs Gaynor Lintott, for personal reasons and appointed in her place Colonel Michael Dudding whose exemplary service dominated the next decade.

To quote from the Resolution passed by the Court on 26 January 2012:

"Past Master Dudding became Clerk in uncertain times for the Company. His renowned managerial skills steered the Company to the success, respect and status it now enjoys as a Modern Livery Company. He is an admired and respected Clerk amongst his peers. He has made many suggestions to the Court for improving the Company's ways: it now punches above its weight as a Modern Company. He has given enthusiastic support to the City of London Corporation, ensuring that the Company participates in the Lord Mayor's Show; to the successful Company Apprentice Scheme. As a dedicated, fair and courteous Clerk, Mike Dudding embodied the spirit of Livery and was a shining exemplar for the Company motto 'Service with Integrity'".

The process of finding a successor to take over from Mike Dudding started in early 2011 with the formation of a Selection Committee chaired by the Master, Rory Jackson, and which included the Wardens and representatives from Past Masters, the Court and the Livery. There was a strong field of candidates but the unanimous decision of the Committee was to recommend the appointment of Hugo Summerson and at its meeting on 27 July 2011, the Court, on a proposal by the Master, "Resolved that the employment of Dr. Hugo Summerson FRICS as Clerk (designate) from a date to be determined, be endorsed."

THE MASTER'S MARK

As with earlier years, the opening decade of the new century reflected the energy and dedication to the Company of many people. In particular, individual leadership and wisdom from each Master was decisive in keeping the Company in good shape and enhancing its status. It is therefore entirely fitting to close this Chapter by briefly recalling each Master's year of office, as recorded in the citations awarded by the Court. In every instance these contributions were preceded by, and also followed, years of solid work, safeguarding the Company's interests and reputation.

Mr Philip Marcell (2001/02)

Master Marcell declared his year to be one of consolidation, intent on increasing the strength, stability and depth of the Company, bringing to fruition the legacy of earlier initiatives. He focused particular attention on establishing good Company governance, developing the almoner scheme, increasing member participation at company functions, and acting as Company ambassador, particularly in City activities. These culminated in record attendance at the Company's Mansion House banquet that year. He was responsible for the refurbishment of the officers' robes at his expense and greatly strengthened the West Ham Sea Cadet Unit where he was elected President from 2005 to 2012.

Mr David Wright (2002/03)

Master Wright presided over the celebrations to mark the silver jubilee of the grant of Letters Patent to the Company. He was thus the public "face of the Company" in one of its most important years, meeting representatives of royalty, distinguished guests and dignitaries at numerous prestigious events. He funded Company newsletters to provide members with information. Within the Company he strengthened all aspects of its activities, including finances, fellowship, charitable giving and its associations with the City and Armed Services, as well as inaugurating the apprentice scheme. He was a champion of the Almoner scheme and subsequently rendered distinguished service in that role for many years, as well as championing the need for wheelchair access in livery halls.

Mr Donald Kirkham (2003/04)

Master Kirkham concentrated his energies on the drive to expand membership and to involve new and more members in the charitable, educational and social activities of the Company. With this objective, he set in place strategic plans and restructured the fines payable on admission to encourage new members. He promoted the appointment of liaison officers to enhance the Company's links with the Armed Forces. At the same time he ensured that financial management was placed on a sound footing for the future, and that proper attention to the Constitution safeguarded the Company's heritage and reputation.

Sir Clive Martin (2004/05)

Master Martin embodied a unique wealth of leadership and management experience, having been Lord Mayor of the City of London in the Millennium year, Senior Alderman, distinguished soldier, Chairman and Chief Executive of several organisations and a charity advocate. He led by example and was an outstanding motivator. These characteristics encouraged members of the Company to participate in livery affairs with enjoyment and pride, and to support worthy activities and charities. By gifting a significant endowment to promote the Company among all ranks of the Staff and Personnel Support Branch (Army) he demonstrated his own pride in this association. As Company ambassador, Master Martin enhanced the Company's esteem, through his extensive involvement in civic affairs and connections in the City and worldwide.

Mr Jeffrey Greenwell (2005/06)

Master Greenwell declared his intention of promoting social cohesion as a unifying force within the Company, the profession and the Livery generally. This ambition led to an active social programme with record attendances, with increasing numbers of members taking part in Company affairs as volunteers. Under his leadership the Company took the first steps to becoming incorporated by Royal Charter, set up more affiliations and, of great practical significance, resolved a contentious VAT dispute. He was particularly noted by members and guests for the gracious charm with which he presided over distinguished events.

Mr Richard Sermon (2006/07)

Master Sermon pledged to promote "Integrity in a Global Marketplace". Carrying this into action, his extensive contacts ensured the global market was represented by eminent leaders as guests and speakers at Company events. Thus he was widely recognised as a distinguished ambassador, in respect of the many City, civic and Armed Forces organisations associated with the Company. Through this, the Company's reputation and esteem were also enhanced. He had the honour of signing the Petition for the grant of a Royal Charter. Master Sermon brought characteristic dignity and distinction to every role, including his later eminence in the office of Sheriff.

Mrs Adèle Thorpe (2007/08)

Master Thorpe had the honour of presiding over the Company's celebrations of the grant of the Royal Charter. These were many and involved much preparation and ceremonial, regarded with interest by the Royal Household, the City and the livery movement generally. Master Thorpe excelled in her attention to discharging these responsibilities with distinction. She complemented this profile by devoting her year of office to promoting the Company wherever possible, and brought unstinting enthusiasm, professionalism and friendship to the events she attended as Master. She was particularly successful in raising money for charity, raising record sums for a number of good causes, through such events as a highly successful charity auction. Master Thorpe involved almost every Liveryman on a personal basis at "Meet the Master" events, held regionally as well as in London. Her year ended with the accolade of being the first woman to be elected as chairman of her Past Masters' Year Group.

Mr Francis Spencer-Cotton (2008/09)

Master Spencer-Cotton brought passion and commitment to consolidating sound governance and professionalism in all the many activities the Company had fostered. He led the Holistic Review of the issues facing the Company at that time, and was indefatigable in ensuring the recommendations of this work were carried through successfully. He maintained and strengthened links with the Armed Forces, and enthusiastically promoted charitable and educational involvements. He was particularly supportive of the services given by the Company's Chaplain and Almoner and of the social value of the contribution the Company was making to Rokeby School and the Newham night shelter.

Mr Robin Eve, Deputy (2009/10)

Master Eve had a long and distinguished record of public service, particularly in the civic governance of the City as Chief Commoner in 2000. His knowledge and experience made for a particularly fruitful relationship between the Company and the City Corporation, culminating in his achievement of official recognition for the Financial Services Group, where the Company was a significant founder member. He challenged many conventions with integrity and personal conviction, and initiated significant changes to enhance administrative efficiency and effectiveness in each organisation with which he was associated. Within the Company he increased financial transparency and secured economies, without compromising standards, and, amid some controversy, inaugurated changes to reduce significantly the costs of being Master.

Commander Rory Jackson Royal Navy (2010/11)

Master Jackson brought a dash of naval verve to his year, which saw the Company's links with the Armed Services significantly strengthened. Senior leaders from these Forces were guests and speakers at Company events, and Master Jackson led reciprocal visits, most notably the first presentation of the Marwood Award at the Lord High Admiral's Parade at the Royal Naval College, Dartmouth in the presence of HRH Prince Michael of Kent, and a visit to Barrow-in-Furness for the launch of HMS *Ambush*. The Company's reputation as a modern and progressive Livery Company benefitted from the illustrious guest lists Master Jackson assembled. Internally, his gregarious and enthusiastic style encouraged many members, and his cool head was impressive when facing a number of unexpected challenges requiring decisions.

Mr Ian Richardson (2011/12)

Master Richardson led the Company in a year of momentous national events. In the Diamond Jubilee of Her Majesty the Queen, Master Richardson had the honour of delivering the Company's loyal greetings. He was in attendance at the livery luncheon at Westminster Hall held in honour of Her Majesty, where he was accompanied by youthful representatives of the Company's schemes for supporting the wider community interest. The 2012 Olympic Games and Paralympic Games were acclaimed as successes for London and the City, and offered opportunities for showcasing the livery's contribution to its world class effectiveness. Master Richardson led the Company's contribution with characteristic style and initiative, drawing on the many leadership roles he had undertaken. Company events were enlivened by his interests in jazz and fine dining, which combined innovation with tradition.

All these Masters have delivered "Service with Integrity", showing high level leadership and skilful management of diverse skills and talents.

By the heritage and many contributions described in this history, the Company is proud that it has earned a reputation as a leading Modern Company. It faces the future with confidence in sound foundations and resilient traditions of service.

CHAPTER FOUR

THE CHARITABLE TRUST

By Past Master Jeffrey Greenwell

INTRODUCTION

One of the primary functions of Livery Companies is to provide financial support to needy and worthy causes. Every Liveryman is encouraged to make regular donations that are invested by Trustees to provide an income for distribution as assistance to students and as donations to charities. In this respect this Modern Company is no different to the more ancient companies formed in the Middle Ages.

THE TRUST DEED OF 1978

On 26 July 1978 the Company established a Charitable Trust by a Trust Deed (Reg. No. 276233) signed by Master John Wedgwood, Senior Warden John Phillips, Junior Warden Stanley Eley, Kenneth Jacques, Peter Newton, Dennis Roberts, Roy Harris and Sylvia Tutt. The Deed was executed pursuant to a resolution of the Court passed on 15 December 1977 whereby a Trust Fund was created with an initial payment of £100 and with the following objects:

(a) the relief of poverty of members of the profession of Chartered Secretaries and Administrators or any other recognised profession, those dependant upon them and in particular of members of the Company and their dependants;

(b) the advancement of education in any manner which is now or hereafter may be deemed by law to be charitable of persons desiring to practise the profession of Chartered Secretaries and Administrators or any other recognised profession or to be qualified for professional or administrative posts in national, public or local authorities and in commerce, industry and finance and to provide or contribute towards the provision of all requisite facilities in connection therewith;

(c) to award to persons intending to become Chartered Secretaries and Administrators or to practise any other recognised profession exhibitions tenable at any educational establishment approved by the Managing Trustees;

(d) to assist in their general or professional education persons who are preparing for, entering upon or engaged in the profession of Chartered Secretaries or Administrators or any other recognised profession by the provision of books, the payment of fees and the defrayment of travelling or maintenance or by such other means as the Managing Trustees may think fit;

(e) to award prizes in connection with examinations of the Institute of Chartered Secretaries and Administrators or of any other recognised professional institutions;

(f) to establish and maintain libraries and other facilities and services to assist and benefit persons who are engaged in or endeavouring to qualify for the Institute of Chartered Secretaries and Administrators or any other recognised profession;

(g) doing all other things which shall be necessary to the attainment of the above objects but not otherwise.

The Managing Trustees were to be not less than four nor more than eight persons all of whom were to be members of the Company. They were given the usual powers of trustees to invest funds, keep proper accounts and to regulate their proceedings.

The Company continued to make payments to the Trust Fund after the initial establishment in 1978. A further £200 was paid in 1979 and in 1983 the Court agreed to execute a four-year Deed of Covenant to pay £350 a year (less basic rate tax). In 1982 Past Master Wedgwood reported to the Court that the first bursary had been awarded to Mr CT Foo and five prizes of £50 had been awarded.

THE SECOND TRUST DEED

An important change was made in 1983. It was felt that the original objects were too narrow and focused mainly on education. To enable the Trustees to support wider objects and, in particular to support charities in the City and Inner London Boroughs, a new Declaration of Trust was executed on 7 July 1983 by Messrs John Wedgwood, Dennis Roberts and Geoffrey Gardiner. This was to be known as the General Charitable Trust Fund (Reg. No. 288487) and the purposes of the Charity were to be such charitable purposes as the Master, Wardens and Court of Assistants shall appoint. The power to appoint Trustees was vested in the Master, Wardens and Court of Assistants while leaving the power to appoint Trustees of the 1978 Deed with the Trustees themselves. This and the apparent creation of two Funds would cause administrative difficulties in the future, as will be mentioned later.

THE RANK XEROX BENEFACTION

In 1986 it was reported to the Court that Rank Xerox had provided a grant of £6,000 towards the cost of the Annual Lecture and on the matter of prizes that the Trustees were proposing to award 15 prizes, for the academic year 1985, covering England, Wales and Ulster. In 1990 the Trustees awarded a bursary of £1,500 to Mr DJ Robertson to study for an MBA at Henley. In 1991 it was recorded that funding support from Rank Xerox appeared to have ceased and the Trustees were considering other arrangements. The Company continued to make regular payments to the funds by a covenant in 1992 worth £375 a year and again in 1995 of £500.

PRIZES AND AWARDS

Mention should be made of the creation of specific awards to commemorate the service of Past Masters of the Company. In 1994 a prize to the value of £250 was created to recognise the contribution of Dr Roy Harris to education. In 1999 it was agreed to create the John Phillips Memorial Medal to be awarded to the Best Student of the Year and to be presented at the Company's Annual Banquet. To-day the best performer in each of the two bi-annual examinations receives a cheque for £500 and the best performer overall is invited to the Company's Annual Banquet and receives an engraved medal.

ABOVE: *Liveryman Anthony Hewitt (right) presenting the John Phillips Memorial for 2010 to Mr Frank Bennett (centre) while Mr Chris Tushingham of Barclays Wealth, Isle of Man looks on (left).*

LEFT: *Master Dr. Roy Harris.*

The winners of the medal have been:

1998	Mrs Jan Cargill
1999	Miss Toni Scammel
2000	Mr Matthew Youngs
2001	Mr Ian Hazlegrave
2002	Mr J Selden
2003	Captain Darren Carrick
2004	Mrs A Matthews
2005	Mr TC Goodman
2006	Mr Alastair Grey
2007	Miss Emma Roche
2008	Miss Lin-Marita Sen
2009	Mr Craig Owen
2010	Mr Frank Bennett
2011	Mr Joe Woodward
2012	Mr Mark Tanguy

Many of the prizes and awards have been to personnel in the Armed Forces as described in Chapter Six. Early bequests included a legacy of £10,500 from the estate of Past Master Constable which enabled a prize to the value of £500 to be awarded annually to "The Royal Air Force Officer under 21 on initial entry to the Royal Air Force College who during initial officer training demonstrated the greatest potential for further development by producing the best overall performance in both leadership and professional studies during the year". A bequest from Past Master Eley enabled a prize to go to the best Army officer in the ICSA examinations each year.

A prize was established in memory of Sir Edward Howard who had been the sponsoring Alderman when the Company was founded. This prize was awarded to the best-performing undergraduate on a course at the Business School of the University of East London.

Winners of the prize have been:

2001	Miss Outi Isopuro
2002	Ms M Tolba
2003	Mr Matthew Moore
2004	Miss D Kapdee
2005	Mr Suhail Mohmed
2006	Mr Desmond Carey
2007	Ms Sylwia Pajor
2008	Ms Bertha Fiattor
2009	Ms Natalie Chung
2010	Ms Lena Steinmetz
2011	Ms Julianne Lotz
2012	Mr Umair Lodhi

More recent awards have been the William McKenzie Memorial Prize in memory of William McKenzie who was President of the Institute in 1971 and awarded to a student at Edinburgh Napier University.

Winners have been:

2004	Miss Clarke
2005	Ms Mhairi Glen
2006	Ms Samantha Curtis
2007	Ms Samantha Curtis
2008	Ms Lee McLeod
2009	Ms Jennifer Ucha Placke
2010	Mr David Moir
2011	Not Awarded
2012	Not Awarded at the time of writing

And in the last few years new awards have included the Daphne Durban Memorial Prize and Trophy endowed by Past Master Durban awarded to the top graduate of the Royal Navy Fleet Air Arm; the Past Master Sir

RIGHT: *Past Master Sir Clive Martin presenting his Award to Corporal Samantha Brown, 2007.*

Clive Martin Award for the officer or soldier who has contributed most to the work of the Branch in an operational environment; the Past Master Sermon Award for the officer or airman of the RAF's Personnel (Support) Branch adjudged to have made the most outstanding contribution in an operational environment, the Dennis Glover Memorial Prize, endowed by Court Assistant (and Treasurer of the Charity) Julie Fox and her sister, Susan Bowden in memory of their father, to a student at City University, London, for Company Law; the Prudence Donaldson Wright Memorial prize at Bournemouth University School of Health and Social Care to study at Memorial University of Newfoundland; and the Past Master Marwood Award to the best Logistics Branch officer passing out from Britannia Royal Naval College, Dartmouth each year. Much more detail on the awards to the Armed Forces is given in Chapter 6.

THE LONDON CHAMBER OF COMMERCE AND INDUSTRY COMMERCIAL EDUCATION TRUST

A notable collaboration of the Charity has been with the London Chamber of Commerce and Industry Commercial Education Trust (LCCI-CET). In June 1997, thanks to the efforts of Past Master Finn, an Agreement was reached with the Commercial Education Trust whereby for each of the following 5 years the LCCI-CET paid to the Charity the sum of £25,000 for the purpose of commercial education projects. The money was used to fund scholarships, annual bursaries, additional prizes as well as the annual Rivers Lecture. Although the original gift eventually lapsed, the LCCI-CET has continued to support the annual Rivers Lecture which has proved to be a significant event in the City's calendar with distinguished speakers addressing contemporary issues as described in Chapter 5.

THE INSTITUTE OF CHARTERED SECRETARIES AND ADMINISTRATORS

The Trustees have always focused on the importance of helping students of the Institute, and regularly discuss with its education staff how best to do this. With the Institute moving from direct examinations to granting exemptions for graduates from collaborative university courses approved by the Institute, the Trustees in 1998 established twelve Livery Company Scholarships of £1,000 each where the Institute had established collaborative courses. In 2011 the Trustees agreed to help prize winners become members of the Institute by offering grants to cover the initial cost of moving from Grad ICSA to ACIS. In part this was funded by reducing the value of the prizes from £1,000 to £500, which recognised that the monetary value of the prizes exceeded the value of comparator prizes in higher education.

FUNDING THE TRUST

As has been mentioned, the Trust has received its funds from a variety of outside sources as well as the initial donations from the Company when the Trust was first established. The mainstay of the annual income has come, of course, from regular contributions by Liverymen and Freemen. Each new Liveryman is encouraged by the Master and Wardens to enter into an arrangement to gift-aid an annual contribution to the Trust and to make this by standing order. The Company is fortunate that so many of its members have done so. Members are also encouraged to consider leaving a legacy to the Trust in their wills. A notable legacy came to the Trust in 2006 when Mrs. Joan Harris, the widow of the late Past Master Harris, left her residuary estate amounting to in excess of £800,000 to the Trust. Sponsored events by the Company's Apprentices and donations from surpluses generated by social events organised by the Company's

LLG represent welcome additions to the Fund. Generous gifts of capital by deceased Liverymen and the regular donations by current Liverymen have created a capital fund of £1,281,427 as reported in the Trust's accounts for 2011.

In 2012, a Deed of Variation to the will of the late Past Master Tutt allows £50,000 to be paid to the Trust.

CHAIRMEN AND SECRETARIES

The Chairmen and Secretaries of the Trust were always members of the Court and a full list is given in Appendix 3. Notable among the Chairmen is Kenneth Jacques who held the chair for 13 years from 1990 to 2003.

In 2012 the work involved in running the Trust had greatly increased and it was decided that the role of Secretary to the Trust should be taken over by the Assistant Clerk to the Company, Erica Lee, on a salaried basis with the Trust paying the Company for the equivalent of one day's work a week.

THE 2011 POLICY REVIEW

In 2011 the Trustees reviewed the Trust's policy for making grants and reported to the Court as follows:

> "whilst no charitable object is completely ruled out, we decided that our funds should normally be used in support of:

(a) educational awards for success in the examinations of the ICSA and in collaborative courses between ICSA and several universities;

(b) support for Apprentices of the Company in their ICSA studies;

(c) education and social welfare in the City of London and the Inner London Boroughs;

(d) the charities nominated annually by the Lord Mayor of the City of London and by the Master of the Company;

ABOVE: *Junior Warden John Murray and Liveryman Christina Parry at a presentation at the University of East London.*

(e) charities relating to current or former members of the Armed Services and awards for members of those branches of the Armed Services with which the Company has affiliations.

Other than awards within those categories, the Trust will not normally now give support:

(a) to individuals;

(b) to national charities (as opposed to local ones which are focused on the above objectives); nor

(c) to independent schools (except where a donation would be of benefit to deserving individuals, rather than adding to a school's general fund)."

ABOVE: *Lord Mayor Nick Anstee receiving a donation to the Lord Mayor's appeal from Master Robin Eve.*

MODERNISING THE TRUST DEEDS

The Trustees have also kept under review the governance of the Trust. Mention was made earlier of the differences between the two Trust Deeds of 1978 and 1983 and in particular the relationships between the Court and the Trustees. Because the procedure for the appointment of individual trustees varied for each Trust, in 2006 the Trustees applied for, and the Charity Commission granted, an Order enabling the Trustees to make amendments to the Deeds to bring into line the procedure and the eligibility for new trustees. Under the power granted by the Charity Commission's Order, Clause 7 of the 1983 Declaration of Trust was amended enabling the Trustees, rather than the Court, to appoint and remove trustees. In addition it was provided that Trustees need not be

Members of the Court so long as they were Members of the Company.

Both Trusts remained in being and in theory two sets of accounts should have been maintained, but for a number of years only one set of accounts was kept. In 2009 Past Master Kirkham reported that, when a nil return was submitted for the 1978 Deed, the Charity Commission challenged this and suggested that the 1978 Charity could be removed from the Register of Charities. The Trustees agreed to remove the Charity from the Register accordingly. This apparently simple step did have one unintended consequence in that the detailed provisions for regulating meetings, setting the quorum and retirement of trustees set out in the 1978 Deed were lost. In October 2010 the Trustees incorporated as amendments in the 1983 Declaration of Trust the relevant clauses of the 1978 Deed.

In 2012 the Trustees carried out a far-reaching survey of the Trust. With the assistance of Court Assistant Christopher Hallam and Liveryman Stephen Gilbert, the Trustees approved a new Deed to re-establish the Trust with modern provisions representing changes to charity law and best practice and which reflect best practices of a modern Company.

In the past eight years, including the Lord Mayor's Annual Appeal and charities supported by Masters, over 100 charities have been supported by the WCCSA Charitable Trust. These include charities supporting the armed forces, educational and environmental projects, the homeless, churches, young people, art and music.

Well over £200,000 has been contributed in that time. It is expected that the Company as an active part of the Livery movement will continue to expand its philanthropic and charitable activities.

CHAPTER FIVE

EDUCATION, EDUCATION, EDUCATION!

By Past Master Ian Richardson and Others

CANNOCK SCHOOL

Education was a topic of concern from 1994 onwards. That year the Court received a report from a committee, consisting of Past Masters Jacques and Roberts and Court Assistant Bristow, which had been asked to examine the feasibility of an association between the Company and Cannock School at Chelsfield near Orpington, the Headmaster of which was a member of the Company - Liveryman Keith Lawrey. The Committee recommended that since the School seemed to be heading for closure or merger, the Company should not get involved. The Court agreed with the recommendation but also agreed that after a suitable interval, a search should be made for an educational establishment where the Company could have a meaningful relationship. Association with a Sixth Form College or University was commended.

The School did indeed close but with the benefit of hindsight, the opportunity at Cannock School was perhaps one which the Company should not have missed as, not least, the School had substantial grounds! However the financial obligations of owning the School, or turning it into another business would have been considerable as well as an immense time commitment for involved Liverymen. The Company did not have a sufficiently strong capital base, or inclination, to accept risks of this magnitude.

THE EDUCATION COMMITTEE

In 1997 under the guiding hand of the Master, Geoffrey Finn, an Education Committee was formed. Initially, its principal purpose was to manage the Company's support for the Institute's professional education programme, particularly through grants and prizes.

In 2001 Court Assistant Thorpe, then Chairman of the Education Committee, submitted to the Court draft objectives for the Committee and was given approval for a leaflet to be issued to all Liverymen setting out ways in which they could engage in the educational field to the benefit of the Company's standing. When explaining the proposed objectives, she readily conceded that there was a risk that the work of the Committee might be seen to be encroaching on the functions of other Committees and on the work of the Institute, but the programme was a long-term venture and needed time to show if it could succeed in gaining the commitment of Liverymen to the promotion of education.

The response to the leaflet was heartening leading to a database of 43 volunteers and donations amounting to £1,500 towards educational initiatives. One of these initiatives was supported by Liverymen Suzanne Davison and Arthur Denny for "Young Enterprise", a national scheme aimed at improving teenagers' understanding of business. Sadly many of the proposed initiatives were not pursued because of a lack of adequate staff resources in both the Company's office and on the Committee.

The Company awards prizes (funded through the Company's Charitable Trust) for the best performing student each year in the management/business studies courses run by various UK universities in collaboration with the Institute. There are also prizes for the best performing students in the bi-annual exams of the Institute itself as outlined in the previous chapter.

ABOVE: *Casting for recovery – a charity supported by the Company which enables sufferers from breast cancer to learn fly-fishing. Company Secretary: Court Assistant Patricia Day.*

The remit of the Committee has also expanded to include the Company's work with its own Apprentices, who receive the support of an Apprentice Master, some financial support with examination fees and study materials and the "fellowship" of regular meetings of an informal Apprentices Group. More of this later on in this chapter.

Another important role has been to offer pro bono help in governance etc to charities with a turnover of less than £100,000.

More recently the Committee has taken on responsibility for *Integrity*, the Company's annual magazine, the web-site and other Information and Communication Technology (ICT) matters. To reflect this the Committee was named the Education and Communications Committee.

ROKEBY SCHOOL

Some 16 years after the Court had agreed not to assist Cannock School, the Clerk, Colonel Michael Dudding (who was also a Deputy Lieutenant of Greater London with particular responsibility for the

London Borough of Newham), suggested that the Company should consider some form of support for Rokeby School in Newham which was going through a particularly difficult time, having been classified as a "failing school" by the Office for Standards in Education "Ofsted" and having been put into Special Measures. Schools in Special Measures are given additional support from the Local Authority and are subjected to frequent inspections to monitor the progress being made to improve performance.

Rokeby School is a comprehensive school for 11–16 year-old boys, run by the Local Authority, in Stratford. At that time, it had approximately 940 pupils. Its catchment area was (and, regrettably, still is) one of the most deprived in England. In Newham, 55% of children meet the criteria for free school meals and 85% of students do not have English as a first language.

Members of the Company visited the school in February and March 2003 and it was agreed in principle to develop a closer relationship. Court Assistant Ian Richardson had an existing connection with East London Business Alliance "ELBA" (a government and business-supported not-for-profit organisation, charged with encouraging regeneration and business support for the East End), through his employer's previous support of ELBA with employee volunteering and professional advice. It was therefore agreed that he would progress these ideas with ELBA and Rokeby School.

In June 2003, ELBA made a presentation to the Committee, suggesting ways in which Livery Companies in general could help ELBA to achieve these objectives in the East End and also ways in which ELBA could help this Company develop the relationship with Rokeby.

At Ian Richardson's request, ELBA spoke to Mark Keary, Head Teacher at Rokeby, and identified the following areas of possible support from the Company:

(a) one person to join the Governing Body of Rokeby (recognising that this was an extremely challenging role, with the Governors having to meet every two weeks to deal with all the issues which were arising from the Ofsted report);

(b) coaching/mentoring of key staff on performance management issues;

(c) work experience for students.

But at the first meeting with the Head Teacher in December 2003, the Company was advised that the school no longer needed an independent Governor as the pressure was on finding more parent Governors. However the Head Teacher wanted to progress the idea of mentoring staff and also wanted to find ways in which the Company could help fund various initiatives. Progress was slow with meeting dates being set and then cancelled. Meetings with other members of staff were offered (and held) but as Ian Richardson reported to the Education Committee "it was clear to me that there was a lack of continuing communication between the leadership team and the staff on these matters or indeed between each member of staff that I saw."

The leadership team was under huge pressure and although meetings took place occasionally during 2004 there was no meeting with the Head Teacher until April 2005. Perhaps as a result of poor communication, a student who had been invited to join our float in the Lord Mayor's Show failed to turn up and a promised team to support the fundraising City Dip, for the Lord Mayor's Charity, was not recruited. In view of the lack of any real progress in the discussions, Ian Richardson and the Committee began to question whether the Company would be able to give the School the support it needed.

However, in July 2005, the school was released from Special Measures and made a request for specific areas of funding to reward and recognise improvements in behaviour by individual students particularly those who had a track record of being "difficult".

The Company continued its support and the "behaviours" project was largely a success (the one notable failure being a "difficult" student who was making surprisingly good progress, until he ran amok one day, climbed a tree in the playground, swore at other students and staff and then shinned down the tree and ran off across an electrified railway line). It was at least an antidote to any Liveryman who felt that working in such a challenging environment could be any more that "two steps forward and one step back" (or worse).

Unfortunately, the poor communication with the School continued, with no meetings or significant conversations between July 2005 and March 2006. The Company had agreed specific actions on mentoring of staff but these did not come to fruition.

Mark Keary resigned in July 2006 and Charlotte Robinson (the Deputy Head with responsibility for Curriculum and Access) was promoted to Head Teacher. In December of the same year Court Assistant Richard Vardy was appointed to the Governing Body.

A team from Rokeby School took part in the City Dip for the first time, as the Company's B team, and raised over £700 for the Lord Mayor's Appeal, which was subsequently followed by a contribution of the same amount from the Company's Charitable Trust to the School.

Communication with the school improved immeasurably. Court Assistant Richard Vardy's presence on the Governing Body obviously helped the information flow but other channels of communication also improved.

Whilst mentoring of teachers (and, indeed, of students) continued to be discussed, it never actually took place. However, several members of the Company made helpful contributions to the School's thinking on performance management. The School continued to supply teams for the City Dip in 2007, 2008, 2009 and 2010, the swim in 2009 contributing to the record-breaking sum raised by the Company that year, the best of any Livery Company.

The Company's Charitable Trust has continued to support the school, with a contribution of £5,000 towards the fee for the School's accreditation as a Mathematics and Languages Specialist School, a contribution towards the School's Eco-Garden and regular funding of the termly awards for student leadership.

Through the Company's connections with the Central Criminal Court (Old Bailey), visits to the Court have been arranged each year since 2009 for the GCSE Law students (which include sitting in on a case, having a Question and Answer session with one of the judges and having a conducted tour of the building, including the cells) before the students spend time with a firm of solicitors (McGrigors) learning about the civil side of the legal profession. McGrigors, (now part of Pinsent Masons), is one of the firms (mainly, but not exclusively, local employers near the school) who are members of the Rokeby Business Support Group. Other members include the Company as well as London City Airport and Tate & Lyle.

The Company also arranged visits to Ronnie Scott's Jazz Club as an incentive/reward for the school's jazz quartet in 2010 and 2011; the Company's Apprentices Group arranged a public speaking competition at the school between teams from the school, the Apprentices and the

Court in 2011; and the Student Leader (Head Boy) of the School was the Company's guest at the Luncheon hosted by Livery Companies for Her Majesty The Queen in Westminster Hall following the Diamond Jubilee service in St Paul's Cathedral.

Through an initial introduction by the Company between the Head Teacher of Rokeby and the Headmaster of City of London School, the highest achieving student in Year 11 (fifth form) of Rokeby in each of the last four years has been awarded a full scholarship to the sixth form of the City of London School.

Ian Richardson was appointed a Governor in December 2007 (and Vice Chair of Governors in 2009); Court Assistant Richard Vardy resigned as a Governor in 2010 and Court Assistant John Ainsworth was appointed in his place later that year.

In addition to the extensive support (and time) each of these Governors has given to the School, Ian Richardson's skills as a Chartered Secretary were particularly useful in advising the school on the legal contracts involved in having a new school built under the Government's Building Schools for the Future programme (a Private Finance Initiative). Not only were the legal contracts complex but the negotiations with the Local Authority and the contractors were equally so. Commercial experience was extremely useful, particularly as Governors had to accept legal responsibility under the contracts.

The new school (in a different part of Newham – Barking Road) opened successfully in September 2010. Regrettably, many major "snagging" and financing issues arose, with, at times, the Governing Body acting alone to deliver the right outcomes for the students.

That said, the new buildings are now working well and the school has gone from strength to strength under the leadership of Charlotte Robinson.

Academically, the results are improving. GCSE results have risen from 16% of the students achieving at least five A^* - C grades (including English and Maths) in 2005 to 65% in 2011. On the non-academic side, the school has excelled in many areas, including football, debating and music. In 2011, the Rokeby Business Support Group also won the Times Educational Supplement's national award for 'Outstanding Business Partnership'.

The School and the Company continue to be jointly committed to the School's prime purpose of delivering the best possible outcomes for the students.

CITY UNIVERSITY

The Company has a long standing relationship with the City University and is represented on the University's Court. The Master of the Company attends the Degree Awarding Ceremony in Guildhall, generally presided over by the Lord Mayor who is the University's Chancellor, and is invited to the University's Annual General Meeting and certain lectures. For many years the Company's representative on the University Court was Past Master Tutt with Past Master Richardson taking over after her death.

THE APPRENTICE SCHEME

In July 1995, a paper put to the Court by the Master (Colonel Cauchi) and the Senior Warden (Mr Grinsted) proposed the formation of a junior branch of membership but the Court decided to take no action at that time but review the matter in 1997.

LEFT: *Apprentices attending a briefing by Marie Curie Cancer Care, January 2012.*

However it was not until 2000 when the Master Elect (Colonel Dudding) prepared the ground by prior consultation with the Company's Committees, Charitable Trustees and Hon. Clerk and the Clerk to the Chamberlain's Court in Guildhall. A detailed scheme for submission to the Court of Aldermen was approved by the Court in February 2001; Aldermanic approval followed a few months later and the first Apprentices, Mr David Taylor apprenticed to Court Assistant Eve and Miss Sarah Giles, apprenticed to Court Assistant Hughes, were admitted by indenture in 2003.

Sarah Giles got married and went to New Zealand with her husband for a couple of years. On return to this country she no longer wanted to be part of the apprentice scheme as she had decided not to continue with the Institute's examinations.

David Taylor successfully followed the path envisaged, passing the Institute's examinations and becoming a Freeman in 2007. As described in Chapter Six, he took part in an exchange with an Officer from the Royal Navy. David, then working as a Company Secretary in a quoted company, was clothed with the Livery in 2010, in a fitting coincidence by the then Master, his old Apprentice Master, Robin Eve. David has commented "Being an apprentice of the Company served me well and has opened doors to a range of novel and unique opportunities; it has brought me friends and contacts throughout the profession, and I would thoroughly recommend both the scheme and the Company to any aspiring Chartered Secretary".

John Rowland-Jones is another scheme alumnus, apprenticed in 2005. John was admitted to the Livery in 2008 and became the first former apprentice to become a Court Assistant in 2010.

Court Assistants Day and Lock have made great personal efforts to ensure the Apprentice Scheme has been of benefit to those involved. Apprentices enjoy a programme of lectures, workshops and events intended to support their studies and careers and benefit from the guidance of senior Chartered Secretaries. In return they join in sponsored activities to raise money for charity. Networking is now the contemporary term for fellowship, and apprentice events provide opportunities geared to friendship and support as well as learning.

Court Assistant Lock recalls that he took over running the Apprentice Scheme in 2008 after the very successful start by Court Assistant Day. He developed a programme that would:

(a) supplement the Apprentices studies and professional experience;

(b) provide professional and personal support;

(c) enable the Apprentices to contribute to the achievement of the objectives of the Company through gaining an insight into the City and how it worked and;

d) aid the Apprentices on completion of their studies to become effective Freemen and Liverymen of the Company.

Court Assistant David Lock said "he wanted the group to feel special and appreciate that there were opportunities to contribute, and pleasure to be had, from getting involved in the Company, City and in the profession". In each of the 5 years the Apprentices were given in-depth insight into key City organisations such as the Shrievalty, the operation of the Lord Mayor's international programme and Southwark Cathedral. On the professional side, the Apprentices meet Company Secretaries in various roles speaking about their organisations and current challenges. There were "enhancing career and career opportunities" evenings given by head-hunters, Liverymen and speakers from various sectors such as charities and education, and social events ranging from dinners in the Mess of the Honourable Artillery Company (thanks to Liveryman Graham Oxenham) to summer socials at Vinopolis and Tower 42.

David feels he has gained "professional satisfaction from working with the group through seeing the advancement of individual Apprentices, their success in examinations and admission to the Company as Freemen and Liverymen". In October 2012 former Apprentice Steve Owen succeeded Court Assistant Lock as organiser of the programme.

MANSION HOUSE SCHOLAR

For three years, the Company gave financial support to a Bulgarian student, Miss Bilyana Apostolova, to study for an undergraduate degree in Economics and Government at the London School of Economics as part of the Mansion House Scholarship Scheme. Bilyana also took part in many of the Company's Apprentice activities with Court Assistant Stephen Bristow acting as her quasi Master.

ABOVE: *The Mansion House Scholarship (left to right: The Clerk, Master Richard Sermon, Ms. Bilyana Apostolova, Sir John Stuttard, Lord Mayor and Stephen Bristow).*

OTHER EDUCATIONAL LINKS

In 1997, the Company joined the Livery October Group Vocational Education Committee, an intra-livery companies organisation which aimed to assist companies build relationships with schools, particularly in the poorer London Boroughs neighbouring the City. However the organisation seemed to become more of a "talking shop" than an executive body and by 2004 had been wound up.

At the instigation of Past Master Marwood the Company also presents prizes at the West Kent College although no formal association has been inaugurated.

The Company has also been a member of the City and Guilds of London Institute.

THE LONDON CHAMBER OF COMMERCE AND INDUSTRY

In 1997 Past Master Finn was successful in establishing a link with the LCCI-CET. The Trust gave our Charitable Trust a grant of £25,000 per annum for disbursement to educational bodies to advance students' knowledge of business.

The enormous benefit this gave the Charitable Trust in its grant-giving is recognised with immense gratitude. In particular, the then Secretary to LCCI-CET, Mr Robin Booth, is thanked for his personal support for this arrangement over many years.

THE RIVERS LECTURE

From 1988 the Annual Lecture was run by the Charitable Trustees as a charitable event with the first lecture being held at City University with sponsorship from Rank Xerox. In 1994 the Court took the view that it should become a Company function aimed at enhancing the prestige of the Company in the City. This has meant that prestigious speakers had to be found. and that his/her diary matches the availability of a Hall.

In 1996 Court Assistant Sermon suggested a revised format for the event and that perhaps it could be merged with the Rivers Lecture which had been abandoned by the Institute when the endowed sum expired.

Peter Rivers was a member of the Institute for almost fifty years. He served with distinction as a member of the Council from 1957 to 1973. He was elected President in 1970, an important year in which the merger of the Corporation of Secretaries and the Institute was smoothly and

The Rivers Lecture, 2011 in Drapers' Hall being addressed by The Lord Wilson of Dinton.

successfully accomplished. He devoted a great deal of his life to charitable purposes, and the Institute's Educational Trust and Benevolent Fund both benefited from his support. He also made a generous provision for an annual series of lectures the first of which was held on 2 May 1972 at the Royal Institute of International Affairs at Chatham House. Lord

LEFT: *The Master, Wilfred Hammond, greeting Mr Ken Livingstone.*

Redcliffe-Maud spoke on the "Indispensability of the Administrator". Peter Rivers died in 1977.

The first Lecture in the new format was held in Saddlers' Hall immediately after a Court meeting on 17 October 1996. It was chaired by the Rt. Hon. The Lord Cuckney, sponsored by Wrightson Wood Associates Ltd and followed by a supper.

The first Lecture after the link with the LCCI-CET was made was in 1998. The Master (Rear Admiral Carine) was instrumental in reviving collaboration with the Institute and moving the venue to Drapers' Hall which became a favourite venue in succeeding years. A list of past lecturers and their subjects is shown in Appendix Four.

The value of the Lecture as a means of enhancing the status of the Company in the City was well demonstrated in 2000. The Master (Mr Hammond) had persuaded Mr Ken Livingstone to be the speaker and just two days before the Lecture, Mr Livingstone declared himself as a candidate to become Mayor of London independent of the Labour Party. The Rivers Lecture became "the hottest ticket in town" and Drapers' Hall was full. Mr Livingstone gave such a persuasive speech that the audience, who surely would have been overwhelmingly sympathetic to political parties other than Labour, gave him a standing ovation!

Education, as befitting a modern company, is very much in the forefront of the Company's activities.

CHAPTER SIX

THE ARMED FORCES

By Past Master Commander Rory Jackson Royal Navy

INTRODUCTION

Most Livery Companies have always had strong links with the Armed Forces and the Worshipful Company of Chartered Secretaries and Administrators is no exception. Indeed perhaps helped by the number of Masters and Liverymen who served in the Armed Forces, this Company has stronger links than most.

The Charitable Trust has always looked benignly upon the various Service Charities and in 2011 agreed that "Charities relating to current or former members of the Armed Services and Awards for members of those branches of the Armed Forces with which the Company has affiliations" was one of five areas where the Trust funds would normally be used.

The Trust also created prizes or awards to commemorate the service of Past Masters of the Company. A legacy from the estate of Past Master Constable enabled a prize of £500 to be awarded each year to a Royal Air Force young officer who had done exceptionally well during initial training. A bequest from Past Master Stanley Eley enables a prize to be awarded to the best Army candidate in the ICSA examinations each year, although sadly because of the small number of soldiers sitting the examinations it has not been awarded for some years.

As will be seen later in this chapter, prizes and awards to the Armed Forces continue to this day.

HONORARY FREEMEN

Although job titles have changed over the years, currently officers holding the positions of Chief Naval Logistics Officer in the Royal Navy, Director Staff and Personnel Support in the Army and the Air Commodore A1 (Personnel Support) in the Royal Air Force become ex-officio Honorary Freemen for the duration of their appointment. Honorary Freemen have included:

Royal Navy

Rear Admiral David Allen CBE
Rear Admiral John Musson
Rear Admiral Nick Wilkinson CB
Rear Admiral Richard Lees CVO
Rear Admiral Peter Dunt CB
Rear Admiral Roger Lockwood
Rear Admiral Michael Kimmons CB
Vice Admiral David Steel CBE

On leaving the Navy Roger Lockwood became Chief Executive of the Northern Lighthouse Board. In July 2008, the Master, Adèle Thorpe, held the Master's Weekend in the Isle of Man. Also in the Isle of Man was

ABOVE: *The Master's Weekend, Isle of Man, 2008.*

HRH The Princess Royal, Patron of the Board with Roger Lockwood in attendance. Roger joined the Company for a group photograph on the steps of the Nunnery at the annual Tynwald Garden Party.

Hon. Freeman Peter Dunt was later promoted Vice Admiral and Hon. Freeman David Steel was promoted Vice Admiral and appointed Second Sea Lord in October 2012.

Army	Major General John Kinahan CB
	Major General Leonard Bartlett CB OBE
	Major General Bryan Bowen CB
	Major General Paul Bray CB
	Brigadier Colin Geal OBE
	Brigadier Neil Mackereth
	Brigadier Richard Leighton
	Brigadier Valerie Batchelor OBE
	Brigadier John Wolsey OBE
	Brigadier Max Marriner CBE
	Brigadier Nicky Moffat CBE
	Brigadier Paul Burns

General Bray was the last Paymaster-in-Chief of the Army. Brigadier Mackereth was a Fellow of the Institute and remains a Freeman of the Company.

Royal Air Force	Air Vice-Marshal Terry Sherrington CB
	Air Commodore CG Winsland OBE
	Air Vice-Marshal Mike Dicken
	Air Vice-Marshal Andrew Burton OBE
	Air Vice-Marshal Andrew Collier CBE
	Air Vice-Marshal Steve Chisnall
	Air Commodore Nigel Beet OBE
	Air Commodore Colin Smith
	Air Commodore Nigel Beet CBE

ABOVE: *Air Commodore Nigel Beet receiving the Freedom of the City of London, 2011.*

Andy Burton was a Fellow of the Institute and on leaving the Royal Air Force became Bursar of Sevenoaks School and was clothed with the Livery in his own right in 2005.

On 31st October 2011, Air Commodore Nigel Beet received the Freedom of the City of London under the auspices of the Company. He and his wife Becky and Rear Admiral Mike Kimmons, a previous Hon. Freeman, were entertained to lunch after the ceremony in the Guildhall Members Private Dining Room where they were greeted by the Chief Commoner, Deputy and Liveryman Richard Regan.

THE ROYAL NAVY

Formal Letters of Association between what was then known as the Supply and Secretariat Branch of the Royal Navy were signed, appropriately, at Watermens' Hall on 14 March 1988. Rear Admiral Brian Brown CBE, the Chief Naval Supply and Secretariat Officer, who later became the first Supply Officer to be appointed Second Sea Lord, and Captain John Musson RN, Commanding Officer of the Royal Naval Supply School, signed on behalf of the Royal Navy with the Master, Ronald Bounds and Hon. Clerk, George Challis, signing on behalf of the Company. Also present was Commander Roger Lockwood RN who would later become the Chief Naval Supply Officer and an Hon. Freeman of the Company.

THE DEFENCE MARITIME LOGISTICS SCHOOL

The School is based in HMS *Raleigh*, a "stone frigate" just outside Torpoint in Cornwall. Since 1989 the Company has presented silver medals and latterly cheques to the top qualifying officer on the Initial Logistics Officer Course and the Petty Officer who has the highest professional assessment on the Petty Officer Writer Qualifying Course.

Year	Officer	Rating
1989	Lieutenant Mike Bath RN	Petty Officer R Galpin
1990	Lieutenant Andrew Keith RN	A/Petty Officer DC Bale
1991	Lieutenant Chris Bennett RN	Writer I Graves
1992	Lieutenant David Watts RN	Leading Writer Mark Cox
1993	Sub-Lieutenant Sandra Watts RN	Petty Officer Lynne Ogden
1994	Lieutenant Rachael Scandling RN	Petty Officer Ian Blakeman
1995	Lieutenant MDJ Dicks RN	Leading Writer Simon Hubbard
1996	Lieutenant Alexandra Watts RN	Acting Petty Officer Karl Burke
1997	Sub-Lieutenant Mark Cox RN	
1998	Sub-Lieutenant Simon Hubbard RN	Leading Writer Christopher Banks
1999	Lieutenant Jude Terry RN	
2000	Sub-Lieutenant Karen Ledward RN	Petty Officer Richard Perfect
2001	Lieutenant Michael Welch RN	Petty Officer Anthony Quant
2002	Lieutenant Rachel Cunnell RN	Petty Officer Ian Wilson
2003	Lieutenant Karen Shortland RN	Petty Officer Damien Millington
2004	Sub-Lieutenant Emma Searle RN	Petty Officer Writer Mark Henderson
2005	Lieutenant Frances Coles-Hendry RN	Petty Officer Linda Gavin
2006	Lieutenant Nicole Bassett RN	Petty Officer Garry Braddock
2007	Lieutenant Katie Thomas RN	Leading Logistician Natalie Bywaters
2008	Lieutenant Andy Akerman RN	Petty Officer Chris Donkin

LEFT: *James Carine presents HMS Raleigh Award to Lt. Katie Thomas.*

2009	Lieutenant Lauran Castleford RN	Petty Officer James House
2010	Sub-Lieutenant Joanne Rowe RN	Petty Officer Michael Read
2011	Lieutenant Oliver Hinton RN	Petty Officer Stuart Merriman

Other Companies, such as the Cooks and the Innholders, also make awards and HMS *Raleigh* sometimes lays on a tour or a boat trip down the Hamoze, or something similar. In 2007, the awards were presented by the Junior Warden and the visit was to the Damage Control Trainer. This is a mock-up of a ship's compartment which has been holed and the damage control parties have to prevent flooding. By the time they have finished they are literally up to their necks in water. Sadly, non-Service visitors can only watch but even this was too much for one of them, who fortunately for the City's reputation, was not a Liveryman. The model moves and this visitor felt seasick!

THE DAPHNE DURBAN AWARD

In 2008 Mr Donald Durban, Master 1990/91, donated a sum of money to the Charitable Trust to endow an annual award in memory of his wife Daphne to be given to the Fleet Air Arm officer who was the best Military Aviation Studies Degree Student in the year. Donald had served

ABOVE: *Presentation of the Daphne Durban Award by Past Master Donald Durban, 2008.*

as an officer in the Fleet Air Arm during the Second World War and in 2008 his nephew, Rear Admiral Simon Charlier, was Rear Admiral Fleet Air Arm.

The first award was made in August 2009 at the Royal Naval Air Station (RNAS) Yeovilton in the presence of Past Master Durban and family members.

Year	Winners
2008	Lieutenant Andrew Bird RN and Lieutenant Luke Edwards RN
2009	Lieutenant Mark Gilbert RN awarded at RNAS Culdrose
2010	Lieutenant Christopher Jones RN awarded at RNAS Culdrose
2011	Lieutenant Richard Swales RN awarded at RNAS Yeovilton
2012	Lieutenant Adam Dean RN awarded at RNAS Yeovilton

THE DAVID MARWOOD AWARD

In 2010, Past Master Marwood, at that time the Senior Past Master, endowed a sum of money to the Charitable Trust to provide an annual award of £400 to the best officer passing out of the Britannia Royal Naval College, Dartmouth to enter the Logistics Branch of the Royal Navy. David donated this prize to mark his own boyhood desire to be a Naval Officer (Paymaster Branch) and his lifelong interest in the sea. The recipient was to be awarded the prize at Lord High Admiral's Divisions, the Lord High Admiral being then HM The Queen but currently HRH The Duke of Edinburgh.

The first Award was made at Lord High Admiral's Divisions by David Marwood in April 2011 in the presence of HRH Prince Michael of Kent.

The winners to date have been:

Year	Winner
2011	Lieutenant Michael Payne RN
2012	Sub-Lieutenant Matthew Cullen RN

ABOVE: *Presentation of The David Marwood Award, 2011.*

HMS *TRAFALGAR*

The Company became affiliated to HMS *Trafalgar* in 2006. *Trafalgar*, the fifth Royal Navy vessel to bear that proud name, was a nuclear-powered hunter killer submarine built at Barrow-in-Furness and launched by the wife of the then Chief of Defence Staff, Lady Fieldhouse, in 1981. The Commanding Officer at the time of signing the Letters of Association was Commander Peter Green RN who some years later was in command of HMS *Ambush* when Letters of Affiliation were signed between that boat and the Company.

Liveryman Julia Bradley recalls visiting the submarine in August 2006 when *Trafalgar* was alongside in Portsmouth. The submarine had just returned from a long deployment and Julia particularly remembers how many of *Trafalgar*'s acoustic tiles were missing. Many ladders were ascended and descended and airlocks entered and exited before meeting in the Wardroom where the Logistics Officer, Lieutenant-Commander David Johnson and First Lieutenant, Lieutenant-Commander Stuart Blackburn answered questions before adjourning to a slightly larger

ABOVE: *Past Master Marwood and Beadle, Mr Terence Young, aboard HMS* Trafalgar, *2006.*

shore-side Wardroom for lunch. Afterwards, in complete contrast, the party toured HMS *Victory*!

In October 2006, Commander Green and five of the ship's company were the Company's guests at the Installation Dinner in Saddlers' Hall.

A second visit was made to the submarine when she was alongside in Devonport in September 2008.

Finally, a group from the Company attended the De-Commissioning Ceremony at Devonport in December 2009. The Company made a financial contribution to ensure that the party that followed was a successful one!

HMS *AMBUSH*

After HMS *Trafalgar* paid off, Commodore (later Vice Admiral) David Steel suggested an affiliation with HMS *Ambush*, the second of the Astute Class nuclear-powered hunter killer submarines building at Barrow-in-Furness. This was eagerly accepted and in December 2010, a small group led by the Master travelled to Barrow for the official naming ceremony/

LEFT: *The launch of HMS* Ambush *(left to right: Liveryman Hallam, The Master, Senior Warden Richardson and the Clerk).*

rollout and launch by Lady Ann Soar, the wife of the Commander-in-Chief. The rollout was VERY slow as it took over two days for the submarine to reach the water!

The formal Letters of Association were signed at the Royal Charter Luncheon held in Butchers' Hall in July 2011. Signing the document on behalf of the Navy were Admiral Sir Trevor Soar, Admiral the Lord Boyce, Admiral Sir James Eberle and the CO HMS *Ambush*, Commander Peter Green. The Clerk to the Butchers' Company, Commodore Tony Morrow RN, had the White Ensign flying above the Hall!

THE IAN MOLYNEUX AWARD

The first *Ambush* Liaison Officer during part of the construction period was Lieutenant-Commander Ian Molyneux RN, the Weapons Engineer Officer. He was a member of the submarine's team in the Naval Field Gun competition at HMS *Collingwood*, a shore establishment near Gosport. It is very rare for a submarine ship's company to take part and the team performed well perhaps helped by the encouragement from Liveryman John Galpin a former Commander in the RNR, Liveryman Bill Hughes and the Clerk. Afterwards the Company sent a cheque for £50 to pay for beer for the team.

Tragically, when on secondment to HMS *Astute*, Ian was killed trying to subdue a sailor who had run amok with a rifle during the submarine's visit to Southampton. Ian was subsequently awarded a posthumous George Medal.

The Court agreed to award an annual prize to the Rating who had contributed most to making *Ambush* a happy boat and that this would be known as the Ian Molyneux Award. The first award was made in September 2011 by the Master when a group from the Company visited the submarine when she was alongside in Barrow.

Year	Winner
2011	Chief Petty Officer Colin 'Tiny' Small
2012	Petty Officer John Lewis

BALTIC MEDAL 1854-1855

Past Master Marcell presented the Company with a Baltic Medal awarded to Paymaster (later Paymaster-in-Chief) Henry Gibson. The Medal is always placed in front of the senior naval officer present at the Company's formal lunches and dinners. A fuller account of Henry Gibson's career is given in Chapter Eight.

VISITING ROYAL NAVAL SHIPS IN LONDON

The Company has been extremely fortunate in receiving invitations to naval ships visiting London. In return, our Liaison Officer, Past Master Marcell and the Clerk generally entertained the various Logistics Officers to a meal in the City.

Additionally the Clerk invited Liverymen visiting ships to donate between £15 and £20 each to naval charities.

In January 1999, a group from the Company visited HMS *London*. A magnificent silver model of the White Tower in the Tower of London belonging to the ship now has a place of honour in the Royal Regiment of Fusiliers Officers' Mess in the heart of the Tower itself.

In July 2006, Robin Eve and his wife Ann represented the Master at a Reception on board HMS *Albion* to celebrate in the presence of Her Majesty The Queen the 250th Anniversary of the Marine Society and its merger in 2004 with the Sea Cadet Corps. Robin and Ann recall that the ship should have been HMS *Ocean* but due to an outbreak of an infectious disease, *Albion* had been given less than a week's notice to take over! The evening finished with a Royal Marine Band Beating Retreat.

Some four years later Robin and Ann were guests of Commander Jackson at Greenwich for the 10th Anniversary of the Britannia Association, with another Royal Marine Band Beating Retreat prior to dinner in the Painted Hall.

In November 2006, 10 members of the Company were among several hundred guests conveyed by boat from Greenwich Pier to the aircraft carrier HMS *Illustrious* for a reception on board. The highlight of the evening was when the vast lift used for transferring aircraft from the flight deck to the hangers was lowered to reveal the Band of the Royal Marines from the Royal Naval College, Dartmouth.

Also in 2006, a group from the Company visited HMS *Grafton* and, in 2007 HMS *Ark Royal*. In November 2008 the Master, Francis Spencer-Cotton went on board HMS *Illustrious* to hear a presentation by the First Sea Lord, Admiral Sir Jonathan Band, on "The Royal Navy Today and Tomorrow".

Liveryman Geoffrey Woodward recalls visiting HMS *Westminster* with the Master and some other members of the Company in December 2008. In 1944/45 he had been trained in what was then a new specialisation "Radar Plot" so new that there was not even a badge to sew on to his uniform to indicate he had been trained. Would there be anything on the ship he would even vaguely recognise? The answer was "not a lot" as in Geoffrey's day the radar aerial was turned by hand crank with one hand, whilst calibrating the range with the other, all the time squinting at a small dimly lit cathode tube.

2008 also saw a visit to HMS *Exeter*. Two more visits were made to *Illustrious* in May 2009 when the ship was again in London and then some 18 Liverymen visited the ship when she was alongside in Portsmouth where they were briefed by Commander Alec Parry RN and his team on all aspects of logistics. The ship could sail for anywhere in the world at just 48 hours notice.

In the same year a group from the Company also visited the frigate HMS *St Albans*.

In July 2010, the Master, Robin Eve, and the Clerk attended the Logistics Branch Dinner held in HMS *Collingwood* and a group from the Company visited HMS *Richmond*.

WEST HAM SEA CADETS

An affiliation with the West Ham Unit of the Sea Cadet Corps, Training Ship "Thunderer", was established in July 2005 when the Commanding Officer, Lieutenant (SCC) Mark Weston and the Vice Chairman of the Support

LEFT: *Master Commander Rory Jackson talking to Sea Cadets at West Ham.*

Committee, Derek De Buick, were the Company's guests at a Livery Luncheon and were presented by the Master, Sir Clive Martin, with a cheque for £750 towards the purchase of a new minibus.

Past Master Marcell was asked to serve as President of the Unit and did so from 2005 to 2012 offering advice and financial support from outside sources. He is to be succeeded by another former naval officer, Liveryman Brian Gopsill.

In May 2011 the Master, Commander Rory Jackson, accompanied by the Clerk and Past Marcell visited the unit and formally presented the Letters of Association. The Cadets and the Clerk were much impressed that the Master of a Livery Company could tie a bowline!

Many readers will have seen the Cadets at the Company's Banquets in the Mansion House where they provide a Guard of Honour.

EXCHANGES

In 2010, the first exchange in the work-place between a naval officer from the Logistics Branch and a member of the Company took place. Lieutenant Dan Poole RN joined the Group Secretariat of HSBC plc for four weeks thanks to Liveryman Ralph Barber, the Group Company Secretary. Apprentice David Taylor also spent six weeks with the Royal Navy including the first week at sea in the Mediterranian with HMS *Cumberland* joining at Malta and disembarking in Greece. On his return to HMS *Raleigh* he was invited to undertake a project on "How to attract and incentivise officers to training roles at the Logistics School" which concluded with a presentation to the Chief Naval Logistics Officer and some of the staff of HMS *Raleigh*.

He fondly recalls flying a Merlin helicopter off the deck of HMS *Ark Royal* with all going well until the simulator crashed!

Although the Senior Service was the last of the three Services with which the Company formed an affiliation, the links are probably now the strongest and this is reflected in a letter from Admiral Sir Mark Stanhope

GCB OBE ADC, the First Sea Lord, to Colonel Michael Dudding on the latter's retirement as Clerk in December 2011. He commented on the close relationship between the Company and the Logistics Branch of the Royal Navy and thanked him for all that he and the Company had done to foster and strengthen the relationship.

THE ARMY

THE ROYAL ARMY PAY CORPS AND ADJUTANT GENERAL'S CORPS (STAFF AND PERSONNEL BRANCH)

On 27 March 1979, through the good offices of Liveryman Major Kenneth Vink, the Master, Mr John Phillips CBE QC, met the Paymaster-in-Chief of the Army, Major General John Kinahan and his Deputy, Brigadier AT Skinner, to discuss a formal association between the Company and the Royal Army Pay Corps.

This was followed up by a visit by the Master and Clerk, Mr Ron Simmonds, to the Royal Army Pay Corps (RAPC) Training Centre at Worthy Down and on 6 March 1980, Letters of Association were signed at the Duke of York's Headquarters, Chelsea. The Master, Stanley Eley,

LEFT:
Signing the Letters of Association with the Royal Army Pay Corps, 1980.

who had served with the Corps during the Second World War, and the Clerk signed on behalf of the Company and the Colonel Commandant, Major General K Saunders and the Paymaster-in-Chief Major General Kinahan signed for the Army.

Major General Kinahan was later enrolled as a Freeman of the City of London sponsored by the Master, Stanley Eley, and Hon. Liveryman Sir Lindsay Ring. Later that year a small party from the Company visited Worthy Down when a bronze statuette of a Paymaster was presented to the Company. A gift of a Company's embroidered Coat of Arms was presented to the Corps.

Later at a Passing Out Parade of the RAPC Apprentices, with the salute being taken by General Sir Timothy Creasy KCB OBE, Commander-in-Chief UK Land Forces, the Master presented the first of the silver medals to the Outstanding Apprentice of the Year in A level studies. The Company has continued to present silver medals for exceptional performance ever since.

Year	Winner	
1980	Apprentice Sergeant P.G. Rodford	
1981	Apprentice Sergeant P.E. Musson	
1982	Apprentice Tradesman J.E. Cronin	
1983	Apprentice Sergeant D.R. Lewis	
1984	Apprentice Tradesman Leslie Yuen	
1992	Apprentice Tradesman LJ McKeown	
1995	Second Lieutenant Emma Cooper	
1998	Warrant Officer I Carrick	
1999	No award made	
2000	Second Lieutenant Emma Cooper	Staff Sergeant Montana
2001	Second Lieutenant Danny Reid	Warrant Officer David Hazelden
2002	Second Lieutenant Tracy Prouse	Warrant Officer David Wood
2003	Second Lieutenant Tracy Wright	Staff Sergeant Catherine Munroe
2004	Second Lieutenant Barry Cooke	Warrant Officer Andy Vincent
2005	Captain P Ashman	Second Lieutenant NM Ledger
2006	Second Lieutenant Lydia Ratcliffe	Private Michelle Barber

2007	Second Lieutenant Lisa Keevash	Private Jeffrey Bates
2008	Captain Kirk Reynolds	Private Aaron Stelmach-Purdie
2009	Second Lieutenant Richard Ayre	Private Pratheesh Vaniyan
2010	Captain Justine Williams	Warrant Officer Terence Clasper
2011	Second Lieutenant Henry Lidgley	Private Andrew McLaren

The RAPC was absorbed as the Staff and Personnel Branch into the Adjutant General's Corps in 1992 and as a result new Letters of Association were exchanged on 3 November 1995 at, rather aptly, Armourers' Hall prior to the Livery Dinner. Signing on behalf of the Company was the Master, Clifford Grinsted, and for the Army, the Director General, Major General Michael Regan and Director, Brigadier Neil Mackereth FCIS.

Some years later the Clerk noticed that the collection of military helmets in the entrance to the Hall did not include a contemporary model. The Staff and Personnel Support Branch were persuaded to donate one and through the good offices of Liveryman Gerald Garnett (a Past Master Armourer and Brasier) it was presented at a lunch attended by the Masters of the two Companies, their Clerks, the Director and Chief of Staff of the Branch and Gerald Garnett.

In 2001 Master, Colonel Michael Dudding, presented the Branch with a Long Service and Good Conduct Medal of a founder member of the Army Pay Corps dating back to the 1890s. The medal is now displayed in the Corps Museum.

In the same year the Master also arranged for a small group of Liverymen to visit the 2nd Battalion, Royal Regiment of Fusiliers (in which he had served as a company commander) at their barracks in Rutland. The group was briefed on the various roles and weapons of the Battalion and fired some of the weapons. Liveryman Commander John Galpin was pleased to record that the Senior Service outshot the representatives of the other services on the 30 metre range!

The highlights however were when they were invited to don all the kit and perform the classic "section attack" manoeuvre (extremely tiring) and a long evening at the Officers' Mess bar hearing what it was really like at the sharp end.

In 2003 a party from the Company visited the Royal Regiment of Fusiliers training on the Ranges at Lydd.

In 2005 the 25th anniversary of the affiliation with the Staff and Personnel Branch was celebrated by Beating Retreat and Dinner at Worthy Down attended by 21 Liverymen and 31 members of the Branch. Court Assistant Rory Jackson was one of the 21 and recalls that the evening was a very special one and blessed with good weather. He also remembers being taken by a very senior Army officer down a series of long corridors to be shown a photograph of Worthy Down when it was a Royal Naval Air Station!

In September 2008 a group of Apprentices spent a weekend at Worthy Down which included live firing and cooking in the field. The weekend must have done some good as one of the Apprentices, John Rowland-Jones, is now on the Court!

THE SIR CLIVE MARTIN AWARD

In 2005 at the end of his year as Master, Sir Clive, a former Lord Mayor of London, made a donation to the Charitable Trustees of an endowment to cover an annual award for the most significant contribution by an officer or soldier of the Adjutant General's Corps (Staff and Personnel Support Branch) to administration in the field. The recipient is selected by a panel of Branch officers and a member of the Company, initially Liveryman Colonel Terry English and currently Liveryman Colonel Clive Drake. The Award is not earned lightly.

Year	Winner
2006	Corporal MW Gardner
2007	Corporal Samantha Brown
2008	Corporal Craig Shaw
2009	Corporal Cecil Carter
2010	Corporal Michael Borysenko
2011	Corporal Kieron Challand
2012	Warrant Officer Rupert England

THE TERRITORIAL ARMY

April 2008 saw the start of a year of celebration to mark the contribution of Territorial Army soldiers past and present across a century of service. On 15 May following a Service at St Paul's Cathedral, the Company held a Reception followed by lunch at Dyers' Hall for some TA members of our affiliated Branch. The

occasion was noteworthy for first, the excellent homely fare provided by the Dyers' cooks and secondly, the bravado performance on the piano for the toasts by Past Master Grinsted.

THE BIG CURRY LUNCH

Each year the Company's Charitable Trustees support the Lord Mayor's Big Curry Lunch at Guildhall in aid of the Army Benevolent Fund. The Masters of the Livery Companies are lined up by a Regimental Sergeant Major in alphabetical order of Companies rather than by seniority. This

ABOVE: *The Master talking to HRH The Duke of Kent at the Big Curry Lunch, 2012.*

must be the only time that the Masters of the Chartered Accountants and Chartered Secretaries find themselves alongside the Master Clothworker and way ahead of the Master Mercer! More about the Livery Company's order of precedence is given in Chapter 10.

THE ROYAL AIR FORCE

THE PERSONNEL (SUPPORT) BRANCH

A formal association with the Branch has been maintained since 1986 when formal Letters of Association were signed on 19 May at Armoury House. Air Marshal Skingsley CB and the Head of the Administrative Branch, Air Vice-Marshal RA Mason CBE, signed on behalf of the Royal Air Force and the Master, Leslie Croydon and the Hon. Clerk, George Challis on behalf of the Company. The Company was presented with two silver Loving Cups by the Royal Air Force to mark the occasion.

The Company presents annual awards to the best students on the Personnel (Support) Officers' Basic Course (POBC) and the Personnel (Support) Airmans' Basic Course (PABC). Originally the Administration Branch was based at RAF Halton and the Company representatives would be entertained in the Officers' Mess in the magnificent Halton House built by Alfred Rothschild, a bachelor, in 1883 for weekend entertaining. More recently the Branch has been located to what had been the Royal Navy's School of Navigation HMS *Dryad* but re-named MOD Southwick Park when the Navy left.

Winners have been:

Year	POBC	PABC
1998	Flying Officer Sally-Ann Rowlands RAF	Senior Aircraftsman Lynn Coffill
1999	Flying Officer Adrian Portlock RAF	Senior Aircraftsman Paul Lamont
2000	–	–
2001	Flying Officer Emma Marshall RAF	Senior Aircraftsman Rachel Nice

ABOVE: *Master Michael Dudding at RAF Haltern, 2001 (Liveryman Air Vice Marshal Burton second from the left).*

2002	Flight Lieutenant Steve Parker RAF	Leading Aircraftsman Rachel Hewlett
2003	Flying Officer Julie Perrett RAF	Leading Aircraftsman Julie Armstrong
2004	Flying Officer Julie Mann RAF	Leading Aircraftsman Joan Ochwodho
2005	–	–
2006	Flight Lieutenant Victoria Fuller RAF	Leading Aircraftsman Gary Jones
2007	Flying Officer Lottie Gunn RAF	Leading Aircraftsman Rebecca Smith
2008	Flying Officer Katie Strickland RAF	Senior Aircraftsman Adam Hill
2009	Flying Officer Angela Button RAF	Leading Aircraftsman Joseph Wrigglesworth
2010	Pilot Officer Beth Cullen RAF	Senior Aircraftsman Michelle Bicknell
2011	Flying Officer Barry Dunn RAF	Leading Aircraftsman Nicholas Knight

THE GROUP CAPTAIN JOHN CONSTABLE MEMORIAL PRIZE

After a distinguished career in the Royal Air Force, John Constable became the Secondary of London and Under Sheriff at the Old Bailey and was Master in 1998/99. Very sadly he died on 19 November 1999 only a few weeks after his year of office had ended. A prize in his memory is awarded to the officer under the age of 21 at entry to RAF Cranwell who has demonstrated the greatest potential for further development by producing the best overall performance in both leadership and professional studies during the year.

2001   Flying Officer Adam Watts RAF
2002   Flying Officer RC Briggs RAF
2003   Pilot Officer SR Harth RAF
2004   Acting Pilot Officer DM Lowes RAF
2005   Pilot Officer Adam Grant RAF
2006   Pilot Officer Christopher Gonzalez RAF
2007   Pilot Officer Michael Highmoor RAF
2008   Pilot Officer Thomas Wallington RAF
2009   Pilot Officer Adam James RAF
2010   Pilot Officer James Roy RAF
2011   Pilot Officer Michael Robbins RAF

THE RICHARD SERMON AWARD

In 2009 Past Master Sermon made a donation to the Charitable Trust to fund an award to the officer or airman of the Personnel Branch considered to have made an outstanding contribution to the effectiveness of the Royal Air Force in an operational environment.

Winners have been:
2009   Sergeant Donald Reynolds
2010   Flight Lieutenant Gary McIntosh RAF and Senior Aircraftman
        Hamza Majid
2011   Flight Lieutenant Beverley Gill RAF

AFFILIATION WITH THE BASE SUPPORT WING, ROYAL AIR FORCE ODIHAM

The first visit to RAF Odiham was in May 2009, the first highlight being an inspirational talk by the then Station Commander, Group Captain Turner, on the role of the Chinook Force in Afghanistan. Because the sand in Afghanistan accumulates on a Chinook it can acquire an extra 400kg of weight in 60 hours of flying.

Liverymen were impressed that a Chinook could be scrambled in around 90 seconds especially as it took most of the visitors that time just to work out which way the flying helmet should be worn let alone actually getting it on!

The Company's inaugural visit to RAF Odiham, 2009.

175

And that was the second highlight of the day – an actual flight in a Chinook but over the peaceful Hampshire countryside rather than the deserts of Afghanistan!

The Letters of Association between the Company and the Base Support Wing were signed at the Court ,meeting on 27 January 2011 with the Master, Commander Rory Jackson, signing on behalf of the Company, and Wing Commander Justin Fowler RAF, Commanding Officer of the Wing signing on behalf of the Air Force. Witnessing the ceremony was Air Marshal Ian Macfadyen CB, then Constable of Windsor Castle, and our principal guest at the Livery Luncheon that followed.

2011 saw a further visit to Odiham with Past Master Tutt flying in a Chinook – perhaps, but this cannot be confirmed as she never revealed her age, the oldest woman to do so.

VISITS TO RAF STATIONS

In 1996, the then Master, Clifford Grinsted, a former Royal Air Force pilot in the Second World War, accompanied by the Wardens flew in a Tristar

ABOVE: *Signing the Letters of Association between the Company and RAF Odiham, 2011.*

over the North Sea to witness a refuelling exercise. That year also saw visits to Strike Command Headquarters with the AOC, Air Chief Marshal Sir William Wratten accepting an invitation to be the principal guest at a Livery Luncheon held later that year in the Barber Surgeons' Hall.

A year later Hon. Freeman Air Vice-Marshal Sherrington invited the Master, Geoffrey Finn, and a small number of Liverymen to visit RAF Waddington, near Lincoln. The visit was memorable in that the group travelled from RAF Northholt in an aircraft of the Queen's Flight, with white-gloved stewards offering excellent refreshments. Liveryman John Galpin recalls "The complete hash I made in the take off and landing simulator but which the Master carried out perfectly!" After briefings from the two operational flying squadrons based at RAF Waddington, the group enjoyed the return flight to RAF Northolt.

ABOVE: *A Company visit to RAF Marham, 2008.*

In 2003 a party from the Company visited RAF Innsworth and the then Master, David Wright, was a guest at a dinner in Admiralty House in Whitehall hosted by the Chief of the Air Staff, Air Chief Marshal Sir Peter Squire.

Liverymen have also visited RAF Marham twice, and RAF Shawbury. In July 1999, a group visited RAF Leeming where the Officer Commanding the Administration Wing was our future Hon. Freeman, Wing Commander Nigel Beet RAF.

In 2011, as guests of Hon. Freeman Air Commodore Colin Smith, a party went to RAF High Wycombe for a briefing on the work of Air Command.

CONCLUSION

From the initial contact with the Army in 1979, just three years after the formation of the Company, links with the Armed Forces have grown considerably over the years and today are as strong as they have ever been.

CHAPTER SEVEN

THE LIVERY LIAISON GROUP

By Past Master Francis Spencer-Cotton and Others

THE GROUP

The Minutes of the Court meeting held on 14 July 1988 refer to a paper circulated by the Master, Dennis Roberts, headed "Participation by the Livery". The paper is no longer in the archives but it is surmised that it discussed how to involve Liverymen in arranging certain events and providing help at functions for example by acting as Stewards at the Banquets held at the Mansion House. The idea was approved by the Court at its meeting held on 13 October. Thus was born the Livery Liaison Group ("LLG").

The first meeting of the LLG took place in the Irish Chamber in Guildhall Yard on 17 March 1989 chaired by the Junior Warden, Donald Durban. Other than the Junior Warden, the LLG membership was to be drawn from Liverymen not on the Court.

One member of the original LLG was Liveryman Derek Taylor who travelled regularly from Wakefield to attend not just the LLG meetings but also almost every other Livery activity.

One of the early duties of the LLG was to provide Liverymen at the Company's stand at the Livery Exhibition held in Guildhall.

In September 1994, the Court endorsed proposals by the LLG and its Chairman, Junior Warden Clifford Grinsted, that in future the LLG should elect its own Chairman to serve for three years. The Junior Warden would remain an ex-officio member to ensure adequate liaison with wider Company affairs. One third of LLG's members would retire at the Annual Assembly each year. The Chairman would be required to present reports in person about the LLG's activities at two Court meetings a year.

On 14 November 1994 Francis Spencer-Cotton was elected the first Chairman under the new terms of reference with Liveryman Mollie Harris as Secretary/Treasurer. Mollie was to serve many years in this role and in recognition of this, and her unstinted support for all Livery events, was one of the first recipients of the Company's Meritorious Service Awards.

A full list of Chairmen and Secretaries is shown below:

Chairman
1994 to 1997   Francis Spencer-Cotton
1997 to 2001   Thelma Wilson
2001 to 2002   Sydney Donald
2002 to 2004   Charles Ledsam
2004 to 2007   Julia Bradley
2007 to 2010   Sir Jeremy Elwes
2010 to 2012   Jo Whiterod
2012   Richard Reger

Secretary
1992 to 2002   Mollie Harris
2002 to 2003   Yvonne Barnes
2005 to 2007   Sir Jeremy Elwes
2007 to 2010   Kerry Porritt
2010 to 2012   Mandy Webster
2012   Yvonne Barnes

Treasurers have included Liverymen Yvonne Barnes, Julia Bradley, André Confavreux, Mike Davis, Ivan Whittingham and Trevor Partridge.

In 1995 a float of £150 (increased to £500 in 1999) was authorised by the Master to meet general expenses and in 1998 it was agreed that the LLG's accounts would be open to inspection by the Hon. Treasurer and incorporated in the main Company accounts from 2001/02. A simple accounting system was made complicated when the Company registered for VAT.

Members of the LLG were authorised to wear a distinctive ribbon with a bar to denote membership. A fine of £25 was also imposed but rescinded a few years later!

Some of the Members have progressed to Master.

THE EVENTS

BLETCHLEY PARK

Liveryman Julia Bradley recalls that in 2006 when members of the Company met at Bletchley Park, one of them nearly sent the whole building up in flames. He had ordered a toasted sandwich for his lunch and caused the toaster to go up in flames, exploding the sandwich and setting off the fire alarms. The restaurant was closed and the building evacuated to await the fire engines. Heroically the firemen entered the building before deciding that the danger had passed, but they needed to do the usual safety checks. The visit was then able to proceed rather later than planned. Luckily toasted sandwiches were not popular during the Second World War.

ABOVE: *The Company visit to Bletchley Park, 2006.*

THE TOWER OF LONDON

Adèle Thorpe, the Company's second female Master, was determined that during her year, the majority of speakers at Company events would be women. One of these was Moira Cameron the first ever female Warder at the Tower of London. In 2009 Moira very kindly invited members of the Company for a private tour of the Tower and to witness the Ceremony of the Keys after the Tower had closed to the public. It was a very dark night with a new moon giving a ghostly atmosphere. Liveryman Mandy Webster recalls how well Moira conveyed the terror of facing imminent death as the condemned were led up from the Tower to the public scaffold in what is now the garden at Trinity House.

There had been concern over costs so the LLG had arranged a fish and chip supper in the Yeoman Warders' Mess. Total cost of the evening – just £5.

THE JOHN RUTTER CHRISTMAS CONCERT

The Christmas visit to the Albert Hall organised by the LLG has become something of a fixture in the Company's calendar. Attendance peaked

ABOVE: *The John Rutter Christmas Concert, Royal Albert Hall, 2011.*

in December 2011 when more than 60 Liverymen and their guests enjoyed lunch at Imperial College followed by a wonderful afternoon of Christmas-themed music played by the Royal Philharmonic Orchestra. Liveryman Jo Whiterod still admires the organisational skills of the RPO's Jo Thompson who kept finding "one more ticket" for a show that was sold out!

HOTELS AND HOSPITALS

The LLG has organised tours of some of the most historic and famous hotels in London including Royal Horseguards, Radisson Grafton, the Pelham, the Waldorf and St Pancras. Most of the tours included that wonderful, but neglected, meal: afternoon tea.

Perhaps one of the more unusual visits was to the Old St. Thomas's Hospital Operating Theatre in 2010. 19 Liverymen and their guests toured the Museum which contains an amazing collection of surgical instruments, specimens etc illustrating the history of surgery. The centrepiece is the old operating theatre itself built in 1822 with an 1830 wooden operating table. LLG treasurer, Mike Davis, volunteered to be a patient for a lower leg amputation – were the LLG accounts that bad? The surgeon was assisted by Court Assistant Bish Lis. Happily 19 two

ABOVE: *The Company visit to Sutton's Hospital in Charterhouse.*

legged members exited the theatre for a supper in the nearby Wheatsheaf
hostelry.

More recently the LLG organised a visit to Sutton's Hospital in
Charterhouse, a former Carthusian monastery and now almshouses.

FINE DINING

Food features in most LLG events! Two outstanding occasions were in
February 2003 when a Dinner was organised by the LLG in the House of
Commons hosted by Michael Portillo. So popular was this event that the
venue was changed to the Churchill Room which had seating for 96, all
of which was taken up. Then in October 2007 there was another excellent
Dinner in the House of Lords in the Attlee Room hosted by the Rt. Hon.
The Lord Hodgson of Astley Abbots.

CHURCHES AND MUSEUMS

Visits to churches have included Southwark Cathedral, Evensong tour and
supper at Westminster Abbey and a tour of the Bevis Marks Synagogue.

Museums have included the Horniman, the Polish Armed Forces Museum, Foundling Museum, Tate Britain, the Wallace Collection and a private tour of the Queen's Gallery.

CONTINUOUS PROFESSIONAL DEVELOPMENT (CPD)

In 2012 the LLG received requests to provide CPD opportunities for Liverymen but preferably twinned with social events. Thanks to Adrian Waddingham of Barnett Waddingham and Wyn Derbyshire of SJ Berwin, the LLG was able to hold two "teach ins" on pensions and law, each followed by a reception with plentiful food and drink. The rumour that some of the retired members of the Company just attended the social half is entirely untrue!

THE LLG AFLOAT

In 2001 the LLG organised a visit by boat to the Royal Naval College at Greenwich. Their guide was the then Master, Philip Marcell, who also arranged for the party to have lunch in the undercroft of the Painted Hall. In 2008 Liveryman Tony Davis, who was also Master of the Honourable

ABOVE: *HQS Wellington, Livery Hall of the Master Mariners' Company.*

Company of Master Mariners, hosted an LLG visit to his Livery Hall, the Headquarters Ship Wellington moored by the Embankment in the River Thames. Gin and tonics on the Quarterdeck were followed by a tour of the ship and lunch in the Court Room which had once been the engine room. Tony Davis completely denied the rumour that HQS Wellington was actually aground on discarded champagne bottles! More recently the LLG has arranged a tour of London on land and water by a DUKW known more colloquially as a Duck.

Not on water but very impressive was the visit to Freemasons' Hall organised by Liveryman Ray Fox.

THE WHITECHAPEL BELL FOUNDRY

Visits to this working bell foundry in the East End were organised in 2004 and 2011. The tour, given by the owner, is a fascinating one and finishes with an excellent buffet supper in the Georgian house which forms part of the factory premises.

CONCLUSION

Over the years the LLG has gone from strength to strength organising up to half a dozen low cost events a year ranging from Arab horse racing at Brighton, visits to the Magic Circle, Kew Gardens, the Travellers' Club, the College of Arms, gunsmiths, fish smokers, Central Criminal Court and the Royal Opera House to name but a few.

The LLG has also participated in City Dip, helped organise social weekends outside London mostly in the United Kingdom but also Antwerp and Bruges; and provides ushers and other support at the Company's more formal functions.

The LLG has played a huge part in the Company's life – every modern company should have one.

CHAPTER EIGHT

THE COMPANY'S TREASURES

By Master Charles Ledsam

INTRODUCTION

Although the Worshipful Company of Chartered Secretaries and Administrators has only been in existence since 1976, its 70 plus "Treasures" all have fascinating stories to tell. This chapter records some of the highlights.

There is in existence an album with beautiful photographs of the Company's treasures and a brief description of each item. This album, which at the time of writing is almost full, was presented by Colonel Michael Dudding in 2001 on completion of his year of office as Master. A second album was later presented by Adèle Thorpe, Master 2007/08, in recognition of her year in office and will record more recent treasures.

How has the Company acquired its treasures? In some cases these have been given in memory, in celebration or as gifts in recognition of the ties and links that individuals or organisations have had with the Livery.

Some of the Company's treasures have been donated by Masters, some by other members of the Company and some by other organisations such as the Armed Forces, with whom the Company has developed significant relationships in administrative branches. Some of the silverware was new at the time of presentation, whilst other items are much older than the Company itself.

The majority of our treasures are on display in the Guildhall. Others are on display in the Company's office, including the Royal Charter. However the remainder are safely boxed up and stored for use at banquets, lunches and other special events and sadly are not therefore on regular display.

Not all the items have been silverware. Amongst the more unusual items is a Crimean War Medal belonging to Paymaster Henry Gibson RN. This is dated 1854-55 with a "Baltic" clasp and was purchased in an auction by Philip Marcell, Master 2001/02. Henry Gibson joined the Navy as an Acting Paymaster on 28 June 1838 but does not appear to have joined the service until January 1845 being confirmed as Paymaster in October 1846 subsequently serving in HM Ships *Volcano*, *Driver* and *Hercules*. He joined HMS *Ajax* in December 1854 which was deployed to the Baltic during 1855. Future appointments included Paymaster to the Coast Guard Divisional Headquarters at Cork and Paymaster in HM Ships *Formidable* and *Asia*. He was promoted to the rank of Paymaster-in-Chief on 17 May 1870.

In 1982 David Marwood, Master 1981/82 and our Senior Past Master at the time of writing, gave a silver mounted cut glass ship's decanter to celebrate his year in office. He also donated a silver gilt pendant badge on a chain for use by the Master's Lady. This is currently used by the Master's wife or consort if a lady on formal occasions.

At a Court meeting held at the Irish Chamber on 4 April 1985, Ken Jacques, Master 1982/83, presented a silver plated tray to mark his year in office. The intention was that the name and date of each Master be engraved on the tray. There is sufficient room for each Master until 2024.

LEFT: *The Jacques' tray.*

All Livery Companies embrace the role of dining as a forum for cementing relationships and furthering the economic and charitable causes which they support. Tradition plays a large part and so it is at formal dining events that Worshipful Companies can not only admire but derive innate pleasure from using their many bequeathed items of plate and other Treasures.

Within the Company we are indeed fortunate, despite our very relative youth, to have already amassed several unique and valuable items, many of which are used several times a year at formal events such as Lunches and Dinners. More information about these items is given below.

LOVING CUPS

Founder Master John Wedgwood, Master 1977/78, presented a Loving Cup in 1977 during his term of office. This was first used at the Inaugural Livery Dinner on 5 April 1978 at Apothecaries Hall.

In 1981 two Loving Cups were presented by Thomas Mason (Master 1980/81). A further one was presented in 1985 by Liveryman Harry

ABOVE: (LEFT) *One of the Loving Cups presented by Past Master Ted Mason.* (RIGHT) *The Loving cup presented by Liveryman Henry Rawlings.*

Rawlings, who had been a founder member and staunch supporter of the LLG in its early days.

In 1985, the Company was fortunate to be presented with two more Loving Cups by the Royal Air Force. Ten years later in 1995, Geoffrey Finn, Master 1996/97, presented a Loving Cup, hallmarked Birmingham 1927.

Two of our more modern and unusual Loving Cups were designed and made by Smith & Harris, well known Hatton Garden silversmiths. These were commissioned by Past Masters Jeffrey Greenwell and Francis Spencer-Cotton respectively.

Jeffrey Greenwell (Master 2005/6) wrote: "The Loving Cup which I presented to mark my year as Master was commissioned from Smith & Harris of Hatton Garden as a Loving Cup to be used at Company functions.

"Advice from Smith & Harris was that so many cups used by livery companies are former racing trophies which have been re-engraved and were not intended to be used as loving cups. They suggested that I revert to an Elizabethan design with a stem meant to be grasped in one hand rather than two, and with a spiral engraving to ensure that a greasy hand would have a better grip! The resulting design reflects this advice".

Francis Spencer-Cotton, Master 2008/09, continues "when I got around to thinking about my gift to the Company at the end of my year as Master I remembered the Loving Cup which Jeffrey had given and which I so admired as it was a true Loving Cup. So many I have seen at various functions have two handles like sporting trophies, whereas it should be in the form of a Chalice. I thought that I would like to donate an identical cup to the one Jeffrey presented so that the Company had a matching pair. I telephoned Jeffrey to ask him if he would allow me to copy his donation and was delighted when he said that he welcomed my suggestion.

At the Installation Dinner following the Court meeting and Livery Assembly I had the honour of sitting at the top table alongside the new Master, Robin Eve. To my delight the Loving Cup I had earlier presented was placed on the table in front of me and then looking to my right further along the table, Jeffrey was sitting there, with his cup similarly placed. The effect was just as I had anticipated and I am very grateful that Jeffrey was so accommodating when I sought his permission. I often go into the Guildhall Club to look in the cabinet where both cups reside and have also taken friends in to show them and have told them the story of how it all happened."

CANDLESTICKS

A pair of silver gilt Candlesticks, hallmarked 1860, were presented in 1981 by Liveryman Cyril Ridd to celebrate his Golden Wedding and 50 years as a member of the Institute.

A Banner, embroidered mainly by Mrs Joyce Judd, wife of a Liveryman, with the Company's Coat of Arms, was presented by Ken Jacques, Master

ABOVE: *The Ridd candelabra.*

191

1982/83. Ken was also one of the founding Trustees of the WCCSA Charitable Trust from 1978 until 2010.

GOBLETS, BEAKER AND INK-STAND

In early 1979 John Phillips, Master 1978/79, presented the first silver goblet for use at formal dinners. This was followed by three silver goblets being presented by Mr Ken Jacques on 22 March 1979 at the Mansion House Dinner. These are modern ones hallmarked Sheffield 1977/78. The Livery Company knows them as the "Neepsend" goblets as Neepsend is both an area of Sheffield and the name of the Company where Ken Jacques was employed. They are used by the Master, Senior and Junior Wardens regularly at Dinners.

In 1986 three more goblets were presented by Past Master Croydon for use by the Armed Forces guests. In 1995 Past Master Cauchi presented one more goblet for use by the principal guest.

David Wright, Master 2002/03, and his late wife Prue proved to be most generous as well in presenting a variety of items. These included 4 silver champagne goblets similar to those presented by Past Masters Jacques and Hammond. The goblets were to be used by the Master's

ABOVE: (LEFT) *The Neepsend goblets.* (RIGHT) *The Phillips goblet.*

ABOVE: (LEFT) *The Cauchi goblet.* (RIGHT) *The Croydon goblets.*

Lady, the Founder Master (or most Senior Past Master present at a function) and the Immediate Past Master. The fourth could be allocated at the discretion of the Clerk.

Other items donated have been a silver beaker, which was presented by Dennis Roberts (Master 1988/9) to celebrate the 800th anniversary of the Mayoralty in 1989.

A silver ink stand (hexagon-shaped with two quills) was presented to the Company by Court Assistant Roy Harris (who was to become Master in 1991/2) in 1981.

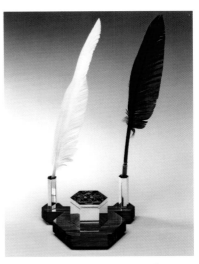

ABOVE: *The Harris ink-stand.*

GAVEL AND STAND

Rear Admiral James Carine, Master 1997/98, presented a gavel and block, made out of wood from HMS *Victory*. He wrote "Towards the end of my naval career I was guest speaker at a dinner held by naval auxiliaries on the main gun deck of HMS *Victory* on a wild stormy night similar to the weather often endured by those who served in blockade duties off Ushant during the Napoleonic Wars. Instead of a traditional Trafalgar Night celebration, I was asked to speak about Lady Emma Hamilton who was

ABOVE: *The Master, Charles Ledsam, bidding farewell to Terence Young as Beadle, 2012.*

probably the most vilified woman of the early 1800s and died in poverty with an unmarked and lost grave in France. However I pointed out it was she who personally nursed Nelson back to health in Naples after the Battle of Aboukir Bay and, had she not done so, it is most unlikely Nelson would have been at Trafalgar and changed the course of European history.

"At the evening's end, I was given the gavel and stand made from the timbers of HMS *Victory* and used at that dinner. When I was Master, we had no gavel for use at meetings or social occasions and I could think of no better home for it."

A new gavel and block has recently been presented by the former Beadle, Terry Young BEM, in celebration of his twelve years as Beadle. Terry had commented that he felt the original one did not attract the required attention of the Court!

SILVER MACES

Past Master Carine also presented the Company with a mace for the Beadle. He wrote "In my day, led by the Beadle, we processed formally from Founders' Hall, where we later returned for supper, via Cloth Lane and Smithfield to the Priory Church of St Bartholomew the Great for the Company's annual church service. In my pompous way, I thought we needed a mace on such occasions so I commissioned Smith & Harris of Hatton Garden to design and make a short silver mace which I presented to the Company at the end of my Mastership. My only stipulation was that the name of each Beadle was to be engraved on it in the space provided for that purpose."

John Constable, Master 1998/99, presented a full length silver mace in 1999. This is more often used by the Beadle in processional events.

ARMADA DISHES

There are three silver Armada dishes all engraved with the Company's coat of arms, all donated by Past Masters.

Francis Bergin, Master 1993/94, takes up the tale: "I had always liked the appearance of the Armada dish and its historical association, especially going back to Elizabethan times. They are featured in many museums around the country. Besides, I thought I should follow the example of two of my most distinguished predecessors as Masters of the Company, the late John Phillips, Master for the second time in 1986/87, and Donald Durban, Master 1990/91, both of whom were good friends of mine for many years."

ABOVE: *Armada dishes presented by* (LEFT TO RIGHT) *Past Masters Durban, Phillips and Bergin*

WANDS

During his year in office Stanley Eley, Master 1979/80, presented a Wand, made of ebony, with a silver secretary bird. The bird is interchangeable with the Mace presented by Group Captain John Constable in 1999.

A pair of wands was also presented by Ron Bounds (former President of the ICSA in 1985 and later Master 1987/88). The silver discs engraved with the secretary bird were later kindly paid for by Ron's widow, Margaret Bounds. David Wright recalls Liveryman Harry Rawlings bearing the wands at formal livery events for many years.

ABOVE:
The Eley wand.

GIFTS FROM THE ARMED FORCES

Several of our treasures are gifts from the Armed Forces with which we have close links. These include an Evesham crystal decanter presented by the Royal Navy (Chief Naval Supply Officer) in 1987.

A bronze Paymaster statuette was presented by the Royal Army Pay Corps in 1980 and a silver statuette of an officer of the Adjutant General's Corps was presented by the Staff and Personnel Branch in 2006.

ABOVE: (LEFT TO RIGHT) *"Paymaster", Two loving cups presented by the Royal Air Force.*

As previously mentioned, two more Loving Cups were presented by the Royal Air Force in 1985. These are hallmarked Birmingham 1911 and Sheffield 1933.

TUTT ROSE BOWL

The late Sylvia Tutt, Master 1983/84, chose a silver rose bowl of antique Irish design hall-marked in London 1907. Coming from a lady Master, and indeed the first Lady Master of any Livery Company, she wished her gift to reflect some degree of femininity. A rose bowl signified this aspect very appropriately. "Rose Haven" was the name of her parents' home. Moreover, she wrote in her book *A Mastership of a Livery Company* that "the rose being the emblem of England, seemed to symbolise the especially English character of the Livery Company. The antique Irish design could also be recognised as regarding the fact that the headquarters of the Company were in the Irish Chamber at that time, whilst being hall-marked in London endorses the respect with which the great City of London is universally held".

ABOVE: *The Tutt rose-bowl.*

LONGER CHAIN AND A LECTERN

Past Master Wright's wife Prue presented a longer silver chain to be worn round the neck of the Master's Lady for her badge of office. Traditionally the Immediate Past Master's spouse/consort presents this badge to the incoming Master's consort.

Prue, who loved wood, also presented a splendid oak lectern for use by the Master at Court meetings. This was commissioned from Robert (better known as "Mousey") Thompson, whose business had been in existence in Kilburn, Yorkshire for over a century. All items of furniture made by his company include an engraved mouse. The name of the craftsman can be identified by the unique characteristics of the mouse, for example having longer or shorter whiskers!

Another lectern, more suitable for use when standing up, had earlier been presented to the Company by Bob Simmonds, its first Hon. Clerk.

THE STORY OF THE SECRETARY BIRD CANDELABRUM

In 2010, the Company took delivery of a splendid candelabrum made by Hatton Garden silversmiths Smith & Harris.

Mentioned elsewhere in this History, one could be forgiven for thinking that Smith & Harris is a fourth or fifth generation company so prolific has been its contribution not only to our collection but to the 'treasure collections' of Livery Companies across the City and indeed the gift cabinets of ambassadors and dignitaries across the world. Whilst only a fledgling company

it was commissioned by Margaret Thatcher's first administration to supply diplomatic gifts for Downing Street visitors.

Although an ancient craft going back many centuries, the silversmith's art enjoys a buoyant and thriving existence in London today albeit at the bespoke and quality end of the market.

Gareth Harris and Dennis Smith started their business in 1981 but would readily forgive a visitor to their workshop for thinking its roots lay in Dickensian London; they do – its Hatton Garden premises have been occupied by a silversmith since at least 1820.

The task of making a candelabrum for the Company was one that Gareth Harris relished. "It typically takes several months from sketching a design, (based on an outline sketch of the Founder Master John Wedgwood), to delivery of the finished candelabrum which costs on average between five and eight thousand pounds although of course one can spend less and considerably more" says Gareth.

"The Company's candelabrum took us around five months but not of continuous work. There are necessary breaks while, for example, components are cast and then there's the polishing, finishing and engraving work to be done. It's a very bespoke process and the Secretary Bird which provides the focal point of the commission was one of the more exciting challenges we have faced."

The Secretary Bird is an African bird of prey. "It's not an especially attractive bird but when we modelled it for this candelabrum we obviously employed a degree of artistic license, not just to enhance its visual appeal but to ensure its safety from breakage. The bird in the wild has a very delicate spiked plumage on the back of its head which looks wonderful in context but would be wholly impractical in a cast model" said Mr. Harris.

"First a wax model of the bird was painstakingly hand-made. This was then covered in plaster and a small feeding tube attached and the whole model was left to dry. Once dried, it is heated to a temperature where the wax melts and can be drained from the mould. Molten silver was then poured into the mould and left to cool until solid after which the plaster was carefully unpacked to release the silver bird. Many hours of hand finishing are then required to sculpt the perfect bird we see today."

Gareth Harris explains that his craft is not just about yielding pleasure today. "It's about longevity. We expect a candelabrum such as this to enjoy hundreds of years of use, and so at every stage we do all we can to ensure strength. A heavy and flared base is an essential starting point so that should somebody catch the candelabrum with their coat tails, it won't topple over. In the unlikely event that is does or if it is accidentally dropped, the most delicate points are the arms and therefore we hone these out of solid silver. Economies can be made by using a hollow tubing for the arms but we are loath to do this. The WCCSA candelabrum has arms of solid triangular silver and these are very strong."

The Company wishes to thank Paul Stanyer who talked to Gareth Harris about the Secretary Bird Candelabrum. Paul's father, Eric, was a long-time member of the Institute.

LEFT: *Liveryman Stuart Carmichael and Liz Scott.*

The funds for the Candelabrum were provided by a most generous legacy from the late Liveryman Stuart Carmichael, who tragically died on his wedding day, and equally kind contributions from his fiancée Liz Scott; Mrs Jeanette Wedgwood, widow of the late John Wedgwood; and Liveryman Richard Pugh.

Careful inspection reveals it is a truly astonishing work of craftsmanship with an attention to detail that is in total harmony with the aims and objectives of the Company.

Following donations from Mrs Jane Campbell, widow of late Court Assistant Donald Campbell, and Past Master Wright, it is hoped to commission a matching candelabrum shortly.

GOWNS FOR THE MASTER, WARDENS AND CLERK

One of the Company's most valuable groups of items is the gowns worn by the Master, Wardens, Clerk and Beadle at ceremonial events. These were recently restored and renovated thanks to the generosity of Past Master Marcell.

CONCLUSION

In October 2010 the then Master, Robin Eve, gave the Company a beautiful bespoke box to display the Founder Master's Second World War campaign medals which had been presented by the Founder Master's son, David. He then endorsed the Clerk's statement that, other than the second candelabrum, no more treasures were needed at present due in part to lack of storage space and in part due to the ever increasing cost of insurance. This policy could of course change if the Company ever acquires its own premises.

ABOVE: *The Founder Master's medals.*

CHAPTER NINE

THE ROYAL CHARTER

By Past Master Clifford Grinsted

INTRODUCTION

The idea of creating a Livery Company, for members of the Institute of Chartered Secretaries and Administrators, was conceived in the mid 1970's, to fulfil a wish at that time by senior officers of the Institute to cement the close association which had developed between the City of London Corporation and the large number of members of the Institute already in practice in the City.

The founding fathers took the necessary steps and the Company came into being on 3 November 1976, to be followed by the grant of Livery on 19 July 1977. A constitution was required and at great speed a minimal one was produced comprising 1,750 words recorded on 10 pages of A4 sized paper.

The said constitution was to remain in force and unquestioned until January 1994 when at a meeting of the Court under the chairmanship of Master Francis Bergin, it was resolved that a Long Term Planning Committee be established with the widest possible remit to look at, and make recommendations, for the future of the Company. The Committee, under the chairmanship of Past Master Croydon, undertook intensive research and study and towards the end of the year the Committee produced its report containing a large number of recommendations of a substantial nature for the future conduct of the Company. (see Chapter Two).

THE 1999 CONSTITUTION

In the succeeding months, and well into 1995, the Court took its time in examining and testing each of the recommendations and eventually the conclusion was reached that each was worthy of support, whereupon the Court resolved that they should be implemented.

Inevitably these proceedings brought into focus the inadequacy of the Company's 1977 constitution. As the result of many observations made at subsequent meetings of the Court during the years 1996/97, and as each recommendation became fulfilled, the necessity for a new constitution became ever more evident, culminating in a resolution that a study be undertaken with the object of justifying a proposal that a new constitution to meet the needs already identified, and fit for the 21st century, be commissioned.

Past Master Grinsted was invited to undertake the study, with the help of a working party, and in June 1997 his report was presented to the Court strongly recommending the commissioning of a new constitution. A decision was deferred but at a subsequent Court meeting on 29 January 1998, under the chairmanship of Master James Carine, the Court resolved to proceed and, having been invited to do so, Past Master Grinsted accepted the commission to write the new constitution and to conduct it through its various stages. He was assisted by a small working party and also had the help of Past Master Roberts as a mentor.

The work began with a blank sheet of paper and, by the study of other relevant models, unique drafting, and consultation with eminent and learned officers of the Corporation, including the Comptroller and City Solicitor, and the City Archivist, a final and substantial draft of the new constitution, comprising Ordinances and Standing Orders in excess of 10,000 words, and recorded on 21 pages of A4 paper, was published, and presented to the Court for approval.

After time for study, the formal approval of the Court was given on 15 October 1998 whereupon the officers of the Company signed a Petition addressed to the Lord Mayor and Court of Aldermen and sponsored by Alderman Clive Martin (later Sir Clive, Lord Mayor and Past Master) praying for approval of the new constitution. The customary and formal process of examination and consultation, over a period of months, then began, and continued until 25 May 1999 when, at a meeting of the Court of Aldermen with the Lord Mayor in the chair, the Court of Aldermen was pleased to grant its approval, and thus what came to be known as the 1999 constitution of the Worshipful Company came into being.

From that time onwards, and for the next nine years, and under the direction of each succeeding Master, aided by the Clerk, Colonel Mike Dudding, the 1999 constitution proved to be a most effective bible, as a source of guidance and regulation for the proper conduct of the affairs of the Worshipful Company, as it entered into the 21st century. Yet always, and particularly at times when the large number of developments which had inspired the creation of the 1999 constitution began to become a reality, it encouraged the Court to set its aspirations even higher towards the ultimate objective set out in both the 1977 and 1999 constitutions "to apply, when to the Court of Assistants the time shall seem meet, to Her Majesty in Council for a Charter of Incorporation".

THE ROYAL CHARTER

As early as October 2005 reports were being tabled, amongst others, on the legal status of the Company, the achievement of the Company's maximum permitted membership, the expansion of its charitable activities, the structure of the Company within the City and elsewhere, the greater involvement of the membership in good and worthy social and public works, and the Company's support for the world of Livery generally. All of these aspirations, and others, promoted a greater interest in the stature of the Company for the future, and at a meeting of the Court held on 20 July 2006, under the chairmanship of Master Jeffrey Greenwell, the Court decided to take the next step, by harnessing the experience already gained by Past Master Grinsted and authorising him to develop a case for an application to the Privy Council for the grant of a Royal Charter. At the next following meeting of the Court on 5 October 2006 the commission given to Past Master Grinsted was reaffirmed, and thus began a two-year exercise of mammoth proportions and intensity.

The Court had asked for a complete review of the 1999 Constitution in which all Court members were invited to make suggestions. Out of some 150 suggestions less than half a dozen were incorporated into the final version. It was clear that the Ordinances and Standing Orders of 1999 constitution provided a firm base on which to build, and that these would be the principal source and inspiration for those that were to become a part of the Royal Charter.

The writing of the Charter itself was virgin territory and could not have been accomplished without the skilled oversight and counsel of Mr. Alex Galloway CVO, who at the time was the Clerk to the Privy Council. When, upon his retirement, his responsibilities were taken over by Mrs Ceri King, Deputy Clerk to the Privy Council, the same professional degree of guidance and counsel continued until there emerged a first draft of the Charter that had the prospect of acceptance by the Privy Council, subject to the exercise of the royal power and prerogative.

A second document, but of equal importance to procure acceptance of the Company's application, was the preparation of the Humble Petition to Her Majesty. The language to be used was distinctive, in the manner used for all Loyal Messages, but at the same time it had to convey the depth of desire and the persuasive arguments felt by the Company in seeking to become enriched as a professional body and in stature by association with the Royal Grant. Thus the acquisition by the Company of a legal status of its own, independent of the membership, was seen as a primary motive, enhanced by the claim the Company could make to being financially sound and morally strong.

A critical element of the procedure to be followed was the evidence of solid support required to underwrite the Humble Petition, and to be an assurance that opposition was unlikely to arise. It was desirable that, if possible, supporters should themselves be incorporated by Royal Charter and able to speak with authority, and that at least one of them should be an appropriate Government department. Acceptability of the supporters by the Privy Council was also a requirement to be borne in mind, and thus began a carefully managed exercise of approach, consultation, challenge, persuasion and acceptance. Each approach had a particular objective of its own, and it is relevant to record that because its role and its authority was to be enshrined in the Charter and in the Ordinances, the fullest consultation took place with the City of London Corporation in the persons of the Court of Mayor and Aldermen of the City. When, at the end of the exercise several months later, Past Master Grinsted was able to report all objectives achieved, the Court of the Company acknowledged a deep debt of gratitude to the following:

The Institute of Chartered Secretaries and Administrators
The Worshipful Company of Saddlers
The Worshipful Company of Weavers
The Charity Commissioners
The College of Arms
The Secretary of State for Business, Enterprise and Regulatory Reform
The Court of Mayor and Aldermen of the City of London

Thursday 4 October 2007 will be remembered as a milestone in the history of the Company when the Court, having approved the pleadings to be made, and upon a proposal from the Master, resolved with acclamation that as Petitioners they most humbly prayed that Her Majesty be graciously pleased to exercise Her Royal Prerogative to grant a Charter to the Petitioners in the terms of the draft submitted or in such other terms as may to Her Majesty seem proper. Whereupon the Petition was signed by the Master, Richard Sermon, the Senior Warden Adèle Thorpe, the Junior Warden Francis Spencer-Cotton and the Clerk Michael Dudding.

On 11 October 2007 and accompanied by the several supportive documents, the Petition was delivered into the hands of the officers of the

Privy Council and entrusted to their examination and to the judgement of the Council and Her Majesty.

During the next few weeks, with admirable speed and efficiency, borne out of the intense preliminary preparations made in the fullest co-operation with Past Master Grinsted, the officers of the Council became engaged in procedural matters requiring formal close study of the draft Charter and Ordinances, reaffirmation from the appropriate Government departments, the verification of supporters, publication of the Petition in the London Gazette, and the preparation of the appropriate documents for presentation at meetings of the Privy Council.

The first presentation of the Petition and draft Charter took place at the November meeting of the Privy Council when, in accordance with custom, Her Majesty referred the draft Charter, incorporating the Ordinances, to a committee of the Council for their consideration and recommendation. While that process was taking place the first thoughts were being given to the manner in which, if granted, the Company should receive the Charter, and for that purpose the Master, now Mrs Adèle Thorpe, set up a small working party, under the chairmanship of Immediate Past Master Richard Sermon, to assist Past Master Grinsted in the development of his conception of a Church Service of Consecration and Thanksgiving to be held in one of the City Churches followed by Dinner in one of the more prestigious Livery Halls.

The festive season of 2007 thus passed in a spirit of high expectation which was fulfilled when it was announced that the Charter and Ordinances were to be commended to Her Majesty for approval at the February 2008 meeting of the Privy Council. It was at that meeting, duly held on 12 February 2008, that Her Majesty The Queen in Council ordered the Right Honourable the Lord High Chancellor to cause a warrant to be prepared for Her Majesty's signature for passing under the Great Seal a Royal Charter to the Company. There followed arrangements for the delivery of the Charter to the Crown Office for affixing of the Great Seal of State. Thus the Company was to receive its Royal Charter, and preparations began in earnest both as to its composition as an article for display in future years, and the manner in which it should be received.

ELIZABETH THE·SECOND

by the Grace of God of the United Kingdom of Great Britain and Northern Ireland and of Our other Realms & Territories Queen, Head of the Commonwealth, Defender of the Faith:

TO ALL TO WHOM THESE PRESENTS SHALL COME, GREETING!

WHEREAS a humble Petition has been presented unto Us by the Master and Wardens of the association formed in the year of our Lord One thousand nine hundred and seventy seven under Letters Patent issued by the Lord Mayor of London as a Livery Company of the City of London and known as "The Worshipful Company of Chartered Secretaries and Administrators" (hereinafter called "the former Company") praying that We might be pleased to grant to it a Charter of Incorporation for the object of promoting and supporting good governance and the highest standards of administration in the private public and not-for-profit sectors and the better discharge of responsibilities under such regulations and with such powers as to Us might appear meet and expedient: AND WHEREAS We have taken the said Petition into Our Royal Consideration and are minded to accede thereto: NOW THEREFORE KNOW YE that We by virtue of Our Prerogative Royal and of Our especial grace certain knowledge and mere motion have granted and declared and by these Presents do for Us Our Heirs and Successors grant and declare as follows:

1. (a) The persons who are now the members of the former Company and all such persons as may hereafter become members of the Body Corporate hereby constituted shall forever hereafter be one Body Corporate and Politic by the name of "The Worshipful Company of Chartered Secretaries and Administrators" (hereinafter referred to as "The Worshipful Company") and by that name shall have perpetual succession and a Common Seal with power to break alter and make anew the said Seal from time to time at their will and pleasure and by the same name shall and may sue and be sued in all Courts and in all manner of actions and suits and shall have power to do all other matters and things incidental or appertaining to a Body Corporate

   (b) The Arms Crest Supporters and Badge granted and assigned unto the Master Wardens and Court of Assistants of the of the former Company of the City of London by Letters Patent under the hand and Seal of Garter King of Arms bearing date 6 May 1980 shall be transferred to the said Worshipful Company on the date on which this Our Charter shall take effect and We do hereby give and grant unto the Worshipful Company Our Royal Licence and Authority that it may thenceforth bear and use the said Armorial Ensigns according to the Laws of Arms the said transfer being first recorded in Our College of Arms otherwise this Our Licence and permission to be void and of none effect

2. In this Our Charter and in the Ordinances unless the context otherwise requires the following words shall have the following meanings:—
"the Court" shall mean the Governing Body of the Worshipful Company;
"the Ordinances" means the Ordinances set out in the Schedule hereto or the other Ordinances for the time being in force;
"the Members" mean the Freemen and Liverymen of the Worshipful Company for the time being as defined in the Ordinances;
"the Institute" means the Institute of Chartered Secretaries and Administrators;
"Special Resolution" means a Resolution passed by not less than two-thirds of the members of the Court present and voting at a meeting of the Court and a Resolution passed by not less than two-thirds of the Liverymen present and voting at a General Meeting of the Liverymen of the Worshipful Company of which not less than twenty-eight days notice shall have been given to those entitled to such notice specifying the substance of the Resolution and the intention to propose it as a Special Resolution

SERVICE WITH INTEGRITY

The working party began its deliberations in earnest and, among its first decisions it reaffirmed the wish of the Court that the Charter be reproduced by a calligrapher on vellum, and thereafter photographed and framed. This work was delegated to the care of Windsor Herald at the College of Arms who co-operated fully with the Company's wishes, and later honoured the Company by his presence as the bearer of the Charter during its consecration and presentation at the Thanksgiving Service. During this time the Charter, when completed by the calligrapher and before framing, was delivered, together with the Ordinances, to the Crown Office for the affixing of the Great Seal of State. The affixing of the Seal represented the final act of incorporation, which meant that for evermore it would be known that the Company was reborn and received Royal patronage on 24 July 2008.

THE SERVICE OF CONSECRATION AND THANKSGIVING

The working party was quick to adopt the plan tabled by Past Master Grinsted for a Service of Consecration and Thanksgiving in the presence of eminent guests and the Livery. After much planning, on 11 September 2008 in the Church of St Michael, Cornhill, and in the presence of a great congregation embracing the Livery, high officers of the Corporation headed by the Lord Mayor (locum tenens), Masters of other companies and other eminent guests, the Royal Charter was carried in procession into the Church and laid on the altar. There then followed in solemn ceremony, and in the presence of the Right Reverend and Right Honourable Richard Chartres, Bishop of London, the Charter was consecrated by the Company's Chaplain, and then received by The Lord Fellowes who, as the Queen's representative, presented it to the Master with a charge to preserve and guard it, and to ensure that it would be used forever to provide counsel and wisdom in all the deliberations of the Company.

For posterity it should be recorded that the Church Service included a short exposition on the history and purpose of Royal Charters given by Mr. Alex Galloway CVO and formerly the Clerk to the Privy Council, a

CLOCKWISE: *Windsor Herald handing the Royal Charter to the Hon. Chaplain at the start of the service. The scene in the Church of St Michael, Cornhill. Lord Fellowes presenting the Royal Charter to the Master on behalf of HM The Queen.*

Bible reading taken from the Book of Exodus, Chapter 18 vs 19-23, read by the Company's youngest Apprentice, Miss Eleanor Lang, the Anthem "I was glad" by Sir Hubert Parry sung by the Choir, an address from the Bishop of London, and the singing of the Company's own hymn written by Past Master Grinsted.

THE COMPANY HYMN

In this moment of Thanksgiving
When our hearts are filled with praise,
When we recognise Thy mercies
Found surrounding all our ways.
Lord, we come in humble spirit
And, as supplicants, we plead,
Make us worthy of Thy blessing,
Hon'ring Thee in every deed.

Like the scribes of Holy Scripture
As with pen and gift of word,
They recorded times most wondrous
So that they be truly heard.
Let us too as willing servants
Seek with skill and honesty,
True fulfilment of our pleading
Service with integrity.

For this Company's past we thank Thee,
For its future we beseech,
Members drawn to highest service,
Giv'n to those they seek to reach.
Grant us, Lord, in goodly measure
Gifts you gen'rously bestow,
May we use them for thy glory,
Serving Thee while here below.

WORDS: CLIFFORD H. GRINSTED
MUSIC: BLAENWERN

212

At the end of the Service, and to conclude the evening, the congregation, headed by the Master and the Lord Mayor (locum tenens), led by Honourable Artillery Company Pikemen, Musketeers, drummer and flautist, and a mounted escort from the City Police, processed to nearby Drapers' Hall. Dinner was then served to 270 guests and, to conclude proceedings, both the Master and Sir David Howard Bt (Lord Mayor locum tenens) commended all those who had worked tirelessly to achieve such a magnificent and prestigious result and occasion.

In a symbolic gesture a special award was presented to Past Master Grinsted in recognition of his unique service to the Company as author and producer of both the 1999 constitution and the Royal Charter, and the act of commemoration, which award he dedicated to all who had supported him unreservedly and who would forever share with him the joy of this historic achievement.

ABOVE: *The Master presenting Past Master Grinsted with a silver salver at the Royal Charter dinner.*

PERSONAL REMEMBRANCES OF THE CHARTER CELEBRATION

By Adèle Thorpe – Master at the time

———◆———

I could sense the sigh in the words "let's try again" as much as Clifford Grinsted could probably sense the gritted teeth behind my smile. It was the rehearsal of the ceremony for the Charter celebration and he wanted everything to be perfect. I had to take a step forward at a particular part of the ceremony. The first time my step was too big, the second time it was too small. Everyone involved with the ceremony stood around in St Michael's Church. All waited to be summoned. All were in awe of Clifford. All did as we were told. All practised to death every tiny element so that it would be all right on the night.

I had very little to do with the run up to the celebration itself, Richard Sermon and his Charter Committee dealt with all the details and I was kept informed of the decisions they had made and occasionally asked for my opinion.

Court Assistant Donald Campbell was responsible for publicity and filming in the Church. Brian Sole devised a seating plan in a Church where pillars restricted views of the chancel. The Clerk master-minded the planning for the dinner.

At one stage the committee decided to spend a large sum on an additional dessert wine which was rather special and in replying, with my views as a teetotaller, I said I really did not have a view one way or the other on the wine as long as we had the chocolate crème brûlée I was really looking forward to. The reply came back that they had changed the dessert for a plain fruit brûlée as it would go better with the top class wine!

By the time the actual day came I had just started a new job and was very reluctant to take more time off than absolutely necessary. I put my pen down from taking minutes of a two-hour meeting a mere 25 minutes before I appeared changed into full evening dress, having collected my daughter Katy on the way, to a church about a mile away trying desperately not to look rushed and harassed. I had put on long evening gloves which I thought rather elegant, but Katy glared at them and asked if I intended doing a strip tease during the service. When in a response to asking his opinion Past Master Kirkham said "I think the dress is elegant enough without any additional adornment" I realised Katy was probably right and removed them (just them).

The service went off like a dream. Windsor Herald in full dress uniform holding the ornate, calligraphed and framed (and extremely heavy) Charter. He continued to carry it in our procession and has subsequently mentioned to me that his back has not been the same since! You could have heard a pin drop during Alex Galloway's speech and Lord Fellowes' formal script which contrasted with Richard Chartres, the Bishop of London's sermon which was hilariously received. He talked of us achieving the triple – as Chartered Secretaries receiving a Royal Charter and Richard Chartres being there. My Senior Warden, Francis Spencer-Cotton, as throughout my year, gave me just the smile or pat on the back to give me the confidence I needed, as I took exactly the right-sized step forward. Taking the oath of allegiance to the new Charter and the Queen on behalf of the Company was a very emotional moment.

There was a complicated mini dance of switching places as we left the doorway of the church to comply with protocol. Apparently the Lord Mayor (even a locum tenens) takes precedence over the Bishop in the streets of the City of London whereas the Bishop takes precedence within the church building itself.

The procession through the streets from St Michael's to Drapers' Hall was a memory treasured by many. There are probably still about twenty Japanese tourists wondering what they had photographed. Our elegant and erect sword bearers, Sir Jeremy Elwes and John Murray were both also secretly armed with umbrellas - just one of the contingency plans which luckily we did not need. There were fully uniformed Pikemen and Musketeers, the mounted police, then the very long procession. My Master's fur-trimmed black gown contrasted very nicely with the reds of the Lord Mayor locum tenens, David Howard, on one side and the Bishop of London's white ceremonial robes on the other. There then came the Masters of several other companies, and every city dignitary you could

think of from the Lord Fellowes, representing the Crown, to the Remembrancer, to the Chief Commoner, to the Recorder of London, the Chamberlain and many others, then followed by our own Liverymen and their guests all in uniform or white or black tie. With about 270 of us, it was quite a spectacle!

I was told that the end of the procession lost the start of it at one point, but where I was it was difficult to get lost – I just had to follow the rear of a horse. The horses appeared to have had a rather unpleasant meal before the walk. Certainly samples of it appeared from time to time both in gasses and more solid form, making the journey on the cobbles in stilettos one of the more difficult roles I performed in my year as Master.

TOP: *The procession to Drapers' Hall.*

ABOVE: *The procession nearing Drapers' Hall.*

216

The Pikemen on guard as we entered Drapers' Hall were magnificently solemn and statesmen-like and, therefore, I was not expecting a wink from one of them. I did a double take until I realised both the Master Draper and the Clerk to the Information Technologists, both friends, were on duty that day. Drapers' Hall was full to capacity and the catering staff really pushed the boat out with the meal, but when the dessert came I could not believe it. Everyone else had, as expected, the plain crème brûlée and yet the catering staff delivered me a chocolate one which Past Master Richard Sermon had arranged for me. If I had not been feeling nervous or emotional enough before this, coming very shortly before my speech it nearly tipped me over. Is it any surprise that a couple of years later I was one of his main supporters in his campaign to be elected Sheriff.

The Master had a lot of things to do that night and people to speak to and therefore my official consort, daughter Katy at 21 and down from university, was more or less left to fend for herself. I was immensely proud of her as she sat at the top table between the Bishop of London and the Lord Mayor locum tenens chatting away non-stop to both of them. I cannot think where she inherited the chatting from, as I am such a quiet shy individual. It was wonderful that she was able to share this special evening with me.

Clifford had done so much work in helping pushing our application for a Charter through all the different hurdles and in getting the ceremony correct. A few weeks before this rehearsal, unbeknownst to him I wrote personally to

LEFT: *Dinner in Drapers' Hall..*

each of the Court members asking if they would consider making a personal donation for us to buy a "thank you" for him. Every Court member responded to me, some with more than the minimum I had suggested and with Robin Eve's contacts, he was able to acquire for us a wonderful engraved silver salver that was presented to Clifford on the night. It was very difficult to keep this secret, particularly when Clifford was unimpressed about where he had been seated for the dinner, not realising that he needed to be seated there to make it easy to come up and collect the gift about which he knew nothing. Clifford was delighted on the evening with this gift and he has subsequently advised the Company that he will leave it to the Company. So we all pray that we will not see the salver again for a good many years.

After the solemnity of the ceremony, I lowered the tone in the evening by starting my speech with a somewhat corny joke. "It is always nerve racking talking after a dinner, but on an occasion such as this – well I spent most of the dinner not enjoying my food as I was worrying about spilling it. Irving Berlin wrote a song about just such an occurrence when the waiter tripped and covered him in pudding. You may know it - pudding on my top hat, pudding on my white tie, pudding on my tails."

I proceeded to talk about the vital importance of history and tradition and needing to have vision to adapt to the future and how this evening and these celebrations were a perfect merger and celebration of both.

I ended quoting George Bush who said "I think we are all agreed, the past is now over" and continued "Like the Monty Python parrot, our unincorporated association is dead, demised, passed on, no more, ceased to be, expired. It is an ex-unincorporated association." I then asked all members to join me in the toast to our rebirth as a Charter Company and to the array of distinguished guests.

The next day typing up my minutes, I wondered if I had dreamt all this, but my sore feet from the new shoes told me otherwise. Following the event there were the photos and the memories of so many people who called, wrote and e-mailed to tell me it was an extraordinary occurrence that they will always remember. I am proud to have played my little part in the early history of the Company.

CHAPTER TEN

AT THE HEART OF THE CITY

By Past Master Sir Clive Martin

This chapter describes aspects of the City and illustrates the extent of the contribution made by the Company. Individual Liverymen and the Company as a whole are outward looking towards civic responsibilities, in addition to supporting the work of the Institute of Chartered Secretaries and Administrators.

What is meant by the City? In a westerly wind, an international flight into Heathrow is sometimes accompanied by an announcement that the City of London can be viewed from the starboard windows. A glance reveals the whole of London laid out below.

ABOVE: *The City of London at Night.*

By most citizens of the UK, the City is thought to be the square mile, but to overseas visitors it is likely to be the whole of London. From a financial services standpoint, the City can be viewed as the hub of global financial services. The word City can be expanded or contracted according to context.

The Company was granted the Royal Charter of Her Majesty Queen Elizabeth in the fifty-seventh year of Her Reign and effective from the twenty-fourth day of July in the year two thousand and eight. Referring to object 3 (d) the following applies:

"To further interest within the Worshipful Company in the history, traditions and customs of the City of London and to … support the Lord Mayor Aldermen and Corporation … and all worthy objects of Livery within the City of London".

In this context Corporation is a convolution of the Right Honourable The Lord Mayor, the Right Worshipful the Aldermen and Commons in Common Council assembled.

Throughout its existence, the Company has supported the City on a broad front and can justly claim to be at the Heart of the City. With special interest in governance, it is not surprising that Liverymen have been and many are elected members of the City government, the Corporation.

For the reader unfamiliar with the nature of the City and livery, the following short narratives listed above are intended to demonstrate the unique nature of the City and the Livery Companies.

CITY OF LONDON

Some several thousand years ago, the first settlers might have sailed and rowed up the Thames, seeking a suitable landing. Most of the estuary shoreline was mud. Eventually, on the north bank, they found a gravel landing between two small hills. These hills were subsequently named Corn Hill and Ludgate Hill. A stream, the Walbrook, ran between them and there was a navigable river upstream, the Fleet River. The first bridge across the Thames was where the London Bridge is today.

Readily accessible by sea and conveniently situated between the Mediterranean and northern Europe, it was natural for London to become an important trading centre. The Romans recognised the importance of Londinium's location and by the eighth century, Venerable Bede was describing London, in the language of his time, in these terms. "London is a trading emporium to which traders come by land and sea to conduct business".

William of Normandy recognised London as an important trading centre, for him a source of wealth. Also, he realised that many of his fellow countrymen were trading profitably between London and France.

ABOVE: *The City seen from the south.*

Thus he decided to grant a charter to the citizens of London, the original being in the care of the Corporation to this day. King William was not popular, however. He needed to be careful and to keep an eye on London. He initiated the construction of the White Tower, on the City boundary. During the construction he lived at Barking Abbey.

By the turn of the second Millennium, the City had consolidated its position as the leading international trading centre, arguably one of the nation's greatest financial assets, contributing vast sums of money to the national Exchequer. New York trades huge volumes of business by virtue of the size of the United States, but London has had greater volumes of global trading.

Accelerated by the so called "Big Bang" in the 1980s, whereby restrictions on financial trading activities were removed, the City has achieved critical

ABOVE: *The Lloyd's building.*

mass. International companies feel compelled to have City representation and in many cases, their head offices. Nearly all languages are spoken in the City and the time zone favours London's location. The City is far from complacent however, realising that other financial centres are keen to take the crown.

CITY OF LONDON CORPORATION - DELIVERING A WORLD CLASS CITY

At the heart of the City is the City of London Corporation, an outstanding governing body, whose responsibilities and interests are extensive, within the square mile and beyond. These include police, port health, the quarantine centre at Heathrow, Billingsgate, Smithfield and Leadenhall Markets, Epping Forest, Highgate Wood, Queen's Park, Burnham Beeches, Hampstead Heath, the Honourable the Irish Society, Guildhall School of Music and Drama, Boys' School, Girls' School and Freemen's School, Barbican Centre and the major charity City Bridge Trust.

ABOVE: *Leadenhall Market.*

Within the square mile, the Corporation is dedicated to providing the best possible environment in which people live and work. Some three hundred thousand people travel daily in and out of the City. Others come regularly from all international financial centres, both home and abroad.

The Corporation also recognises the needs of communities in the adjoining boroughs. Some of the most deprived communities in the land are to be found not far from the city centre. A wide range of support is given by City Bridge Trust and by a range of economic and social initiatives.

A fine example is one which provides opportunities for those about to leave school in the deprived communities to visit the City offices of international and national companies. Approaching enormous glass edifices can be daunting and this initiative provides the opportunity for a chat and a tour with the chairman or other senior executive. This is designed to break the myths, and hence the perceived barriers, thereby encouraging young people to apply for jobs across a range of skills.

The principal task of the Court of Aldermen must be to ensure a succession of well qualified men and women prepared to offer themselves

ABOVE: *A meeting of Common Council in the Guildhall.*

for election as Lord Mayor. Also, with a reduction from about 125 Common Councilmen to 100, Aldermen also share the increasing workload of chairing Corporation committees.

THE LIVERY COMPANIES

At the end of Second World War, there were fewer than 80 Livery Companies, many having lost their halls in the Blitz, subsequent bombing and rocket attacks by the Luftwaffe.

Most of these guilds and companies were of ancient origin, some like the Weavers' Company dating back to 1155. In medieval England, traders banded together to form trade guilds. Their objects were concerned with training apprentices, controlling entry, quality of work and looking after distressed families.

Charity was part of their remit and worship was an important aspect. Hence the word "mystery" was often included in the guild description.

Through fashion and technological development, a few companies have lost or changed their original trade. The Fanmakers' Company for example, has adopted the jet engine industry and ventilation.

After the Second World War it was considered, by some, that Livery Companies not only had their roots in the past but were also becoming out of touch with modern business. Perhaps it was not recognised that below the surface these historic companies were engaged in extensive support in the fields of education, arts and heritage. It was a case of hiding a light under a bushel.

What did emerge from a detailed study of the City and its institutions, was the foundation of what are generally referred to as the modern companies. New companies formed as guilds and in due time achieved livery status, Chartered Surveyors, the Chartered Accountants of England and Wales and of course the Chartered Secretaries and Administrators. By 2012, there were 108 companies, with several others working their way towards recognition.

Several Liverymen of the Company have been Master of other companies including:

Deputy Richard Regan	Master Cutler
Francis Bergin	Master Baker
Sylvia Moys CC	Mistress Plumber to Mr Peter Lerwill
Sir Clive Martin	Master Stationer and Newspaper Maker
Sylvia Tutt	Master Scrivener
Richard Sermon	Master Wheelwright

LEFT TO RIGHT: *Richard Sermon (Master Wheelwright), Michael Dudding (Master Chartered Secretaries and Administrators), Susan Hughes (Master World Trader).*

Tony Davis	Master Mariner
Vernon Knapper	Master Gold & Silver Wyre Drawer
Susan Hughes	Master World Trader
Gerald Garnett	Master Armourer & Brasier
Neville Joseph	Master Wheelwright

LIVERYMEN AND THE CITY OF LONDON CORPORATION

This narrative attempts to indicate how the Company continues to take a significant part in the wider city, through service of its Liverymen to the City's government, as Common Councilmen, Chief Commoners, Sheriffs and Lord Mayors.

Governance being at the heart of the Chartered Secretaries' responsibilities, it is not surprising that many of the Company's Liverymen have served and are serving as elected members of the City of London Corporation.

Two developments took place at the turn of the second Millennium. The franchise has been extended to include representation by limited companies and chartered companies. Representation is proportional to numbers employed but on a weighted scale so that large companies do not have cohorts of nominated electors. The Company qualifies for one vote on the City electoral register.

Another development has been extending the term of elected office for Common Councilmen, from one year to four years. In wards contested regularly, no sooner had a member won a seat than, within a short time, it was necessary to think about the next election.

LEFT: (ABOVE) *Mr Robin Eve, Chief Commoner, receives HRH The Queen Mother.* (BELOW) *Liveryman Sylvia Moys, Common Councilman.*

Being formed by 13 members of the ICSA, the Company supports the Institute by enhancing the profession, particularly by engaging in educational and charitable activities. The involvement of Company Liverymen in the governing body of the City raises the profile of the profession throughout the City and beyond.

In line with the Corporation's work in supporting the neighbouring boroughs, the Company takes a role in community projects. Covered in other chapters are Rokeby School, West Ham Sea Cadets and the University of East London, all being in the London Borough of Newham of which Past Master Mike Dudding was the Representative Deputy Lieutenant and President of Newham Scout District.

Several Liverymen have served as Chief Commoner. This appointment used to coincide with the elected office of chairman of the City Lands Committee. The office of Chief Commoner is now by election of all the Common Councilmen. The workload of Chief Commoner is considerable, ranging across the work of the Corporation, with many meetings, visits inwards and outwards, attendance at a vast range of social and economic initiatives.

COMPANY LIVERYMEN ELECTED TO CITY GOVERNMENT

George Challis CBE	Chief Commoner 1990/91 and 1991/92
Deputy Robin Eve OBE	Chief Commoner 2000/01
Deputy Richard Regan	Chief Commoner 2011/12
Sylvia Moys	Common Councilman 1991-

Past Masters John Constable and George Cauchi have both served as Secondary and Under Sheriff at the Old Bailey.

SHRIEVALTY

In his charter of 1067, King William addresses Geoffrey the Portreeve and William the Bishop, recognising that London already had an effective

ABOVE: *Past Master Richard Sermon receiving the Company's gift on taking office as Sheriff.*

administration. One is left to wonder why William addresses two people? Was it that William the Bishop could read and write whilst Geoffrey was skilled with the sword, a powerful combination! Of recent times, a Sheriff might have carried a sword on ceremonial occasions, but rarely would skill at arms be practised!

Each year on Midsummer's Day, two Queen's Sheriffs are elected in Guildhall, to serve for the ensuing year. Nomination is open to all Liverymen, the total electorate consisting of some 25,000 livery names from the 108 Livery Companies.

A frequent question is why do elections for Sheriffs and Lord Mayor concern the Liverymen, yet ward elections for Aldermen and Common Councilmen are the province of the ward public electorate. There was a time when the whole City elected the Sheriffs and Lord Mayor. However, as the population grew, it became impossible to control the populace on election day. Sometimes, a person might, unexpectedly and unwillingly, be elected to office by acclamation of the crowd! Several alternatives were examined and tested, but eventually it was decided that the only viable solution was for the Livery to form the electorate for the Sheriffs and Lord Mayor.

The two Sheriffs are equal, although usually one is an Alderman and the other not an Alderman. The expressions "lay sheriff" and "aldermanic sheriff", whilst not entirely unacceptable, are not encouraged, because both are equal in every respect. Also, when occasionally both Sheriffs are Aldermen, such informal descriptions are not relevant.

Both Sheriffs operate in close support of the Lord Mayor, occasionally accompanying him or her on overseas official visits. They both share the workload of looking after the judges of the Old Bailey on the one hand and helping the Lord Mayor with his duties, on the other. Informally, they engage with the Lord Mayor in supporting his principal charitable initiative for the year.

Nowadays, the Sheriffs' legal responsibilities are few. However, they still take their seats at the formal opening of Old Bailey terms, but cannot concurrently serve as magistrates.

Increasing pressures on the mayoralty have led to greater opportunities for Sheriffs to share the Lord Mayor's workload, across a range of private and public commitments. This also provides the opportunity for Sheriffs to be heard, as well as being seen!

Confusion sometimes arises with the term High Sheriff in the counties of England and Wales. The Queen's Sheriffs in the City are distinct.

Liverymen of the Company who have served as Sheriffs:

Hon. Liveryman Sir Alexander Graham
Sheriff 1986/87 and Lord Mayor 1990/91

Hon. Court Assistant Sir Roger Cork
Sheriff 1992/93 and Lord Mayor 1996/97

Past Master Sir Clive Martin
Sheriff 1996/97 and Lord Mayor 1999/2000

Deputy, Liveryman Richard Regan
Sheriff 2006/07

Past Master Richard Sermon
Sheriff 2010/11

ABOVE: *"The Lady of Justice" at the Central Criminal Court, Old Bailey.*

MAYORALTY

In 1189 the City of London had its first Mayor, Henry Fitz Ailwyn, who served for 20 years. The Lord Mayor and Aldermen were dealing daily with the challenges of a growing City. They found themselves dealing with some intractable issues, as the following extract from City records shows:

> Letter from the Lords of the Council to the Lord Mayor and Court of Aldermen, stating that the plague was prevalent and increasing in the Netherlands; recommending to their consideration the peril to the City, by means of its continual trade and commerce with that country and requesting them to advise, with as much expedition as possible, upon some course to be offered to the King and Council for the safety and preservation of the City.
>
> 30 September 1617.

The Lord Mayor and Aldermen were in the habit of consulting prominent citizens when considering solutions to problems. Those consulted eventually evolved into the creation of Common Councilmen who soon took over the bulk of Corporation business. However of recent times, with the reduction of numbers of Common Councilmen from some 125 to 100, the Aldermen have shared the committee work load.

The Lord Mayor's schedule is both exhaustive and potentially exhausting. A scan of the diary schedules reveals a kaleidoscope of meetings and visits, ministers, ambassadors, high commissioners, heads of businesses, trade delegations and the panoply of the City, the nation and the world.

The Lord Mayor presides at meetings of the Court of Common Council and the Court of Aldermen. He is Chief Magistrate and enjoys the ceremonial title of Admiral of the Port of London. He is patron of a host of charities.

It might seem strange if the largest international financial services centre did not have its first citizen travelling the world, recognising the huge volumes of business and promoting further reciprocal trade and investment. The Lord Mayor each year devotes nearly 100 days overseas, visiting some 30 countries which account for some 50 major cities. The Lord Mayor is invariably accompanied by senior business men and women. These are official visits supported by national government. They provide access to key members of foreign governments and heads of institutions.

The Company's Charitable Trust always contributes to the Lord Mayor's charity of special interest for the year and participates in the Lord Mayor's Show each November, launching the new mayoral year.

THE FINANCIAL SERVICES GROUP OF LIVERY COMPANIES (FSG)

Twelve livery companies with special expertise in financial services have come together to provide support and advice to the Lord Mayor in his or her overseas promotion programme. The Company is a prominent member, especially since Ian Richardson, Master 2011/12, was the first Secretary of the group. He has now been succeeded by another member of the Company, Liveryman Michael Chitty. A principal objective of the Group is to provide "a network for access to expertise, experiences and issues, to

ABOVE: *Presentation of the FSG booklet to Alderman Ian Luder, 2009.*

provide briefings for the Lord Mayor for outbound and inbound visits".

Through its participation in the Financial Services Group, the Company is strongly in support of the Lord Mayor's overseas programme.

RESTORING TRUST IN THE CITY

For the avoidance of doubt, it should be noted that "Heart of the City" is an initiative launched by the Governor of the Bank of England and the Lord Mayor, in 2000. Under the generic heading of Corporate Social Responsibility, this initiative has grown in scope, its purpose to bring together those Companies who wish to be involved with the neighbouring communities, with those Companies who already have the expertise and experience in community involvement.

Towards the end of his year as Sheriff, Past Master Richard Sermon was invited by the Lord Mayor to lead a group charged with the task of promoting a better understanding of principles of conducting business. From the recommendations emerged the City Values Forum.

CONCLUSION

From its formation in the seventies the Worshipful Company of Chartered Secretaries and Administrators has played an ever increasing part in City life with many of its Liverymen being elected to prominent positions in City governance. The Company was the first to elect a female Master. The Company has forged strong links with the Armed Forces and seen their adopted School move from being in "Special Measures" to being rated "Outstanding". Its charitable activities are appreciated, not only by Lord Mayors, but by a wide range of organisations both within the City and further afield. The Company has a thriving Apprenticeship scheme, supports City University and provides bursaries for students at the Guildhall School of Music. It has been a leading player in setting up and running the FSG.

The case is rested; this Modern Company is surely at the Heart of the City.

APPENDIX ONE

MEMBERS ROLL
AS AT 31 DECEMBER 2012

		Surname	Forenames	Date signing Rolls			Year as Master	Dec'd date if known
				Freedom	Livery	Court		
D	189	Acheson	John Francis	29.01.81	23.04.81			16.08.01
L	440	Adams	Brian	04.05.05	14.07.05			
L	281	Ainsworth	Mervyn John	18.07.91	23.01.92	06.10.05		
F	557	Ajibadé	Mimi	19.07.12				
L	432	Alderman	Roger	10.11.04	28.04.05			
RN	208	Alderton	Robert William	14.07.82	01.10.82			
RN	141	Aldridge	Frederick Mungo	05.07.79	05.07.79			
L	463	Allcock	Charmian	09.05.06	19.10.06			
RF	167	Allflatt	Colin John	17.10.79	16.01.80			
L	174	Alton	Martin Bernard	01.07.80	01.10.81			
D	140	Annis	Arthur	10.01.79	11.04.79			Pre 2003
L	476	Ashton	Helen Louise	25.09.06	04.10.07			
L	308	Atterbury	John Michael	25.01.96	18.07.96			
L	191	Bailey	Colin Haselden	29.01.81	23.04.81			
L	253	Bailey	John Anthony	09.01.86	10.04.86			
L	535	Baldwin	Michael Peter Anthony	08.06.10	28.10.10			
L	329	Barber	Ralph Gordon	29.01.98	23.04.98			
RF	212	Barker	Barry	14.09.82	06.01.83			
L	100	Barnes	Ronald Jork	03.05.78	18.07.78			
L	356	Barnes (née Wise)	Yvonne	20.01.00	20.07.00			
F	486	Barnett	Gavin George	05.12.06				
D	105	Barrington, Sqn Ldr	Arthur	03.05.78	18.07.78			04.11.05
L	257	Bartlett	Derek William	09.04.87	09.07.87			
RN	342	Bartlett	George Derek Wilson	26.01.99				
D	269	Barton	James Keith	19.01.89	06.07.89			26.12.02
D	166	Bateman	Sir Ralph Melton KBE	17.10.79	16.01.80			00.02.96
L	188	Bates	John Gordon	29.01.81	23.04.81			

		Surname	Forenames	Date signing Rolls			Year as Master	Dec'd date if known
				Freedom	Livery	Court		
HF	525	Beet, Air Commodore	Nigel Philip	29.01.09				
L	517	Begby	Georgina Anne	10.07.08	21.01.09			
L	306	Bennett	Stephen George	12.10.95	18.07.96	*11.10.00		
L	22	Bergin	Francis Joseph	18.10.77	15.12.77	01.10.81	1993/94	
D	241	Bing	Edward George Cyril	11.10.84	10.01.85			18.01.99
L	452	Birch	Paul John	09.11.05	20.07.06			
RF	429	Birrell	Lindsay Norman	16.09.04				
F	471	Birthisel	Stockton Bodie	06.09.06				
L	80	Bishop	Leonard Ernest	07.03.78	03.05.78			
L	360	Blackwell	Valerie Angela	20.07.00	11.10.00			
D	77	Bocks	Julian Cecil	23.11.77	03.05.78			06.12.88
D	123	Bond	Ernest William Hepton	18.07.78	10.01.79			22.10.80
RN	142	Borland	Christopher Michael	10.01.79	11.04.79			
D	4	Bounds	Ronald	03.11.76	19.11.77	03.11.76	1987/88	15.04.90
L	400	Bown	John Reginald	02.10.03	22.04.04			
L	406	Boys	Ruth Ilse	02.10.03	29.01.04			
L	177	Bradley	Julia Anne	01.07.80	02.10.80			
RN	95	Braeman	Henry Martin	11.04.78	18.07.78			
RN	5	Brent	Allan Arthur	03.11.76	19.11.77	03.11.76		
D	94	Brewin	Sydney, Baron of Castlecoole	11.04.78	18.07.78			21.01.09
D	178	Bridgeman	David Archer	01.07.80	02.10.80			09.05.06
D	102	Bristow	Gordon Francis	03.05.78	18.07.78	28.10.93		17.05.01
L	328	Bristow	Professor Stephen Leigh	16.10.97	23.04.98	02.10.03		
L	345	Broad	Janet Mrs	22.04.99	21.07.99			
F	521	Broadbent	Alison Margaret	16.09.08				
L	409	Broomfield	Helen Frances	20.11.03	14.07.05			
D	82	Brown	Arthur Frederick	07.03.78	03.05.78			16.12.06

		Surname	Forenames	Date signing Rolls			Year as Master	Dec'd date if known
				Freedom	Livery	Court		
RF	120	Brunt	Paul David	18.07.78	11.10.78			
L	506	Buckingham	Norman James	01.11.07	19.05.08			
F	561	Buckmaster	Ian	15.11.12				
D	19	Bunker	Sidney	18.10.77	15.12.77	05.07.79		
L	389	Burne	George Frank Henry	04.04.03	02.10.03			
L	233	Burnell	John Geoffrey	12.01.84	05.04.84			
RN	58	Burnhill	Gilbert Christopher	23.11.77				
HF	558	Burns, Brigadier	Paul	19.07.12				
L	410	Burton, AVM	Andrew John	20.11.03	27.01.05			
L	411	Burwood	Krista Mary	20.11.03	06.10.05			
L	401	Buskell	David Alan	02.10.03	15.07.04			
L	361	Butler	Malcolm John Robert	20.07.00	16.07.03			
D	245	Butler	Peter Wallace	10.01.85	04.04.85			20.01.02
L	336	Butlin	Rachel Elizabeth	23.07.98	15.10.98			
L	548	Caldara	Angela Jane	21.09.11	19.07.12			
X		Cameron-Chilshe	Stephanie Dolores					
D	303	Campbell	Donald John	12.10.95	25.01.96	24.10.02		20.10.09
L	262	Carine, Rear Admiral	James	07.04.88	14.07.88	11.10.90	1997/98	
D	92	Carmichael	Stuart Netherwood	07.03.78	18.07.78			29.07.06
D	127	Carter	Herbert George	11.10.78	10.01.79			1988
RF	215	Catchpole	Laurence James	06.01.83	06.10.83			
L	198	Cauchi, Colonel	George Edward	02.07.81	01.10.81	10.01.85	1994/95	
D	301	Challis	George Hubert	19.10.94	19.10.94			20.10.11
L	317	Chapman	Albert	17.04.97	17.07.97			
L	383	Charnley	William Francis	12.07.02	12.07.02			
D	160	Chesher	Remington Charles	31.05.79				18.11.79
L	222	Child	Denis Marsden	07.07.83	12.01.84	01.10.87		
HF	499	Chisnall, AVM	Steven	26.07.07				
L	464	Chitty	Michael Patrick	09.05.06	25.01.07			
L	390	Chopin-John	Rosemary Helen	04.04.03	02.10.03			
D	294	Clare	Hilary	28.10.93	07.07.94			00.03.98
D	6	Clarke	Robin Mitchell	03.11.76	19.11.77	03.11.76	1984/85	29.01.02
D	85	Clements	Gilbert Edward Isaac	15.03.78	03.05.78	11.04.79		00.02.97
RN	66	Clipsham	Michael	08.02.78	03.05.78			
L	395	Cockburn	Pauline Anne	16.07.03	07.10.04			
L	453	Coker	David John	09.11.05	20.07.06			
D	128	Cole	Howard Alfred Albury	11.10.78	10.01.79			00.07.89

		Surname	Forenames	Date signing Rolls			Year as Master	Dec'd date if known
				Freedom	Livery	Court		
L	402	Cole	Simon Lawrence	02.10.03	22.04.04			
RN	207	Coles	Percy Corrie	14.07.82	01.10.82			
RHF	408	Collier, AVM	James Andrew	02.10.03				
F	538	Conde	Jemimah Adebola	08.07.10				
D	65	Conder	Reginald Edward	08.02.78				1978
L	129	Confavreux	André George	11.10.78	10.01.79			
L	137	Conley	Patrick Victor	11.10.78	10.01.79			
D	202	Constable	John Hurn	22.04.82	14.07.82	09.04.87	1998/99	18.11.99
D	86	Cook	Harold Simpson	26.03.78	03.05.78			1990
L	526	Cordrey	Christopher Edward George	23.04.09	01.10.09			
D	187	Cork	Ald Sir Kenneth Russell GBE	30.09.80				13.10.91
D	316	Cork	Sir Roger		23.05.97	10.10.01		20.10.02
L	47	Coulson-Thomas	Colin Joseph	23.11.77	08.02.78			
RN	225	Coverdale	Robert Malcolm	06.10.83	05.07.84			
D	242	Coward	David John	11.10.84	10.01.85			05.12.11
L	349	Cowdall	John	22.04.99	21.07.99			
L	529	Cowe	Robertson	08.09.09	29.07.10			
RN	229	Crabtree	Colin	06.10.83				
L	247	Craike	John Anthony Hedley	04.04.85	03.10.85			
L	483	Cranney	Javed Stephen Philip	07.11.06	04.10.07			
L	413	Crisp	Peter	19.02.04	07.10.04			
D	232	Crook	Ralph Desmond	12.01.84	05.04.84			1995
L	382	Crosse	Noel Mitchell Roumieu	12.07.02	12.07.02			
RF	88	Croston	Leslie Joseph	02.03.78	18.07.78			
L	7	Croydon	Leslie Ronald	03.11.76	19.11.77	03.11.76	1985/86	
L	384	Cryan	Mary Eithne	09.10.02	16.07.03			
F	559	Cummins	William	19.09.12				
RF	283	Curnow	Barry John	09.04.92	20.01.94			
RF	343	Daniels	Roger Michael	26.01.99	06.10.99			
D	255	Das	Lala Prithwisranjan	10.07.86	10.07.86			15.10.99
D	251	Davey	Anthony William Chawner	03.10.85	09.01.86			27.12.10
L	175	Davies	David	01.07.80	02.10.80			
L	330	Davies	Pamela	29.01.98	23.04.98			
L	67	Davis	Anthony Phillip Meredith	08.02.78	03.05.78			
D	68	Davis	Bernard	08.02.78	10.01.79			04.10.96
RF	414	Davis	Ian Michael	19.02.04	28.04.05			
L	365	Davison	Suzanne	11.10.00	01.02.01			

		Surname	Forenames	Date signing Rolls			Year as Master	Dec'd date if known
				Freedom	Livery	Court		
RF	96	Dawe	Roger Meredith	11.04.78	18.07.78	01.10.81		
L	519	Dawes	Peter Graham	10.07.08	23.04.09			
L	369	Day	Patricia Mary	19.07.01	31.01.02	*18.10.07		
L	549	de Freitas	Mary Noëlle	21.09.11	26.01.12			
L	367	de Souza	Ayres Maria Jose	01.02.01	19.07.01	*14.10.10		
L	354	Delacombe, Major	Christopher Rohan	20.01.00	27.04.00			
L	230	Denny, Wing Cdr	Arthur Charles Henry	06.10.83	05.04.84			
F	533	Devine	David John	09.02.10				
L	314	Dingwall, Wing Cdr	Peter Charles	17.10.96	30.01.97	02.10.03		
RN	69	Dipple	Eric Roland	08.02.78	03.05.78			
L	507	Dixon	Susan Elizabeth	01.11.07	23.04.09			
D	206	Dixon	William	14.07.82	01.10.82			00.03.86
RF	396	Dolbear	Jonathon	16.07.03				
L	298	Donald	Sidney Milne	07.07.94	19.10.94	10.10.01		
L	500	Dosoo	George Small Yeo	05.09.07	24.01.08			
RF	430	Downs	Gavin Dalziel	16.09.04				
D	44	Downward	Edwin	23.11.77	08.02.78			15.08.81
L	478	Drake, Colonel	Timothy Clive Lewis	25.09.06	25.01.07			
D	70	Drysdale	Douglas Alexander	08.02.78	03.05.78			00.11.92
L	211	Dudding, Colonel	Michael John	14.07.82	01.10.82	12.10.89	2000/01	
RF	310	Dunn	Peter Richard	18.04.96	17.10.96			
L	179	Durban	Donald Desmond	01.07.80	02.10.80	01.10.81	1990/91	
D	243	Eagles	Edmund John Keble Montrine	11.10.84	10.01.85			01.08.07
RF	264	Eales	Victor Samuel Leslie	07.04.88	13.10.88			
L	484	Earl	Jane	07.11.06	18.10.07			
L	454	East	Heather	09.11.05	05.10.06			
D	45	Edwards	Gordon	23.11.77	08.02.78			10.03.07
RF	259	Eilers	Robert Francis Edward	01.10.87	07.04.88			
D	112	Eiles	Frank Henry	23.06.78	18.07.78			00.03.95
D	3	Eley	Stanley James Sidney	03.11.76	19.11.77	03.11.76	1979/80	05.08.01
RN	265	Elliott	Arthur Raymond	07.04.88	14.07.88			
RF	397	Elwes	Jeremy Vernon, Sir	16.07.03	16.07.03			
RF	110	Elyan	David Asher Gremson	18.05.78	18.07.78			
L	433	Emetulu	Lola Olayade	10.11.04	06.10.05			
L	260	English, Colonel	Terrence Henry	01.10.87	07.04.88			
L	445	Eringa	James Arnold Clarence	06.09.05	04.05.06			

		Surname	Forenames	Date signing Rolls			Year as Master	Dec'd date if known
				Freedom	Livery	Court		
D	106	Essex-Crosby	Alan	03.05.78	18.07.78			17.05.96
L	149	Eve	Robin Anthony	05.07.79	05.07.79	*11.10.00	2009/10	
D	223	Farrier	Roy	07.07.83	06.10.83			03.01.04
D	240	Fearn	Frederick Henry	05.04.84	10.01.85			13.05.10
HL	327	Fellowes	The Rt Hon Lord Robert, GCVO	18.07.96	06.10.04			
D	101	Finden-Crofts	Harold John	03.05.78	18.07.78			28.06.81
D	38	Finn	Geoffrey Stuart	18.10.77	15.12.77	01.10.87	1996/97	11.12.09
D	107	Flawn	Stanley William	03.05.78	18.07.78			08.01.81
RN	161	Fleet	Donald Gordon	05.07.79	05.07.79			
F	555	Fletcher	James Harold	01.02.12				
RN	185	Forbes	Ronald William	02.10.80	02.07.81			
L	418	Foster	Alison Taylor	11.03.04	27.01.05			
RF	119	Foster	Ronald Derek	23.06.78	11.10.78			
L	236	Foulkes	Thomas Michael	05.04.84	05.07.84			
L	428	Fox	Jacqueline Elizabeth Lambert	15.07.04	15.07.04			
L	370	Fox	Julie Nicola	19.07.01	10.10.01	*06.10.05		
L	522	Fox	Raymond Alan	16.09.08	23.04.09			
RF	364	Friend	Alistair Robert James	11.10.00	19.07.01			
D	49	Fullick	Douglas Robert	23.11.77	08.02.78			18.07.79
RF	108	Fullwood	Keith Saxon	03.05.78	18.07.78			
L	378	Gallagher	John Liam	31.01.02	17.04.02			
L	267	Galpin, Commander	John Lawrence	19.01.89	06.07.89			
L	8	Gardiner	Geoffrey William	03.11.76	19.11.77	03.11.76		
RF	57	Gardiner	Leslie Henry	23.11.77	08.02.78			
RF	23	Gardner, Major	Ronald John Dutton	18.10.77	15.12.77	01.10.81		
L	318	Garnett	Gerald Archer	17.04.97	17.07.97			
L	391	Geary	Norman Francis	04.04.03	16.07.03			
D	54	Gerrard (Revd.)	George Ernest	23.11.77	03.05.78			27.01.08
D	338	Gibbons	Peter Russell	15.10.98	26.01.99			27.04.03
L	302	Gilbert	Anne Helen King	20.07.95	25.01.96			
L	455	Gilbert	Stephen Charles	09.11.05	19.10.06			
RN	218	Giles	Adrian Patrick Gordon	07.07.83	05.04.84			
RF	193	Gilhespy	George Alfred	23.04.81	07.01.82			
D	89	Gillies	John Sydney Henry	07.03.78	18.07.78			09.02.93
D	90	Glover	Dennis Frederick	07.03.78	18.07.78			17.04.06
L	81	Goddard	James Theodore	07.03.78	03.05.78			
RF	62	Goddard, Major	Douglas George	23.11.77	03.05.78			

		Surname	Forenames	Date signing Rolls			Year as Master	Dec'd date if known
				Freedom	Livery	Court		
RF	83	Godden	Roger Newton	07.03.78	03.05.78			
F	560	Golderg	Justine Magdalen	19.09.12				
D	219	Gollop	Philip George	07.07.83	12.01.84			06.02.08
L	368	Goodwille	Annika Ida Louise Aman	01.02.01	19.07.01			
L	544	Gopsil	Brian Richard	28.04.11	27.10.11			
L	421	Gough	Roy Russell	13.05.04	07.10.04			
HL		Graham, Ald. Sir	Alexander					
L	501	Gray	John Stanley	05.09.07	24.07.08			
F	512	Green	John Michael	13.12 07				
L	271	Greenwell	Arthur Jeffrey	06.07.89	25.01.90	*23.07.98	2005/06	
RN	20	Greenwood, Major	Arthur Alexander	18.10.77	08.02.78			
L	459	Grigg	Raymond John Charles	07.02.06	05.10.06			
L	200	Grinsted	Clifford Hazelton	01.10.81	22.04.82	09.04.87	1995/96	
D	27	Guilford	Phillip Arnold	18.10.77	15.12.77			00.05.95
F	492	Hadley	Jacqueline Anne	28.06.07				
L	508	Hallam	Christopher Alwyn	01.11.07	24.07.08	*11.10.11		
D	87	Hamilton-Hopkins	Albert	28.03.78	03.05.78			09.06.08
D	130	Hammond	Wilfred Charles	11.10.78	10.01.79	01.10.87	1999/2000	26.03.08
L	307	Hampson	Brian Frederick	25.01.96	17.10.96			
L	377	Hampton-Coutts	Cheryl Jane Mrs	10.10.01	30.01.03			
L	341	Hancock	Ronald George	26.01.99	22.04.99			
L	509	Hankin	David Marsh	01.11.07	19.05.08			
D	103	Harding	Alfred Victor	03.05.78	18.07.78			29.10.96
RF	203	Hardy	John Stuart	22.04.82	06.01.83			
L	288	Hare	Paul Edward	09.04.92	21.01.93			
D	36	Harker	John Angus Makepeace	18.10.77	15.12.77			02.12.99
D	14	Harris	Henry Roy	18.10.77	15.12.77	15.12.77	1991/92	00.08.93
D	194	Harris	Mollie	23.04.81	01.10.81			11.07.11
L	479	Harrison	Jeffrey David	25.09.06	24.01.08			
RN	51	Hart	William Reginald	23.11.77	03.05.78			
D	182	Harvey	Arthur Percy Edmund	02.10.80	29.01.81			21.11.00
L	214	Harvey	Michael Gillingwater	01.10.82	06.01.83			
F	547	Harvey-Bussell	Tracy	18.07.11				
L	524	Harwood	Robert John	13.11.08	28.10.10			
D	31	Hawley	Peter Lewis	18.10.77	15.12.77			09.09.11
D	143	Haynes	Frederick Thomas	05.07.79	05.07.79			01.06.82
L	419	Hayworth	John Sidney Irons	11.03.04	06.10.05			

		Surname	Forenames	Date signing Rolls			Year as Master	Dec'd date if known
				Freedom	Livery	Court		
L	550	Heaton-Smith	Leslie	21.09.11	19.07.12			
L	293	Herbertson	Robert Ian	21.01.93	15.04.93			
L	287	Hewitt	Anthony Roland	09.04.92	21.01.93			
RF	277	Hill	Richard Edward	18.07.91	10.10.91			
L	52	Hill	Roy Howard	23.11.77	03.05.78			
F	516	Hill	Trina Janice	01.04.08				
RF	79	Hillman	Francis Owens	07.03.78	03.05.78			
L	71	Hodgson	Samuel	08.02.78	03.05.78			
L	359	Holder	Claire Alison	20.07.00	31.01.02			
L	304	Holley	Alan Jack	20.07.95	25.01.96			
L	465	Holmes	Colin John	09.05.06	25.01.07			
RN	168	Holt	Leslie Alfred Joseph	17.10.79	16.01.80			
D	59	Honey	William Andrew	23.11.77	08.02.78			00.10.93
L	456	Horrocks	Alison Claire	09.11.05	04.05.06			
RF	116	How	David Alfred George	03.05.78	11.10.78			
L	371	Howden	George Kiplin	19.07.01	31.01.02			
D	173	Howe	Harold Derek	16.04.80	29.01.81			28.04.06
F	554	Huband	Harriet Rosin	14.11.11				
L	224	Hughes	Earle William	07.07.83	12.01.84			
D	34	Hughes	Percy F (* died before signing)	18.10.77				01.12.78
L	311	Hughes	Susan Margaret	18.04.96	18.07.96	11.10.00		
RN	150	Hughesdon	Bernard	Not signed				
L	480	Hunt	Carol Anne	25.09.06	03.05.07			
RN	48	Hutchings	Derek William	23.11.77	08.02.78			
D	144	Hyne	Anthony Jones	05.07.79	05.07.79			07.10.09
L	415	Idowu	Samuel Olusegun	19.02.04	15.07.04			
L	398	Ilsey	Vanessa Indira	16.07.03	29.01.04			
D	239	Insoll	Richard Hallam	05.04.84	10.01.85			02.05.03
L	124	Ivory	James William	18.07.78	10.01.79			
L	170	Jackson	Daphne Diana	16.04.80	01.07.80			
L	319	Jackson, Commander	Rory Fitton Moresby	17.04.97	17.07.97	*10.10.01	2010/11	
D	422	Jacob	Michael Anthony	13.05.04	27.01.05			12.10.06
L	9	Jacques	Kenneth	03.11.76	19.11.77	03.11.76	1982/83	
RF	171	James	Arthur Sheldon Harris	16.04.80	02.10.80			
L	403	Jamison	Simon Frederick Blackwood	20.11.03	22.04.04			
L	551	Jarvis	Gwynne Myfanwy Price	21.09.11	26.01.12			
RF	457	Jenkins	David Peter	09.11.05				

		Surname	Forenames	Freedom	Livery	Court	Year as Master	Dec'd date if known
L	93	Jenner	Martin John	28.03.78	18.07.78			
RF	273	Johnson	Roy Sidney	12.10.89	25.01.90			
L	151	Jones	John Ieuan	05.07.79	05.07.79			
L	196	Jones	Laurence Aubrey	02.07.81	07.01.82			
RN	152	Jones	Michael David	17.10.79	17.10.79			
L	385	Joseph	Neville Anthony	09.10.02	09.10.02			
D	158	Judd	Kenneth Walter	11.04.79	11.04.79		1991	
RN	32	Kearns	Albert Godfrey	18.10.77	08.02.78			
D	213	Keeler	Anthony Edgar	01.10.82	03.05.83			22.03.10
L	472	Keith	Philippa Anne	06.09.06	03.05.07			
L	362	Kenyon	Rodney Frank	20.07.00	01.02.01			
RHF	462	Kimmons, R. Admiral	Michael	04.05.06				
RF	313	Kinch	John Patrick	18.04.96				
RF	309	King	Geofrey William	25.01.96	30.01.97			
D	118	Kirk	Eric Stanton	07.06.78	11.10.78	10.01.85	1992/93	14.01.09
L	217	Kirkham	Donald Herbert	07.07.83	12.01.84	*11.10.90	2003/4	
L	379	Knapper	Edward Michael Vernon	17.04.02	17.04.02			
F	514	Knight née Jackson	Laura Ann Maria	07.02.08				
D	113	Knightley	Albert Arthur	23.06.78	10.01.79			00.01.82
D	145	Korn	John Reginald	05.07.79	05.07.79			29.01.94
L	138	Kramer	Colin Cedric	06.10.78	10.01.79			
L	437	Lance	Mark Richard	09.02.05	20.10.05			
D	122	Lavanchy	Kenneth William Charles	18.07.78	11.10.78			17.02.03
L	326	Lawrence	William Sackville Gwynne	17.07.97	15.10.98			
L	39	Lawrey	Keith	18.10.77	15.12.77			
L	282	Ledsam	Charles Edmund Royden	18.07.91	10.10.91	*21.10.04	2012/13	
D	249	Lee	David Alton	03.10.85	09.01.86			13.07.03
L	546	Lee	Erica	18.07.11	27.10.11			
L	404	Lee	Robyn Jane	02.10.03	29.01.04			
RF	339	Lee-Kelley	Liz	15.10.98	15.10.98			
L	416	Lehmann	Max Andrew	19.02.04	15.07.04			
RN	284	Leigh-Quine	Rodney	09.04.92	21.01.93			
L	270	Lescure	Kenneth	19.01.89	13.04.89			
L	552	Lewis	Sarah	21.09.11	26.01.12			
RF	344	Lilley	David John	26.01.99	30.01.03			
L	117	Lindsay	Maurice Rowland	03.05.78	11.10.78			
RN	99	Lines	Oscar Arthur	14.04.78	18.07.78			
L	355	Lintott	Gaynor Elizabeth Lavinia	20.01.00	27.04.00			
D	279	Lintott	George David	18.07.91	10.10.91			07.04.98
L	332	Lis	Zbigniew Stanislaw	29.01.98	23.04.98	*23.10.08		
D	24	Liss	Hyman	18.10.77	15.12.77			1993
L	527	Littauer	Svend Martin	22.04.09	01.10.09			
F	488	Lloyd	Maureen Ann	06.02.07				
D	131	Loats	Ernest Charles	11.10.78	10.01.79			10.06.97
L	351	Lock	David John	21.07.99	06.10.99	*27.01.10		
D	53	Locke	Michael James Wesley	23.11.77	03.05.78			1982
RHF	394	Lockwood, R Admiral	Roger G	16.07.03				
D	231	Long	Garry	06.10.83	05.04.84			28.06.02
L	248	Louth	John Brian	04.07.85	03.10.85			
L	406	Lovegrove	Ruth Ilse (see Boys)					
RF	380	Lovell	Roger Michael	17.04.02	30.01.03			
RN	321	Mackereth, Brigadier	Neil Anthony	17.07.97	29.01.98			
RN	60	Madden	Ronald George	23.11.77	03.05.78			
RF	347	Maidment	Ian Douglas	22.04.99	21.07.99			
L	381	Mair	Alexander Grant Robertson	17.04.02	09.10.02	*23.10.08		
L	209	Marcell	Philip Michael	14.07.82	06.01.83	28.10.93	2001/02	
L	132	Mardon	John Gale	11.10.78	10.01.79			
RHF	513	Marriner, Brigadier	Simon John Max	24.01.08				
RF	331	Martin	Ilana	29.01.98	23.04.98			
L	268	Martin, Ald'mn, Sir	Clive Haydn	19.01.89	06.07.89	*20.07.95	2004/05	
L	10	Marwood	David Christopher Laborde	03.11.76	19.11.77	03.11.76	1981/82	
X		Mason	Emma Mary Sonya					
L	469	Mason	Kira	09.05.06	19.10.06			
D	11	Mason	Thomas Eric Douglas	03.11.76	19.11.77	03.11.76	1980/81	13.01.90
RF	226	Masters	Michael Roger	06.10.83	12.01.84			
RN	153	Maurice	James Eryr	05.07.79	05.07.79			
L	292	Maydon	Gary	21.01.93	15.04.93			
L	467	McVey	Robert Graham	09.05.06	05.10.06			
D	263	Mead	Frederick Charles	07.04.88	14.07.88			07.06.99
RF	272	Meddins	John Frank	06.07.89	09.04.92			
RF	72	Mellish	Leopold Douglas	08.02.78	03.05.78			
RN	126	Milligan	Derek	06.10.78	10.01.79			

		Surname	Forenames	Date signing Rolls			Year as Master	Dec'd date if known
				Freedom	Livery	Court		
RF	261	Milner	Kevin Joseph	01.10.87	14.01.88			
L	434	Milner-Williams	Charles William Michael	10.11.04	20.10.05			
F	545	Minhas	Tejvinder	28.04.11				
L	438	Moffatt	John Scott	09.02.05	04.05.06			
RHF	541	Moffatt, Brigadier	Nicola Patricia	29.07.10				
L	441	Morrison	Thomas Vance	04.05.05	26.01.06			
D	234	Morton	William Thomas	12.01.84	05.04.84			04.03.93
L	412	Moss	Gordon Edwin	20.11.03	22.04.04			
L	276	Moys	Sylvia Doreen	18.07.91	10.10.91			
RN	305	Muggeridge	John Franklin Charles	12.10.95				
RF	427	Muhwati	Fanuel Chakounetson	01.06.04	14.07.05			
RN	216	Mullally	Michael	03.05.83	07.07.83			
HF	487	Mullen Rev Dr	Peter	25.01.07				
RF	502	Murray	Dominic Pieter	05.09.07	29.01.09			
D	286	Murray	James Wallace	09.04.92	09.07.92	02.10.03		28.03.11
RN	154	Murray	Reginald John Alan	05.07.79	05.07.79			
F	436	Murton	Vivian Marshall	07.12.04				
L	40	Neads	John	18.10.77	15.12.77			
L	33	Needham	Leslie	18.10.77	15.12.77			
D	43	Newman	Geoffrey George	23.11.77	16.04.80			09.02.05
L	353	Newton	Ian Stenhouse	21.07.99	20.01.00			
D	15	Newton	Peter Stenhouse	18.10.77	15.12.77	15.12.77		00.00.82
L	350	Nicholl	Edward James	21.07.99	06.10.99			
D	204	Nixon	Ronald Leslie	22.04.82	14.07.82			15.05.09
L	489	Noakes	David Anthony	06.02.07	04.10.07			
F	539	Norris	Erika Britt	08.07.10				
RF	190	O'Connor	Desmond Ciarran	29.01.81	23.04.81			
RF	136	O'Farrell	Patrick Joseph	11.10.78	10.01.79			
L	493	Ogden	David Michael	28.06.07	24.07.08			
F	556	O'Keeffe	William Francis	01.02.12				
L	417	Osborne	Stephen James	19.02.04	07.10.04			
L	510	Osso	Guiseppe	01.11.07	08.10.08			
RF	228	Ostermeyer	Clifford Henry	06.10.83	12.01.84			
D	133	Owen	George	11.10.78	10.01.79			00.01.04
L	531	Owen	Stephen	11.11.09	27.07.11			
L	322	Oxenham	Graham Francis	17.07.97	16.10.97			
D	30	Page	Derrick William	18.10.77	15.12.77			00.01.83
D	180	Page	Norman John	01.07.80	02.10.80			00.11.85

		Surname	Forenames	Date signing Rolls			Year as Master	Dec'd date if known
				Freedom	Livery	Court		
D	164	Pannett	George John Robert	17.10.79	17.10.79			23.07.11
L	221	Parker	Leonard John	07.07.83	06.10.83			
L	473	Parry	Christina Louise	06.09.06	25.01.07	*11.10.11		
D	21	Parry	Kenneth Ewart	18.10.77	15.12.77	16.01.80	1989/90	05.02.99
L	446	Parsons	Steven Ian	06.09.05	05.10.06			
L	542	Partrdge	Trevor Brian	27.01.11	28.4.11			
L	274	Patterson	Francis Edward	12.10.89	25.01.90			
L	444	Paulson	Mark Dennis	06.07.05	20.07.06			
RF	280	Peake	Adam Charles Edward	18.07.91	23.01.92			
L	388	Pearson	Hugh Michael	09.10.02	29.01.04			
L	481	Pellow	Ian	25.09.06	03.05.07			
L	375	Penton	David Michael	10.10.01	31.01.02			
RN	289	Percival	Betty	28.10.92	21.01.93			
RF	258	Perman	Alec Edward	09.07.87	07.04.88			
L	295	Pert	Royston Clive	28.10.93	07.07.94			
RF	530	Peter	Patricia Anne	08.09.09				
RF	372	Petre	James Oldroyd	19.07.01	12.07.02			
L	296	Phelps	Paul Victor	28.10.93	07.07.94			
D	2	Phillips	John Francis	03.11.76	19.11.77	03.11.76	1978/9 86/7	19.02.98
L	237	Phillips	Mary Eveline	05.04.84	10.01.85			
L	312	Pilgrim	Lorina Mary	18.04.96	18.07.96			
D	41	Pinckney	John Henry	18.10.77	15.12.77			1984
RF	458	Pinkett	Anthony Christopher	09.11.05				
L	392	Piper	Jacqueline Michelle	04.04.03	27.01.05			
F	553	Pitla	Nayesh	21.09.11				
L	285	Platt	Derrick James Branscombe	09.04.92	21.01.93			
L	515	Pointet	David Adrian Jackman	07.02.08	08.10.08			
L	494	Poole	Andrew Philip	28.06.07	24.01.08			
L	35	Poole	John Kenneth	18.10.77	15.12.77			
L	423	Porritt	Kerry Ann Abigail	13.05.04	27.01.05	*14.10.10		
L	520	Power	Benjamin John	10.07.08	23.07.09			
L	460	Prescott	David John	07.02.06	05.10.06			
L	220	Probert	David Henry	07.07.83	12.01.84	23.01.92		
L	238	Pugh	Richard Henry Crommeline	05.04.84	11.10.84	19.10.94		
D	16	Purse	Alfred Turnbull	18.10.77	15.12.77	15.12.77		06.07.00
L	439	Quinn	David John	09.02.05	14.07.05			
L	511	Ramsdale	Robet Alan	01.11.07	24.07.08			

		Surname	Forenames	Date signing Rolls			Year as Master	Dec'd date if known
				Freedom	Livery	Court		
D	139	Rawlings	Ernest	06.11.78	10.01.79			25.01.92
D	97	Reed	Thomas John	11.04.78	18.07.78			05.03.97
D	46	Reeday	Thomas Geoffrey	23.11.77	08.02.78			1997
D	163	Rees	Dennis Albert	05.07.79	16.01.80			18.11.79
D	109	Rees	Mary Elizabeth	03.05.78	18.07.78			07.10.05
RF	91	Reeves-Smith	Leonard Edward	07.03.78	18.07.78			
L	470	Regan	Richard David	20.07.06	20.07.06			
L	358	Reger	Richard Michael	20.01.00	27.04.00			
F	495	Richards	Alison Joanne	28.06.07				
L	333	Richardson	Ian David Lea	23.04.98	15.10.98	*24.10.02	2011/12	
RF	320	Riches	David Kenneth	17.04.97	29.01.98			
D	146	Ridd	Cyril Vincent	10.01.79	11.04.79			19.08.87
D	169	Ring	Sir Lindsey, GBE	17.03.80	17.03.80	16.01.80		21.08.97
RF	420	Ritchie	Ian	11.03.04				
D	12	Roberts	Dennis Howard	03.11.76	19.11.77	03.11.76	1988/89	04.05.10
L	424	Robertson	John	13.05.04	28.04.05			
RN	205	Robinson	Frank Anthony	22.04.82	14.07.82			
L	425	Robinson	Harry	13.05.04	06.10.05			
RN	210	Robinson	Peter James	14.07.82	06.01.83			
L	496	Roche	Jacob Damien John Finn	28.06.07	24.01.08			
RF	497	Rosling	Heather Anne	28.06.07	04.10.07			
L	503	Rowland-Jones	John Richard	05.09.07	11.10.11	*11.10.11		
L	13	Rutherford	William Hood	03.11.76	19.11.77	03.11.76		
L	532	Ruwangu	Emmanuel	11.11.09	28.04.11			
RF	297	Sankey	Christopher John	28.10.93	20.01.94			
RF	334	Saunders	Ruth Judie Frances	23.04.98	23.07.98			
D	244	Sawford	Kenneth	11.10.84	10.01.85			19.10.07
RN	186	Scholfield	Roger	02.10.80	29.01.81			
F	399	Scott	Alan George	02.10.03				
L	278	Scott	David James	18.07.91	23.01.92			
L	540	Sebastion-Smith	Anita Virginia	08.07.10				
D	125	Sequeira	Leslie Joseph	29.09.78	10.01.79			30.03.03
D	407	Serbutt	Robert Frederick Buchan	02.10.03				08.02.08
L	37	Sermon	Thomas Richard	18.10.77	15.12.77	*10.10.91	2006/07	
D	323	Severn	Ronald Craymer	17.07.97	16.10.97			29.07.98
D	176	Shannon	John	01.07.80	02.10.80			19.11.04
RF	184	Shelley	Geoffrey Dennis	02.10.80	29.01.81			
L	376	Shepheard	Geoffrey Arthur George	10.10.01	10.10.01			
RF	291	Sheridan	Thomas Joseph	28.10.92	15.07.93			
RF	254	Shore	Geoffrey John	10.04.86	09.10.86			
D	181	Simmonds	Robert Mayer	01.07.80	01.07.80			00.12.90
L	474	Simpson	Elizabeth Anne	06.09.06	25.01.07			
RF	64	Sinclare	Leslie David	08.02.78	18.07.78			
RF	523	Skeels	Jennifer Elizabeth Caroline	13.11.08	23.07.09			
L	475	Small	Jeremy Peter	06.09.06	19.05.08			
RHF	543	Smith	Colin Michael	27.01.11				
L	442	Smith	Leslie Robert	04.05.05	06.10.05			
L	468	Smith	Linda Gillian	09.05.06	25.01.07			
RF	246	Smith	Sidney William	10.01.85	04.04.85			
L	324	Sole	Frederick Brian John	17.07.97	16.10.97			
RN	78	Somerville	John William	08.02.78	03.05.78			
L	155	Spall	Peter Douglas	17.10.79	17.10.79			
L	199	Spencer-Cotton	Francis	01.10.81	07.01.82	*15.10.98	2008/09	
RF	50	Spooner	Raymond Phillip	23.11.77	03.05.78			
L	98	Springall	Stanley Robert	11.04.78	18.07.78			
L	340	Squire	Angela Elizabeth	15.10.98	26.01.99			
D	147	Steed	Cyril Ernest	10.01.79	11.04.79			16.11.94
HF	528	Steel	David George	23.04.09				
RN	84	Stephens	Malcolm	07.03.78	03.05.78			
D	114	Stevenson	Ivor David	31.03.78	11.10.78			
L	443	Stevenson	Sandra Maureen	04.05.05	20.07.06			
L	290	Stokes-Smith	Keith Reginald	28.10.92	15.04.93			
L	42	Stone	Arthur Edward	18.10.77	15.12.77			
L	485	Stone	Zillah Wendy	07.11.06	26.07.07			
L	299	Strachan	Anthony John	07.07.94	19.01.95			
L	477	Stringer	William Paton	06.09.06	19.05.08			
RF	325	Sumner	Terrence Charles	17.07.97	29.01.98			
L	466	Sylva	Paul John	09.05.06	19.10.06			
RN	121	Symondson	Brian Francis	16.06.78	11.10.78			
F	352	Tallboys	Richard Gilbert	21.07.99	21.07.99			
D	115	Tapping	Donald Alan	11.04.78	11.10.78			13.05.80
L	134	Tate	Heather	11.10.78	10.01.79			
RF	195	Taylor	Brian Eastwood	23.04.81	01.10.82			
L	490	Taylor	David Harvey	06.02.07	29.07.10			
RF	73	Taylor	Dennis Herbert	08.02.78	11.10.78			
D	275	Taylor	Derek James	12.07.90	18.07.91			13.06.09

		Surname	Forenames	Date signing Rolls			Year as Master	Dec'd date if known
				Freedom	Livery	Court		
F	447	Taylor	Richard George	06.09.05				
L	250	Taylor	Roger King	03.10.85	09.01.86			
D	29	Taylor	Stanley Thomas	18.10.77	15.12.77			19.05.06
L	491	Thomas	Andrea Margaret	06.02.07	04.10.07			
D	61	Thomas	Richard Mervyn	23.11.77	18.07.78			2004
L	156	Thompson	Brian	05.07.79	05.07.79			
L	504	Thorne	Anthony Gordon	05.09.07	24.07.08			
L	256	Thorpe	Adèle Loraine	09.10.86	05.02.87	*23.07.98	2007/08	
L	55	Thow	Allan Ramsey	23.11.77	03.05.78			
RF	197	Tomalin	Stanley William	02.07.81	01.10.81			
D	201	Tonks	Harnett John	07.01.82	22.04.82			12.08.03
L	482	Turner	David Charles	25.09.06	03.05.07			
L	363	Turner	Truda Caroline	11.10.00	01.02.01			
D	17	Tutt	Sylvia Irene Maud	18.10.77	15.12.77	15.12.77	1983/84	05.12.11
D	25	Twelvetree	Peter Ian	18.10.77	15.12.77			29.06.84
RF	74	Tye	Jack Ernest	08.02.78	03.05.78			
HF	366	Tyre	Sandra	19.10.00				
L	135	Vanhegan	Donald Frederick Arthur	11.10.78	10.01.79			
RF	405	Vardy	Richard John	02.10.03	02.10.03	05.10.06		
L	505	Venn	Ian	05.09.07	29.01.09			
D	18	Vink	Kenneth Lorani	18.10.77	15.12.77	15.12.77		00.10.86
L	63	Waite	Michael Stephen Timothy	23.11.77	03.05.78			
D	28	Walker	Dennis Bertram	18.10.77	15.12.77			00.03.96
D	373	Walker	Stuart Godfrey	19.07.01	10.10.01			02.11.04
L	536	Wallace	John Charles	08.06.10	28.04.11			
L	252	Walmesley	Keith	09.01.86	10.04.86			
L	518	Walther-Caine	Philippa Tracey	10.07.08	23.07.09			
L	374	Warren	Dorota Maria	19.07.01	31.01.02			
L	534	Webb	Marie-Louise	03.02.10	28.10.10			
L	315	Webber, Commander	Steven John Anthony Maltravers	30.01.97	17.04.97			
L	426	Webster	Mandy Patricia	13.05.04	28.04.05			
D	1	Wedgwood	John Alleyne	03.11.76	19.11.77	03.11.76	1977/78	15.02.04
L	300	Welch	Patrick Alan	07.07.94	19.10.94			
L	448	White	Brian Randolph	06.09.05	04.05.06			
L	461	Whiterod	Joanne Lesley	07.02.06	19.05.08			
L	498	Whittingham	Ivan John	28.06.07	04.10.07			
D	162	Wickstead	Cyril	17.10.79	17.10.79			27.11.12

		Surname	Forenames	Date signing Rolls			Year as Master	Dec'd date if known
				Freedom	Livery	Court		
L	537	Wilcox	Tomas Norman	08.06.10	27.07.11			
L	449	Wilkins	John Keith	06.09.05	04.05.06			
D	76	Williams	Frank	08.02.78	03.05.78			1999
L	386	Williams-Hamer	Gabrielle Mary Mrs	09.10.02	04.04.03			
D	227	Willmott	Ralph	06.10.83	12.01.84			1992
D	235	Wilson	Catherine Thelma	12.01.84	05.07.84			23.03.10
D	165	Wilson	David	17.10.79	17.10.79			
D	26	Wilson	William Stanley	18.10.77	08.02.78			31.12.81
HF	357	Wilson	Richard, Lord Dinton GCB	20.01.00				
L	356	Wise (See Barnes)	Yvonne					
HF	393	Wolsey, Brigadier	John Noel	04.04.03				
L	431	Wood	Alan Peter	16.09.04	14.07.05			
D	104	Wood	Ernest Edward	03.05.78	18.07.78			18.12.78
L	337	Wood	John	15.10.98	26.01.99			
L	387	Woodhead	John Bertram	09.10.02	04.04.03			
L	346	Woodruff	Margaret Susan	22.04.99	21.07.99			
L	183	Woodward	Geoffrey Herbert	02.10.80	02.07.81			
RN	192	Worley	Stanley Francis	29.01.81	23.04.81			
L	450	Worsdall	Sandra Jean	06.09.05	26.01.06	*14.10.10		
D	111	Wosket	Sidney James Barr	03.05.78	11.10.78			1995
L	266	Wratten	Jack	14.07.88	13.10.88			
L	172	Wright	David William Robert	16.04.80	01.07.80	*25.01.90	2002/03	
RF	348	Wright	Matthew William	22.04.99	21.07.99			
L	56	Wykes	John	23.11.77	08.02.78			
RN	148	Young	Cecil Leonard Ronald	10.01.79	11.04.79			
RF	157	Young	Leslie Robert	17.10.79	17.10.79			
L	451	Young	Lorraine Elizabeth	06.09.05	20.07.06			
L	435	Young	Peter Victor	10.11.04	14.07.05			
D	75	Young	Richard Keith	08.02.78	03.05.78			16.04.02
RF	159	Zaidner	Michael Philip	05.07.79	05.07.79			

*Court Assistant as at 31 Dec 2012

D = Deceased; F = Freeman; HF = Honorary Freeman; HL = Honorary Liveryman; L = Liveryman;

RF = Reversion to Freedom confirmed OR have not progresssed to become Liveryman.

RN = Reverted to Freeman, no contact address 2003

X = Did not sign on date due to sign.

MASTERS OF THE COMPANY

1977/1978	John Alleyne WEDGWOOD	1995/1996	Clifford Hazelton GRINSTED
1978/1979	John Francis PHILLIPS	1996/1997	Geoffrey Stuart FINN
1979/1980	Stanley James Sidney ELEY	1997/1998	James CARINE
1980/1981	Thomas Eric Douglas MASON	1998/1999	John Hurn CONSTABLE
1981/1982	David Christopher Laborde MARWOOD	1999/2000	Wilfred Charles HAMMOND
1982/1983	Kenneth JACQUES	2000/2001	Michael John DUDDING
1983/1984	Sylvia Irene Maud TUTT	2001/2002	Philip Michael MARCELL
1984/1985	Robin Mitchell CLARKE	2002/2003	David William Robert WRIGHT
1985/1986	Leslie Ronald CROYDON	2003/2004	Donald Herbert KIRKHAM
1986/1987	John Francis PHILLIPS	2004/2005	Sir Clive Haydn MARTIN
1987/1988	Ronald BOUNDS	2005/2006	Arthur Jeffrey GREENWELL
1988/1989	Dennis Howard ROBERTS	2006/2007	Thomas Richard SERMON
1989/1990	Kenneth Ewart PARRY	2007/2008	Adèle Loraine THORPE
1990/1991	Donald Desmond DURBAN	2008/2009	Francis SPENCER-COTTON
1991/1992	Henry Roy HARRIS	2009/2010	Robin Anthony EVE
1992/1993	Eric Stanton KIRK	2010/2011	Rory Fitton Moresby JACKSON
1993/1994	Francis Joseph BERGIN	2011/2012	Ian David Lea RICHARDSON
1994/1995	George Edward CAUCHI	2012/	Charles Edmund Royden LEDSAM

OFFICERS OF THE COMPANY

Date	Surname	Forenames	Elected	Stood Down
CLERKS				
10.01.77	Barker	Barry	Clerk	03.05.78
03.05.78	Simmonds *	Robert	Hon. Clerk	05.07.84
05.07.84	Challis	George	Hon. Clerk	19.10.94
19.10.94	Hammond	Wilfred	Hon. Clerk	16.10.97
16.10.97	Stewart	Iain	Clerk	29.02.00
29.02.00	Grinsted	Clifford	Hon. Clerk	19.07.01
19.07.01	Lintott	Gaynor	Clerk	12.07.02
12.07.02	Dudding	Michael	Clerk	26.01.12
26.01.12	Summerson	Hugo	Clerk	

* Appointed Hon. Clerk Emeritus on retirement as Hon Clerk

Date	Surname	Forenames	Elected	Stood Down
ASSISTANT/DEPUTY CLERKS				
13.10.77	Simmonds	Robert	Hon. Dep Clerk	03.05.78
16.01.80	Guilford	Phillip	Hon. Assist. Clerk	01.10.81
01.10.81	Hamilton–Hopkins	Albert	Hon. Assist. Clerk	04.07.85
04.07.85	Jones	John	Hon. Assist. Clerk	18.07.96
17.10.96	Lee	David	Hon. Assist. Clerk	31.12.97
13.10.99	Tyre	Sandra	Assistant Clerk	25.10.00
27.01.05	Blackwell	Valerie	Hon. Assist. Clerk	30.06.07
26.01.12	Lee	Erica	Assistant Clerk	

Date	Surname	Forenames	Elected	Stood Down
TREASURERS				
23.04.98	Bristow	Gordon	Hon. Treasurer	20.07.00
20.07.00	Spencer-Cotton	Francis	Hon. Treasurer	19.10.06
19.10.06	Turner	Truda	Hon. Treasurer	30.06.07
04.10.07	Jackson	Laura	Hon. Treasurer	19.12.07
24.01.08	Sylva	Paul	Hon. Treasurer	23.04.09
29.01.09	Jamison	Simon	Hon. Assist. Treas.	23.04.09
23.04.09	Jamison	Simon	Hon. Treasurer	18.10.12
18.10.12	Alderman	Roger	Hon. Treasurer	
CHAPLAINS				
08.02.78	Wallbank Rev Dr	Newell	Hon. Chaplain	31.07.79
25.10.79	Brown, Rev.	Arthur	Hon. Chaplain	18.07.91
09.07.92	Lawson, Rev.	David	Hon. Chaplain	07.07.94
25.01.96	Dudley, Rev. Dr.	Martin	Hon. Chaplain	01.02.01
19.07.01	Mullen Rev. Dr.	Peter	Hon. Chaplain	
ALMONER				
2002	Wright	David William R	Hon. Almoner	
ARCHIVIST				
27.04.95	Coward	David	Hon. Archivist	12.07.02
12.07.02	Sole	Brian	Hon Archivist	
BEADLE				
13.10.77	Abethell	Brian	Beadle	16.10.97
16.10.97	Grant	Paul	Beadle	27.04.00
27.04.00	Young	Terence	Beadle	18.10.12
18.10.12	Theobald	Roy	Beadle	

Date	Surname	Forenames	Elected	Stood Down
CHARITABLE TRUSTS				
10.01.79	Wedgwood	John	Chairman	12.01.84
12.01.84	Phillips	John	Chairman	09.10.86
09.10.86	Roberts	Dennis	Chairman	13.10.88
13.10.88	Gardiner	Geoffrey	Chairman	12.04.90
12.04.90	Jacques	Kenneth	Chairman	30.06.03
01.07.03	Marcell	Philip	Chairman	30.06.07
01.07.07	Kirkham	Donald	Chairman	30.06.09
01.07.09	Richardson	Ian	Chairman	30.06.11
01.07.11	Greenwell	Jeffrey	Chairman	
01.07.02	Carine	James	Hon. Secretary	30.06.05
01.07.07	Fox	Julie	Hon Secretary	06.07.11
06.07.11	Lee	Erica	Secretary	

RIVERS LECTURES

MR. BERNARD HARTY
Town Clerk and Chamberlain, Corporation of London
The Future of Governance of the City of London
Drapers' Hall, July 1998

THE RT HON. THE LORD NOLAN OF BRASTED
ex Chairman Committee on Standards in Public Life
Standards in Public Life
Drapers' Hall, March 1999

MR. KEN LIVINGSTONE
Candidate for Mayoralty of London
The Government of London
Drapers' Hall, March 2000

MR. JOHN BRIDGEMAN CBE TD
ex Director General of Fair Trading
Global Business – Local Consumers
Drapers' Hall, March 2001

SIR HOWARD DAVIES
Chairman, Financial Services Authority
Regulation – Its importance to the future of the Financial Services Industry
Drapers' Hall, March 2002

THE RT HON. THE LORD BAKER OF DORKING

ex Secretary of State for Education & Science

The Future of Universities

Drapers' Hall, March 2003

MR. RICHARD BOWKER

Chairman, The Strategic Rail Authority

The Future for Integrity in a Regulated Society

Ironmongers' Hall, March 2004

SIR JOHN BOURN KBE

Comptroller & Auditor General, The National Audit

Auditing? Is it value for money?

Stationers' Hall, March 2005

THE RT HON. LORD BUTLER OF BROCKWELL KG

Former Secretary to the Cabinet and Master, University College Oxford

Jim Hacker and Sir Humphrey

Drapers' Hall, March 2006

MR. STEPHEN GREEN

Chairman, HSBC

Integrity in Diversity

Drapers' Hall, April 2007

SIR BRIAN BENDER KCB

Permanent Secretary, Department for Business

Science & Risk Management in Government Enterprise and Regulatory Reform

Drapers' Hall, February 2009

MS. JUDITH HACKITT CBE

Chair, Health & Safety Commission

Leadership in Health & Safety – The Essential Role of the Board

Drapers' Hall, March 2009

THE LORD LEVENE OF PORTSOKEN KBE

Member, Court of Aldermen, City of London

The City and International Business

Drapers' Hall, February 2010

THE LORD WILSON OF DINTON GCB

Former Secretary to the Cabinet, Master Emmanuel College, Cambridge

Plain Tales from the Hills: – Former Cabinet Minister's Reflections

Drapers' Hall, February 2011

PROFESSOR DAME NANCY ROTHWELL DBE FRS

President & Vice Chancellor Manchester University

The Role of Universities in 21st Century

Carpenters' Hall, February 2012

ANNUAL BANQUETS

Date	Venue	WCCSA Master	Toast to the Company by	Reply to Guests' Toast
05 April 1978	Apothecaries' Hall	J.A. Wedgwood	Sir Alan Wilson	Sir Alan Wilson
22 March 1979	Mansion House	J.F. Phillips	Lord Mayor: Sir Kenneth Cork	Lord Denning
21 March 1980	Mansion House	S.J.S. Eley	Lord Mayor: Sir Peter Gadsden	Rt. Hon. Sir Graham Page
02 March 1981	Mansion House	T.E.D. Mason	Lt-Col. Colin Cole, Garter King of Arms	Lt-Col. Colin Cole, Garter King of Arms
19 March 1982	Mansion House	D.C.L. Marwood	Major Gen. John Kinahan	Major Gen. John Kinahan
04 March 1983	Mansion House	K. Jacques	Lord Mayor: Sir Anthony Joliffe	Sir Frederick Dainton
23 March 1984	Mansion House	Miss S.I.M. Tutt	Lord Mayor: Dame Mary Donaldson	Lord Templeman
22 March 1985	Mansion House	R.M. Clarke	Lord Mayor: Sir Alan Traill	Alderman H C P Bidwell
21 March 1986	Mansion House	L.R. Croydon	Lord Mayor: Sir William Allan Davis	His Honour Judge T H Pigot
20 March 1987	Mansion House	J.F. Phillips	Lord Mayor: Sir David Rowe-Ham	The Rt. Hon. The Earl of Stockton
08 July 1988	Mansion House	R. Bounds	Lord Mayor: Sir Greville Spratt	Admiral Sir William Staveley
31 March 1989	Mansion House	D.H. Roberts	Lord Mayor: Sir Christopher Collett	Admiral Sir Nicholas Hunt
30 March 1990	Mansion House	K.E. Parry	Lord Mayor: Sir Hugh Bidwell	Mr. J. E. McGee
25 March 1991	Mansion House	D.D. Durban	Lord Mayor: Sir Alexander Graham	The Rt Hon. Lord Alexander of Weedon
03 April 1992	Stationers' Hall	H.R. Harris	Lord Mayor: Sir Brian Jenkins	The Rt Hon. The Earl of Limerick KBE DL
19 April 1993	Butchers' Hall	E.S. Kirk	Lord Mayor: Sir Francis McWilliams	Sir Archibald Forster .
20 April 1994	Mansion House	F.J. Bergin	Lord Mayor: Sir Paul Newall	The Rt. Rev. John Taylor Bishop of St Albans
20 April 1995	Mansion House	G. E. Cauchi	Alderman Sir Alexander Graham	Mr. John B. Zochonis
03 May 1996	Mansion House	C.H. Grinsted	Lord Mayor: Sir John Chalstrey	General Paul A Rader
23 May 1997	Mansion House	G.S. Finn	Lord Mayor: Sir Roger Cork	Sir James Duncan
22 May 1998	Mansion House	J.E. Carine	Alderman Sir Roger Cork	Sir Michael Perry

Date	Venue	WCCSA Master	Toast to the Company by	Reply to Guests' Toast
14 May 1999	Mansion House	J. Constable	Alderman Sir Alexander Graham	Air Chief Marshal Sir Michael Graydon
19 May 2000	Mansion House	W.C. Hammond	Lord Mayor: Sir Clive Martin	Gen. Sir David Ramsbotham
18 May 2001	Carpenters' Hall	M.J. Dudding	Mr. William Punshon	The Lord Watson of Richmond
21 May 2002	Mansion House	P.M. Marcell	Alderman Sir Roger Cork (l.t.)	Admiral Sir Ian Garnett
09 May 2003	Mansion House	D.W.R. Wright	Alderman Sir Richard Nichols (l.t.)	The Rt Hon. The Lord Fellowes
04 June 2004	Mansion House	D.H. Kirkham	Lord Mayor: Alderman Robert Finch	Alderman David Brewer
18 May 2005	Haberdashers' Hall	Sir Clive Martin	Deputy Pauline Halliday	The Lord Rix
10 April 2006	Mansion House	A.J. Greenwell	Sheriff Kevin Kearney	Major Gen. Sebastian Roberts
24 April 2007	Mansion House	T.R. Sermon	Sheriff Richard Regan	Sir Stephen Lander
22 April 2008	Mansion House	Mrs. A.L. Thorpe	Alderman Sir Michael Savory	Mrs Angela Knight
30 April 2009	Mansion House	F. Spencer-Cotton	Sir John Stuttard (l.t.)	Air Chief Marshal Stephen Dalton
19 March 2010	Mansion House	R.A. Eve	Lord Mayor: Nick Anstee	Sir Gavyn Arthur
16 May 2011	Mansion House	R.F.M. Jackson	Alderman Lord Levene (l.t.)	Lord Powell of Bayswater
01 May 2012	Mansion House	I.D.L. Richardson	Alderman Sir Michael Savory (l.t.)	Judge Brian Barker

INDEX